VOLUME FIVE

TRENDS IN POLICING

Interviews with
Police Leaders Across the Globe

Interviews with Global Leaders in Policing, Courts, and Prisons Series

International Police Executive Symposium Co-Publications

Dilip K. Das, *Founding President-IPES*

PUBLISHED

Trends in Policing: Interviews with Police Leaders Across the Globe, Volume Five
By Bruce F. Baker and Dilip K. Das, ISBN: 978-1-4822-2449-8

Trends in Legal Advocacy: Interviews with Leading Criminal Defense Lawyers and Prosecutors Around the World
By Jane Goodman-Delahunty and Dilip K. Das, ISBN: 978-1-4987-3312-0

Trends in the Judiciary: Interviews with Judges Across the Globe, Volume One
By Dilip K. Das and Cliff Roberson with Michael Berlin, ISBN: 978-1-4200-9978-2

Trends in Policing: Interviews with Police Leaders Across the Globe, Volume Four
By Bruce F. Baker and Dilip K. Das, ISBN: 978-1-4398-8073-9

Trends in Policing: Interviews with Police Leaders Across the Globe, Volume Three
By Otwin Marenin and Dilip K. Das, ISBN: 978-1-4398-1924-1

Trends in Policing: Interviews with Police Leaders Across the Globe
By Dilip K. Das and Otwin Marenin, ISBN: 978-1-4200-7520-5

Trends in Corrections: Interviews with Corrections Leaders Around the World
By Jennie K. Singer, Dilip K. Das, and Eileen Ahlin, ISBN: 978-1-4398-3578-4

Trends in Corrections: Interviews with Corrections Leaders Around the World, Volume Two
By Martha Henderson Hurley and Dilip K. Das, ISBN: 978-1-4665-9156-1

Trends in the Judiciary: Interviews with Judges Across the Globe, Volume Two
By David Lowe and Dilip K. Das, ISBN: 978-1-4822-1916-6

VOLUME FIVE

TRENDS IN POLICING

Interviews with Police Leaders Across the Globe

Edited by
BRUCE F. BAKER AND DILIP K. DAS

CRC Press
Taylor & Francis Group
Boca Raton London New York

CRC Press is an imprint of the
Taylor & Francis Group, an **informa** business

CRC Press
Taylor & Francis Group
6000 Broken Sound Parkway NW, Suite 300
Boca Raton, FL 33487-2742

First issued in paperback 2019

© 2017 by Taylor & Francis Group, LLC
CRC Press is an imprint of Taylor & Francis Group, an Informa business

No claim to original U.S. Government works

ISBN-13: 978-1-4822-2449-8 (hbk)
ISBN-13: 978-0-367-86921-2 (pbk)

Library of Congress Cataloging-in-Publication Data
Names: Baker, Bruce F., editor. | Das, Dilip K., 1941-editor.
Title: Trends in policing : interviews with police leaders across the globe/ [edited by] Bruce F. Baker, Dilip K. Das.
Description: 1 Edition. | New York : Routledge, [2017] | Series: Interviews with global leaders in policing, courts, and prison ; Volume 5
Identifiers: LCCN 2016025678| ISBN 9781482224498 (hardback) | ISBN 1482224496 (hardback) | ISBN 9781315390543 (ebk) | ISBN 9781315390536 (web pdf) | ISBN 1315390531 (web pdf)
Subjects: LCSH: Police--Cross-cultural studies. | Police administration--Cross-cultural studies. | Police-community relations--Cross-cultural studies. | Police chiefs--Interviews.
Classification: LCC HV7921 .T74 2017 | DDC 363.2/3--dc23
LC record available at https://lccn.loc.gov/2016025678

Visit the Taylor & Francis Web site at
http://www.taylorandfrancis.com

and the CRC Press Web site at
http://www.crcpress.com

Contents

Series Editor's Preface

The International Police Executive Symposium, in collaboration with CRC Press of the Taylor & Francis Group Publishing, publishes a series titled Interviews with Global Leaders in Policing, Courts, and Prisons. The objective is to produce high-quality books aimed at bringing the voice of the leading criminal justice practitioners to the forefront of scholarship and research. These books, based on interviews with leaders in criminal justice, are intended to present the perspectives of high-ranking officials throughout the world by examining their careers, insights, vision, experiences, challenges, perceived future of the field, and related issues of interest.

True, the literature is replete with scholarship and research that provides the academic interpretation of the field, its practices and future. However, these publications are often in difficult to access journals and are written from the perspective of the academic, with little interpretation or feasible action items for those professionals working in the field. A comprehensive literature discussing the on-the-ground, day-to-day understanding of how police, courts and prison systems work, do not work, and need to be improved is lacking. This series provides "inside" information about the systems as told to respected scholars and researchers by seasoned professionals. In this series, the dialogue between scholar/researcher and practitioner is opened as a guided, yet candid, discussion between the two professionals and provides the opportunity for academics to learn from practitioners, while practitioners also learn from the expression of their experiences, challenges, skills, and knowledge.

Throughout the world the criminal justice field is at cross roads and the time is ripe for change and improvements. Many countries throughout the world have long-standing policies that have been successful for their culture and political climate, or are in need of serious revamping due to budgetary concerns or corruption. Other countries are at a precipice and are beginning to establish new systems. In all of these situations, the international criminal justice field stands to benefit from an accessible, engaging and enlightening series of frank discussions of the leaders' personal views and experiences in the field.

Many volumes are written by academics about criminal justice practitioners, but this series captures the voice of the practitioners themselves. Based on interviews with leading national figures in policing, the judiciary, and corrections, each volume presents their perspectives on their vision, experiences, lessons learned, and future challenges. We are privileged to hear the inside story that is normally hidden from the public and researchers. And being global in scope, the series escapes the silos of our national or Western view of things and exposes the reader to different challenges and approaches within the criminal justice fields. This broader perspective is a matter of serious concern when international crime requires increasing co-operation between jurisdictions, and when international missions require an understanding of local context if their prescriptions are to be appropriate.

This 5th volume in the series of *Trends in Policing: Interviews with Police Leaders Across the Globe*, has no less than 13 police leaders from 5 continents interviewed by some of the leading academics in the field. It is clear that new trends of crime and responses are emerging that were never anticipated when the series began and that the world in which we live is increasingly interconnected with both criminal and policing networks. This volume enables the reader to sit alongside these leaders and hear how they respond to these challenges of our modern world.

It is anticipated that this addition to the series will facilitate discussions within and between countries' police systems to add value to their current operations and future directions. It is hoped that this series will also bridge the gap of knowledge that exists between scholars and researchers in academia and practitioners in the field. It is the intention of the series editor to continue with this series and I invite police scholars, researchers, and practitioners across the world to join in this venture and welcome correspondence on any issues raised by the interviews or regarding future avenues for engagement in this debate.

Dilip K. Das, PhD
Founding President, International Police Executive Symposium
www.ipes.info

Book Series Editor for Advances in Police Theory and Practice—CRC Press, Taylor & Francis Group

Book Series Editor for Interviews with Global Leaders in Policing, Courts, and Prisons—CRC Press, Taylor & Francis Group

Book Series Editor, PPR Special Issues as Books—Routledge,
Taylor & Francis Group

Founding Editor-in-Chief, Police Practice and Research:
An International Journal, PPR
http://www.tandfonline.com/GPPR

Foreword

The interviews that make up this book provide an extraordinary opportunity to peer into the world of police and their policing from the vantage point of senior policing officers from around the globe. The landscapes within which these leaders operate are extraordinarily different socially, politically, and geographically.

Given these different realities one might have expected that these police leaders would have provided very different accounts about assessments of policing. Of course, there are very significant differences, but these are overshadowed by the similarities in the accounts they tell in the pages of this revealing book.

At the heart of these interviews are tensions and contradictions that make the accounts of policing provided here profoundly bittersweet. Sometimes these contradictions are very explicit. At other times they are more implicit. But even then these tensions lurk close to the surface and are not hard to find.

On the "sweet" side one finds leaders who are courageous, persistent, determined, insightful, well-intentioned, knowledgeable, optimistic, hardworking, and committed to high and demanding ideals. On the "bitter" side these accounts recount tale after tale of environments full of very difficult challenges that these officers and their police organizations have been required to confront. Challenges that at times appear almost insurmountable.

The accounts of these "bitter" challenges record policing organizations that are under siege. The sources of this siege are both external and internal. In the accounts, these officers describe the way in which they personally, and through their organizations, have been buffeted by countless waves of change—political, social, and institutional.

The external sources that have buffeted police include difficult fiscal environments, citizens who are disillusioned and sometimes angry and hostile, and institutional contexts that are unsupportive and sometimes crumbling. Internally these sources include concerns about whether the established police vision is appropriate to the new realities of the twenty-first century, problems with morale, frustration that arises when sound programs fail to find traction, and so on.

What makes this book so encouraging, notwithstanding sometimes very dark clouds, is that accounts of crises are balanced with accounts of hope and pride in what is being, and has been, accomplished. This pride, and the countless developments that justify it, is both encouraging and uplifting. In some cases this pride has as its back drop scenes of beleaguered organizations and leaders. Yet even in these trying situations there are senior officers who strive to achieve a quality service of which they and their fellow police officers can be proud.

What is clear from the accounts this volume records is that police and policing across the world is at a turning point. What the officers profiled repeat in interview after interview is that the old vision of policing that police have held to so firmly for so many decades across the globe, and the old organizational forms developed to realize it, is progressively giving way to new visions as Hegel's *Owl of Minerva* takes flight as "the shades of night are gathering."

What this book makes so abundantly clear is that there are many, many fine leaders at the helm of police organizations around the world who are responding with vigor, insight, and considerable wisdom to the challenges of re-positioning police within the twenty-first century. These leaders are constantly scrutinizing policing as they seek ways to improve what police do.

Realizing an emerging ambition of a renewed vision for police and policing that many of these leaders strive to achieve will not be easy. However, if those at the helm of tomorrow's police organizations globally are anywhere near as good as the best of the leaders profiled here we have every reason to be confident that the flight of the police Owl will be strong and high.

Clifford Shearing
Professor, Universities of Brisbane
Cape Town, South, Africa, and Montreal, Canada

Preface

The *International Police Executive Symposium* (IPES) was founded in 1994 to address one major challenge, i.e., the two worlds of research and practice remain disconnected even though cooperation between the two is growing. A major reason is that the two groups speak in different languages. The research is published in hard to access journals and presented in a manner that is difficult for some to comprehend. On the other hand, police practitioners tend not to mix with researchers and remain secretive about their work. Consequently there is little dialogue between the two and almost no attempt to learn from one another. The global dialogue among police researchers and practitioners is limited. True, the literature on the police is growing exponentially. But its impact upon day-to-day policing, however, is negligible.

The aims and objectives of the IPES are to provide a forum to foster closer relationships among police researchers and practitioners on a global scale, to facilitate cross-cultural, international, and interdisciplinary exchanges for the enrichment of this law enforcement, to encourage discussion, and to publish research on challenging and contemporary problems facing the policing profession. One of the most important activities of the IPES is the organization of an annual meeting under the auspices of a police agency or an educational institution. Now in its 17th year, the annual meeting, a five-day initiative on specific issues relevant to the policing profession, brings together ministers of interior and justice, police commissioners and chiefs, members of academia representing world-renown institutions, and many more criminal justice elite from over 60 countries. It facilitates interaction and the exchange of ideas and opinions on all aspects of policing. The agenda is structured to encourage dialogue in both formal and informal settings.

Another important aspect of the meeting is the publication of the best papers presented by well-known criminal justice scholars and police administrators who attend the meetings. The best papers are selected, thoroughly revised, fully updated, meticulously edited, and published as books based upon the theme of each meeting. This repository of knowledge under the co-publication imprint of IPES and CRC Press, Taylor & Francis Group chronicles the important contributions of the International Police Executive Symposium over the last two decades. As a result, in 2011 the United Nations awarded IPES a Special Consultative Status for the Economic and Social Council (ECSOC) honoring its importance in the global security community.

In addition to this book series, the IPES also has a research journal, *Police Practices and Research: An International Journal* (PPR). The PPR contains research articles on police issues. It is an international journal and is distributed worldwide. For more information on the PPR visit http://www. tandf.co.uk/journals/GPPR.

This unique volume, titled, *Strategic Responses to Crime: Thinking Locally, Acting Globally*, includes selected articles that were originally presented by police executives and scholars from several countries who attended the 13th Annual Meeting of the International Police Executive Symposium held in Ayvalik, Turkey, in 2006. However, the articles have been updated and several papers outside of the conference have been added to capture the theme of the book. The volume is divided into four sections, each of which includes perspectives of police administrators and members of the academia from different countries. These chapters encompass topics in law enforcement from operations to organizations including pervading issues that the police confront both locally and globally. The chapters provide a comprehensive survey of police practices across police jurisdictions. This book is a useful reference for practitioners and researchers.

IPES advocates, promotes, and propagates that *policing* is one of the most basic and essential avenues for improving the quality of life in all nations; rich and poor; modern and traditional; large and small; as well as peaceful and strife-ridden. IPES actively works to drive home to all its office bearers, supporters, and admirers that, in order to reach its full potential as an instrument of service to humanity, *policing* must be fully and enthusiastically open to collaboration between research and practice, global exchange of information between police and academics in every country, universal disseminations and sharing of best practices, generating thinking police leaders and followers, and reflecting and writing on the issues challenging to the profession.

Through its annual meetings, hosts, institutional supporters, and publications, IPES reaffirms that *policing* is a moral profession with unflinching adherence to the rule of law and human rights as the embodiment of humane values.

Dilip K. Das, PhD
Founding President, International Police Executive Symposium
www.ipes.info

Book Series Editor for:

Advances in Police Theory and Practice
CRC Press, Taylor & Francis Group

Interviews with Global Leaders in Policing, Courts, and Prisons
CRC Press, Taylor & Francis Group

PPR Special Issues as Books
Routledge, Taylor & Francis Group

Founding Editor-in-Chief, *Police Practice and Research:
An International Journal*, http://www.tandf.co.uk/
journals/GPPR

Editors

Bruce F. Baker is a professor of African security at Coventry University in the United Kingdom. His research and publications cover African policing (http://www.africanpolicing.org), security and justice reform, and local justice and governance. His book, *Security in Post-Conflict Africa: The Role of Non-State Policing* (CRC Press, 2009), won the American Society of Criminology's prize for best book in comparative and international criminology in 2010. He has undertaken research and consultancies in Zimbabwe, Mozambique, South Africa, Rwanda, Uganda, The Gambia, Sierra Leone, Cape Verde, Seychelles, Liberia, South Sudan, Comoros, Madagascar, Ethiopia, Nigeria, and Afghanistan.

Dilip K. Das is the founding president of the International Police Executive Symposium (IPES, http://www.ipes.info) and founding editor-in-chief of *Police Practice and Research. An International Journal.* After 14 years as a police executive, including time spent as chief of police in India, Dr. Das moved to the United States, where he earned a master and doctorate in criminal justice. Dr. Das has authored, edited, and co-edited more than 30 books and numerous articles. He has traveled extensively throughout the world while engaged in comparative police research, and as a visiting professor at various universities to organize annual conferences of the IPES, and as a human rights consultant for the United Nations. He is editor-in-chief of two book series published by CRC Press/Taylor & Francis Group: *Advances in Police Theory and Practice* and *Interviews with Global Leaders in Policing, Courts, and Prisons.*

Contributors

David Baker is an associate professor and head of Criminal Justice, Federation University Australia. Previously, he worked for two decades in Police Studies, Criminal Justice and Criminology at Monash University. His main research interest is public order policing, especially the policing of industrial, social, and political protests. He is the author of *Batons and Blockades: Policing Industrial Disputes in Australasia* (2005). The monograph examines and analyses changes in the way police services in Australia and New Zealand control industrial conflict. He is currently completing a book titled, *Police, Picket-lines and Fatalities: Lessons from the Past*. Baker has written interdisciplinary articles and chapters in relation to police history and reform, police use of force, policing dissent, policing in the South Pacific, the Australian Federal Police, criminal justice institutions and processes, labor history, and workplace relations. He was a member of the International Policing Resort Consortium on the Police Use of Force and is an associate investigator for the Australian Research Council Centre of Excellence in Policing and Security. Baker teaches in the areas of police studies, criminological theory and practice, criminal justice institutions and processes, comparative and international criminal justice, and security.

Michael M. Berlin, JD, PhD, is director of the Criminal Justice Graduate Program and an associate professor at Coppin State University in Baltimore, Maryland. His areas of specialization include constitutional law and criminal procedure, community policing, criminal justice leadership, and management and terrorism/homeland security. Prior to his appointment at Coppin State University, he served as a professor of criminal justice at Baltimore City Community College where he directed both on-campus and Baltimore Police Academy Programs for over a decade. He is an attorney with more than 20 years' experience in private practice and is a former Baltimore Police Officer. Dr. Berlin served as an instructor at the US State Department sponsored International Law Enforcement Academy in Roswell, New Mexico, where he taught thousands of police supervisors from Africa, Asia, Eastern Europe, and Central and South America. He has also served as an instructor for police officers, firefighters, and emergency medical technicians at a US Department of Homeland Security sponsored antiterrorism training in Socorro, New Mexico. He was named Instructor of the Year by the Maryland

Police Training Commission in 2003. His recent publications include *Crime Scene Searches and the Fourth Amendment; The Evolution, Decline and Nascent Transformation of Community Policing in the United States: 1980–2010; An Overview of Police Academy Training in the United States; and an Interview of the Honorable Robert M. Bell, Chief Judge of the Court of Appeals of Maryland (State Supreme Court).*

Marcellus Boles currently serves as the co-chair of the Criminal Justice and Applied Social and Political Sciences Department in the College of Behavioral and Social Science at Coppin State University. Born in Pittsburgh, Pennsylvania, he graduated from Forest Park High School in Baltimore, Maryland. He has a master of science degree in criminal justice from the University of Baltimore and is a graduate of the 116th Session, FBI, National Academy, Quantico, Virginia. After serving 3 years in the US Marine Corps, and participating in the Dominican Republic and Vietnam conflicts, he joined the Baltimore Police Department (BPD) where he served in various capacities during his career, subsequently retiring as a lieutenant colonel. He served as district commander, deputy chief of the Patrol Division, personnel director, and community policing implementation coordinator. He also served as the director and associate director of Mid-Atlantic Regional Community Policing Institute (a collaborative agreement funded by the Department of Justice, Community Policing Services Office). Johns Hopkins University (JHU) was one of the partners and the grantee for this Institute. While at JHU and BPD, he participated in research projects focusing on domestic violence involving police personnel and identification of characteristics of exemplary first-line supervisors (sergeants).

Alexandre Magno Alves Diniz works as an adjunct professor at the Geography Department of the Pontifical Catholic University of Minas Gerais (PUCMinas), Brazil, where he heads the graduate program in Geography. He earned a PhD in geography from Arizona State University (ASU). He has worked as visiting researcher at the Geography Department of McGill University, Montreal (2009). He specializes in human geography and presently researches the geography of crime and violence, and urban and regional geography.

Curt T. Griffiths is a professor and coordinator of the Police Studies Program in the School of Criminology at Simon Fraser University—Surrey Campus. Among his primary research interests are the organizational and operational dynamics of policing, comparative police studies, police performance measures, and improving the delivery of policing services. He has worked extensively with all levels of government, municipal police services, and the RCMP on a variety of projects focused on police performance, building organizational and operational capacities, and the effectiveness of police policies and strategies. He has conducted international studies in Egypt, Netherlands, Japan, and the Commonwealth Caribbean. He has published widely in scholarly journals and is the author of several university-level texts, including *Canadian Criminal Justice* (5th ed., 2015) and *Canadian Police Work* (3rd ed., 2013), both published by Nelson, Toronto.

Garth den Heyer is an inspector with the New Zealand Police with more than 32 years' service. He is also a senior research fellow with the Police Foundation in Washington, DC and a lecturer in Investigation Management and Leadership at the Australian Graduate School of Policing Security, Charles Sturt University, Australia. He is the manager of the National Security for the New Zealand Police, and is responsible for implementing and managing the New Zealand Police's national operational response to natural and civil disasters and national security/counterterrorism incidents. He has a doctorate in public policy from Charles Sturt University, a master's in economics from the University of London, and a master's in security and intelligence from Victoria University, Wellington.

Ann-Claire Larsen is a legal sociologist with a keen research interest in international human rights law. She began her legal studies after completing a PhD in sociology. She now teaches for the School of Law and Justice at Edith Cowan University, Western Australia. Her research is associated with the Centre for Innovative Practice also at Edith Cowan University. Ann-Claire's research topics include criminal justice concerns involving Australia's Indigenous people, women, and children.

David Lowe is a principal lecturer at Liverpool John Moores University's Law School, an academic fellow in one of the UK's four Inns of Court, The Honourable Society of the Inner Temple, and a member of the Liverpool Law Society where he sits on the Criminal Practice Committee. Lowe is also a contributor to the Westlaw's online legal encyclopedia, Westlaw UK Insight, on terrorism-related legislation. Prior to becoming an academic, he was a police officer for 27 years with the UK's Merseyside Police. During his police service, Lowe studied as a part-time student at university where he graduated from Liverpool John Moores University with a BA (Hons) in criminal justice, an LLB, and from Liverpool University with an MPhil where he researched the role of the police in a multiagency approach to crime control. In 2010, Lowe earned his PhD where he researched counterterrorism investigations. His varied police career in uniform and CID posts influenced his research areas. His work in the area of policing, terrorism, and security has been published in a variety of books and journals, with his latest work being in 2013, *Examining Political Violence: Studies in Terrorism, Counterterrorism* *and Internal War.* He has coedited with Dilip Das, *Trends in the Judiciary: Interviews with Judges from around the Globe,* 2014. Following the Edward Snowden revelations, his recent legal research into terrorism-related surveillance and intelligence exchange and balancing the interests of national security with individual liberties is being published in the journal *Terrorism and Political Violence.*

Stephen B. Perrott, professor of psychology at Mount Saint Vincent University in Halifax, Nova Scotia, Canada, was a police officer for 10 years before pursuing his doctorate in clinical psychology from McGill University. His research focuses primarily on the psychology of policing and secondarily on health promotion. Perrott has been a lecturer and workshop leader to the Halifax Regional Police, the Royal Canadian Mounted Police, and the Canadian Police College. He has worked internationally with the Philippine National Police and was project director for the 6-year "Community-Based Policing in The Gambia" initiative. Recent research includes a study investigating the motivational bases of volunteer firefighters, a sexual health research project involving university students across the Canadian Maritime Provinces, and a large-scale survey examining police officer perceptions of reform and of current "hot button" issues. He was a visiting professor at the Royal Melbourne Institute of Technology during 2014–2015.

Diana Scharff Peterson has nearly 20 years of experience in higher education teaching in the areas of research methods; comparative criminal justice systems; race, gender, class, and crime; statistics; criminology; sociology; and drugs and behavior at seven different institutions of higher education. Dr. Peterson has been the chairperson of three different criminal justice programs over the past 15 years and has published in the areas of criminal justice, social work, higher education, sociology, business, and management. Her research interests include issues in policing (training and education) and community policing, assessment and leadership in higher education, family violence, evaluation research, and program development. She has published over 30 articles in areas of criminal justice, sociology, social work, business, management, and higher education, and is the liaison and representative for the International Police Executive Symposium (consultative status) for quarterly annual meetings at the UN meetings in New York City, Geneva, and Vienna including the Commission on the Status of Women in New York City, New York. Most recently, Dr. Peterson chaired and organized the 25th Annual Meeting of the International Police Executive Symposium entitled, *Crime Prevention & Community Resilience: Police Role with Victims, Youth, Ethnic Minorities and Other Partners,* in Sophia, Bulgaria, July 27–August 1, 2014 (27 countries and 43 presenters).

Scott W. Phillips is an associate professor in the Criminal Justice Department at Buffalo State College. He worked as a police officer in Houston, Texas, and for the Office of Community-Oriented Policing Services in the US Department of Justice. He graduated from SUNY—Albany in 2006, and has worked as the Futurist in Residence at the FBI National Academy in Quantico, Virginia. His research interests include police officer decision-making and organizational influences on officers' behavior. His work has been published in *Journal of Criminal Justice, Criminal Justice Policy Review, the International Journal of Police Science and Management,* and *Police Practice and Research.*

Ludmila Mendonça Lopes Ribeiro works as an adjunct professor in the sociology department and as a researcher at the Criminality and Public Security Research Center (CRISP) at the UFMG, Brazil. She earned a doctorate in sociology from the Research University Institute of Rio de Janeiro (IUPERJ). She has also worked as a visiting researcher at the University of Groningen (Holland), as regional representative of Altus—Global Alliance and coordinator of Fundação Getulio Vargas' (FGV), and at the Research and Documentation Center for the Contemporary History of Brazil in São Paulo (CPDOC-SP). Her main publications are related to themes such as the judicial systems of Brazil, Portugal, United States, and Holland; community policing; the effects of crime victimization upon citizenship; and public security policies.

Sebastián Sal is a professor at the University of Buenos Aires, Business School. He earned his LLM at the University of Pennsylvania Law School, USA (1997), and JD at the University of Buenos Aires, Argentina (1988). He was a former judiciary officer (*Secretario*) of the National Criminal Court in financial related matters (1994–2000). From 2000 to 2001, he was an associate of Marval, O'Farrell & Mairal, Attorneys at Law. Since 2005, he has been the coordinator for Spanish-speaking countries of the International Association of Anti-Corruption Authorities (IAACA). He has been a governmental expert for the United Nations Convention Against Corruption (UNCAC) review since 2010 (being appointed by the Argentinean Government). He is an advisor in criminal and constitutional law at the National Argentinean Congress. He has taught at the University of Buenos Aires, School of Economics (graduate and MBA) since 1990. He has been a partner since 2004 at Sal & Morchio, attorneys at law.

Susan Sim is a consulting editor of the *Home Team Journal,* a publication of the Home Team Academy, a multiagency training facility of the Singapore Ministry of Home Affairs. A graduate of Oxford University, she has been a senior police officer, intelligence analyst, and diplomat working for the Singapore Government, and currently serves as chair of the Research

Committee of the National Crime Prevention Council, a volunteer group that works closely with the Singapore Police Force. She is also on the editorial board of *Police Practice and Research*, an international journal that presents current and innovative police research as well as operational and administrative practices from around the world. Sim is an author of *Making Singapore Safe: Thirty Years of the National Crime Prevention Council* (Singapore: Marshall Cavendish, 2011). She has also contributed to the Pearls in Policing Singapore 2012 report, *Homeland Security and Terrorism* (McGraw-Hill, 2013), *Trends in Corrections: Interviews with Corrections Leaders Around the World* (Taylor & Francis, 2015), and has written on suicide bombing and terrorist rehabilitation for the North Atlantic Treaty Organization (NATO) Science for Peace and Security Series. A regular speaker at the NATO Centre of Excellence Defence Against Terrorism in Ankara, Turkey, and vice-president for Asia of The Soufan Group, an international strategic consultancy with offices in New York, Doha, London, and Singapore. She also works on issues related to countering violent extremism.

Rosânia Rodrigues de Sousa works as a researcher at the Fundação João Pinheiro, where she also teaches in the school of government. She earned a doctorate in psychology of work and organizations from the University of Brasilia. Her major research themes are psychology with emphasis in human factors related to work, working mostly with public security, labor, organizational culture, subjectivity, and training.

Perry Stanislas has more than 30 years' experience in policing and security-related matters, with a particular interest in international policing. He was the senior policy advisor for Bedfordshire police in the area of Strategic and Organizational Development and a key leader in the largest development initiative in its history called "Towards 2000." Perry taught for many years at Bramshill Police Staff College and is a specialist in developing and preparing police leaders for change. He has carried out research and written on a broad range of policing matters in leading journals and presented his work at the United Nations and the International Association of Police Chiefs inter alia. He is currently leading research on police and emergency planning for major sporting events and economic crime prevention in large-scale building and construction projects. Stanislas teaches at De Montfort University in Leicester, UK.

Interviewees

Joe Arpaio, 81, has been referred to as "America's Toughest Sheriff." He has served the public for 50 years in a unique law enforcement and diplomatic career. It's a name he certainly has earned as head of the nation's third largest sheriff's office (in Maricopa County, Arizona), which employs over 3,800 people. After serving in the US Army from 1950 to 1953, and as a Washington, DC, and Las Vegas, Nevada police officer for almost 5 years, he went on to build a federal law enforcement career with the Drug Enforcement Agency (DEA). As a federal narcotics agent, he established a stellar record by infiltrating drug organizations on a global scale. His expertise and success led him to top management positions around the world with the DEA. He concluded his 32-year federal career as head of the DEA for Arizona. In 1992, he successfully campaigned to become Sheriff of Maricopa County, Arizona. Since then, he has been elected to unprecedented five 4-year terms. During his tenure as Sheriff of Maricopa County, he consistently earned extraordinarily high public approval ratings. With more than 50 years in law enforcement, Sheriff Arpaio has established several unique programs. He has approximately 10,000 inmates in his jail system. In August 1993, he started the nation's largest 'Tent City' for convicted inmates. Two thousand convicted men and women serve their sentences in a canvas incarceration compound. To date, he has investigated more than 41,000 illegal immigrants, resulting in thousands of deportations. The author of two books, Sheriff Arpaio's persona has been epitomized in television shows and in Hollywood films. It is a remarkable success story that has attracted the attention of government officials, presidential candidates, and media worldwide.

Jean-Michel Blais has more than 26 years of policing experience, having served with the Royal Canadian Mounted Police (RCMP), the United Nations, and presently with Halifax Regional Police. He began his policing career in 1988 with the RCMP in the Québec City area working on various criminal organizations. In 1995, he completed his first tour of duty with the United Nations in Haiti as a civilian police officer. Following his return, he worked in Québec City and Montréal on the Hell's Angels and Colombian drug cartels in Canada, Columbia, and Cuba. He was then transferred to Manitoba as a commissioned officer where he worked in aboriginal, municipal, and provincial policing and was the officer in charge of Major Crimes

Services for the province. In 2004, he was transferred to Adjudications Directorate as a permanent adjudicator and then director of the RCMP's internal disciplinary tribunal. In early 2008, he was assigned to the United Nations Stabilization Mission in Haiti as the Deputy Police Commissioner in charge of operations. Upon his return from Haiti in 2009, he worked as the chief prosecutor for the RCMP's internal disciplinary tribunal. In 2010, following the devastating earthquake that hit Haiti, he returned there to personally lead the recovery of two Canadian police officers and the senior management of the UN mission who had perished in the collapse of the UN headquarters, his former worksite. In 2010, he was transferred to Halifax where he became responsible for labor relations for the Atlantic Region of the RCMP. In 2011, he was promoted to the rank of Chief Superintendent in charge of Halifax District RCMP, responsible for municipal policing services in the areas immediately outside of Halifax Metro. In 2012, after 25 years in the RCMP, Blais retired to become the fourth chief of Halifax Regional Police (HRP) where he works presently, in charge of a 700-person municipal policing service. Chief Blais has two degrees, one in political science and economics from McGill University and another in law from Université Laval and has published several works on international and national police-related topics. He has also lectured extensively on leadership and modern police management.

Horacio Alberto Gimenez has, since 2011, been the head of the Metropolitan Police of the City of Buenos Aires. Before that, he worked for 39 years in the Federal Police, where he retired as Commissioner General. In the course of his career, he has been superintendent of Homeland Security and Federal Crimes Warehouses; director of Homeland Security and the Department of National Security; custody division chief of the Vice Presidential Unit; and cabinet advisor and secretary of the State Secretary of Homeland Security. In addition, he was responsible for the safety of several presidential summits and international meetings (UNASUR, MERCOSUR). Among his other interests, he is a police aircraft pilot, a commercial pilot, as well as a helicopter pilot. He is married and has two children.

Ellison Greenslade was appointed in 2010 as the sixth Commissioner of Police of Bahamas since its independence. He holds a postgraduate certificate in police management and criminal justice and earned an MBA with honors. He is presently engaged in PhD studies in organizational management and leadership studies at the University of Phoenix, Arizona, USA. Commissioner Greenslade was elected as the President of the Association of Caribbean Commissioners of Police (ACCP) in 2010 and was re-elected for three consecutive terms. He is a member of a number of international organizations including The International Association of Chiefs of Police (IACP), and currently serves as a member of the Executive Committee of the IACP and is in his third term in this position.

Ng Joo Hee was the Commissioner of the Singapore Police Force for 5 years from 2010 to 2015. A career police officer for almost 30 years, he started out as a criminal investigator before being posted to the Internal Security Department, where he was involved in counterespionage work. In 1992–1993, he served as a police monitor with the UN peacekeeping mission in Cambodia. On his return, he was tasked to establish and then lead the Special Tactics and Rescue (STAR) Unit, the Singapore Police's elite hostage rescue outfit. He was given his first land division to command in 2001, before moving to the CID as its deputy director. He then took on the job of running the Police Intelligence Department. From 2007 to 2009, he was seconded to the Singapore Prisons Service as its Commissioner, where he was responsible for the effective and efficient operation of all prisons and drug rehabilitation centers in Singapore. Hee joined the Singapore Police Force when he was awarded the Singapore Police Force Overseas Scholarship in 1985. He has an MBA from the Nanyang Technological University in Singapore (1998), and a Masters in Public Administration from the Kennedy School of Government at Harvard University (2001). Hee retired from the police in January 2015 and is currently the chief executive of Public Utilities Board (PUB), Singapore's national water agency. He also holds a concurrent appointment as the deputy secretary (Special Duties) in the Ministry of the Environment and Water Resources.

Doug LePard has been a member of the Vancouver Police Department (VPD) since 1981 and currently commands over 800 frontline police officers in the Operations Division. He previously commanded the Investigation Division. He earned a BA in criminology from Simon Fraser University and certificates from Queen's University and Harvard. In 1996, he created and led the VPD's Domestic Violence and Criminal Harassment Unit, partnering investigators with community counsellors for domestic violence investigations. He has written or cowritten several articles and book chapters on assessing risk in stalking cases, preventing wrongful convictions, serial killer investigations, managing change in police organizations and others. In 2010, his comprehensive review of the Pickton serial killing investigation was released, and he subsequently gave evidence at the Missing Women Commission of Inquiry for an extraordinary 14 days. His review was described in the Inquiry report as "unprecedented" and "a rare exemplar of how you can conduct an internal autopsy and try to figure out what went wrong so that it won't happen again in the future." The Inquiry report also identified the VPD as a "best practice learning organization" and attributed that in part to the leadership of Deputy Chief LePard. He has received many commendations and awards, including an Attorney General's award for service to victims and an award from the Ending the Violence Association of BC "For Outstanding Contributions Toward Ending Violence Against Women in BC." In 2012, he was invested as an Officer of the Order of Merit for the Police Forces by the Governor General of Canada, and, in 2013, he was awarded the Queen's Diamond Jubilee Medal.

J. Thomas Manger has been the chief of police in Montgomery County, Maryland, since February 2004. He began his law enforcement career in 1977 with the Fairfax County (Virginia) Police Department. He rose through the ranks to become Chief of Police in 1998. During his tenure in Fairfax County, Chief Manger received numerous awards including the Silver Medal of Valor. He is credited with reorganizing and expanding the Police Department's Community Policing efforts. His commitment to the highest ethical standards for policing and his enactment of new policies to increase departmental accountability earned significant recognition from the community, including the Fairfax County Human Rights Commission Award for outstanding contributions, and the NAACP's Community Service Leadership Award. In 2012, Chief Manger was inducted into the Montgomery County Human Rights Hall of Fame. He is a graduate of the FBI National Academy, the National Executive Institute, the Police Executive Leadership School at the University of Richmond, and the Senior Executive Institute at the University of Virginia, and he has also completed Harvard University's John F. Kennedy School's Program for State and Local government.

Peter Marshall has been New Zealand Commissioner since April 2011. He was previously commissioner of the Royal Solomon Islands Police Force from March 2009 to February 2011. Commissioner Marshall is a career police officer who joined the New Zealand Police in 1972, and has worked both in uniform and as a detective with the Criminal Investigation Branch. Within New Zealand, he has served as head of the Hawkes Bay Armed Offenders Squad, and area commander in Hastings and Aukland City. Internationally he has been posted to the New Zealand diplomatic missions in Canberra, Australia from 1998 to 2002, and Washington, DC from 2002 to 2004, where he established a New Zealand Police liaison office for counterterrorism. He was then assistant commissioner at the Police National Headquarters in Wellington, before being seconded to the Solomon Islands in February 2007. In May 2008, he became acting commissioner of police in the Solomons, and was officially appointed to the position in March 2009. Commissioner Marshall has diplomas in business studies and New Zealand Policing, and is a graduate of the FBI Academy.

Alberto Melis began his career in law enforcement in Delray Beach, Florida. He spent 24 years there, reaching the rank of captain and working in every division in the agency. He moved on to become the police chief of Lauderhill, Florida. In 2000, Chief Melis moved to Waco, Texas where he became chief of police. He spent 7 years in Waco before becoming the police chief of Douglas, Arizona. Douglas is located on the United States–Mexico border. After more than 40 years in law enforcement, Melis retired from Douglas in 2012. Beyond his practical experience in policing and administrative experience as a chief, he attended the Southern Police Institute at the University of Louisville, and has extensive training in many areas of law enforcement. He earned a bachelor's and master's degree, and is currently living in Waco attending seminary school.

Jon Murphy joined Merseyside Police as a cadet in January 1975, becoming a police officer in the rank of constable in 1976. In 1982, he was posted as a detective to the Criminal Investigation Department (CID) where he served for the next 20 years in various CID departments at the force, regional, and national levels. After completing the Strategic Command Course in 2001, he was posted as head of Operations in the National Crime Squad (NCS) to the rank of assistant chief constable. In this post, he held overall responsibility for all NCS-organized crime national and international investigations into drug trafficking, firearms trafficking, kidnap, extortion, and human trafficking. He returned to Merseyside Police in 2004 as deputy chief constable, but transferred in 2007 to work directly for the UK's Home Secretary when he set up the national Tackling Gangs Action Programme (TGAP). He was then appointed the ACPO National Coordinator for Serious and Organized Crime. In 2010, he returned to Merseyside Police as chief constable, the position he currently holds. In 1995, Murphy was awarded a Fulbright Fellowship for his work researching undercover policing and informant handling with the Federal Bureau of Investigation (FBI) in the United States. For his service to policing, Murphy was awarded the Queen's Police Medal in 2007. During his service, Murphy graduated with an LLB (Hons) in Law from Liverpool University, and in 2001, he graduated from Cambridge University with a postgraduate diploma in Applied Criminology.

Dominic Staltari, APM, a child of Italian immigrants, entered the Western Australian Police Service in 1978 where he was employed 35 years later. In 1983, he became a detective and then worked in various suburban locations and specialized squads, including the armed robbery squad for 4 years. In 1994, he was appointed the officer in charge of the local Criminal Investigation Branch. By 1997, he was made an inspector, and by 2002, he was a superintendent. He reached the pinnacle of his career in 2008 when he became an assistant commissioner over the corruption, prevention, and investigation portfolio. He retired in 2015. During his police career he has seized every opportunity that came his way to improve policing practices at the local level. Over those 35 years, he oversaw numerous changes in policing practices from police carrying firearms and tasers to computerized communication technologies. Dominic attributes his successful, enjoyable, and rewarding career to the personal qualities and values he acquired from his family of origin. That grounding produced a practical-oriented police officer working to achieve peace and order in multicultural Western Australia.

Per Swartz joined the Swedish Police Service in 1972 and retired in 2013 after a distinguished career. He experienced considerable operational and leadership responsibilities during his 40 years of service in the Swedish Police. His leadership in the Swedish Police Service encompassed the roles of area commander at Malmö for 10 years (1994–2004), tactical leader at Skåne (2004–2008), and chief constable of Blekinge province (2008–2012). His formal education background included University Masters of Law (1972), Police Chiefs Education (1973–1975, 1978), and Higher Management (2004). He also undertook some international studies in England and Germany. In the formative years of his police career and prior to his Malmo appointment, Swartz served in eight different police districts, most of them in the southern part of Sweden. During the final 15 or so years of his service, Per has been occupied in reorganization of police areas as well as introducing new methods in the fields of riot policing, community policing, and intelligence-led policing. He has also been active in international development projects in Montenegro, Croatia, Albania, and Slovenia. Swartz has lived in Malmö since 1985. His active community service includes working on the board of the Swedish Police Sports Organization; the last 4 years, he has been the chairman of that organization. During the past 2 years, he has been the chairman for the five Nordic countries for police sports.

Fábio Manhães Xavier is a native of Bom Jesus do Itabapoana, Rio de Janeiro state. He joined the Military Police of Minas Gerais in 1983, where he has held the following positions: commander of Special Operations Company; commander of Cadet Corps of the Military Police Academy; planning and operations officer of the Capital Police Command (CPC); commander of the Police Training Centre; commander of the 22nd Battalion of Police; international instructor of Human Rights applied to police work; delegate to the Police Forces in Latin America and the Caribbean by the International Committee of Red Cross—Geneva (2005 and 2006); deputy chief of the Military Office of the Governor; commander of the 13th Battalion of Police; commander of the Military Police Academy; general coordinator of the Department of Research and Information Analysis and the Development of the National Public Security Secretariat (SENASP)/Ministry of Justice; and the Organizational Development Advisor of Minas Gerais Military Police. Xavier has a Law degree from the Federal University of Minas Gerais (UFMG).

Introduction

These 13 police leaders from the continents of South America, North America, Asia, Australasia, and Europe have between them nearly 450 years' experience in policing from which we can learn. Most of them too, have four decades to look back on and mark the changes that have taken place, and recall the mistakes and successes. By any standards this makes this volume a significant contribution to police leadership, though very much focused on the developed world. It is in this developed world they have all watched a process of professionalism within their organizations and none doubt that the policing they lead is better than it was when they began their careers. It is also more complex, more sophisticated, more information loaded, more efficient, and often larger as an organization due to amalgamations and consolidation. But is it more effective in preventing crime, in responding to call outs, ensuring safety, and solving crime and disorder? That is harder to pin down, not because the leaders are evasive, but because new crime is being defined (e.g., domestic violence, Internet scams), crime priorities constantly change (e.g., child protection has risen to the fore), crime statistics differ (or sadly are massaged), expectations and therefore demands on the police are rising, and downloading leaves the police handling more and more social and mental health issues. Comparisons therefore are difficult.

What is clear from these interviews is that managerialism has taken hold of policing in the last 20 years. "Management" occurs more than 40 times in these interviews. The policies, processes, and structures of big business have penetrated policing. The talk of these police leaders is not that of when they began their careers. Today their concern, as in corporation board rooms, is of strategic plans and corporate vision and values; it is of diversity of customers and the need for that diversity to be reflected in recruitment policies; it is of efficiency and cost reduction and making expensive personnel more productive through computerized systems; it is of resource management and deployment models; it is of internal audits and personnel performance reviews; it is of being proactive rather than reactive to market forces; it is of service delivery and customer satisfaction; it is of targeted strategies aimed at specific outputs and goals; it is of accounting pressures and metrics; it is of accountability to stakeholders and oversight mechanisms; it is of restructuring the business and identifying core business. This is not to say that this is a backward step, but no one can doubt reading this volume that policing has become in the lifetime of the police leaders interviewed, big business.

The business of policing is today, according to these leaders, faced with some "tricky" issues. Though they mention budget cuts and its problems, it is three other areas in policing in the developed world that stand out in the volume. First, what is the relationship of the police to social services; to what extent should they play a social service role, particularly when it comes to the mentally ill and homeless and drug abusers? How is this role to be related to other social service agencies? As other services experience cut back in services, is the police meant to pick up the tag? Some of the interviewees seem positive about this as a role for an agency that is inevitably social in part and is on call 24 hours a day. Others are concerned that they do not have the resources to undertake a significant role and that it is a distraction. Second, what is the relationship to other policing and security services and the criminal justice system? Many of the interviewees are in jurisdictions where there are multiple agencies. Some have established a positive relationship and reap efficiency advantages, but others are struggling to create those links and cooperation. Third, what is the relationship to the government? Though none of the leaders question that they must enforce the laws of the legislature no matter what their personal feelings, many express concern at what new legislation demonstrate about politicians' understanding of what the police can achieve and of what the crime situation is on the ground. Further, there is concern that politicians are still more focused on responding to crime than they are at tackling the causes of crime in social deprivation. All three issues are relational and thus cannot be resolved simply by the police independent of society and the government. That police leaders voice these concerns only demonstrates again that gone are the days when they might see themselves as functioning in isolation unilaterally solving criminal justice problems. Today they see themselves as part of a broad network of agencies and the population at large in providing order and safety, justice and emergency response, and anti-terrorist activity (and an undefined measure of social problem response), even if getting that network to function smoothly is problematic.

Can police leaders of these large complex organizations stay in touch with the populations they serve? Can they manage the external relationships as well as the internal ones? They certainly desire that. They talk in the interviews of "community" 250 times and this is not just about community policing programs. Rather it is about supporting, engaging, partnering, serving, and reassuring the communities. It is concern about their trust, expectations, values, representation, and diversity. Can the call for the focus on the "customer" by leaders really be maintained by all the personnel in such large organizations? Can "partnership" be more than words when the partners are so asymmetrical in strength and resources and professional skills? There is no doubt that these leaders are making a real effort in that regard. But as they would all acknowledge, trust is an unstable mist that can evaporate with one publicized incident of police violence, corruption, or ill-discipline. And how does one get a true representation of the community in the police service or on forums when certain social groups are unwilling to offer themselves? No easy answers are on offer in this volume, for the world outside the police organization proves to be no less complex than the world inside. But if there are no easy answers there are honest and courageous attempts at answers. This may not be a text book, but it is 13 accounts of earnest and inspiring attempts to be leaders of complex organizations in a complex world.

Bruce F. Baker

Dilip K. Das

Doug LePard, Deputy Chief Constable, Vancouver Police Department, Vancouver, British Columbia, Canada

1

INTERVIEWED BY
CURT T. GRIFFITHS

Contents

Introduction

Public policing in Canada is carried out at four levels: federal, provincial, municipal, and First Nations. In addition, there are private security services and para-police services. The latter are generally staffed by officers with Special Constable status. Five Canadian police services—the Royal Canadian Mounted Police (RCMP), the Toronto Police Service, the Ontario Provincial Police (OPP), the Sûreté du Québec (SQ), and the Service de police de la Ville de Montréal (SPVM)—account for just over 60% of all police officers in Canada.

Canadian police services vary greatly in size and in terms of the areas for which they are responsible. At one end of the scale, there are three officer RCMP detachments in many remote northern communities; at the other, there are thousands of officers in the urban centers of Toronto and Montreal.

Royal Canadian Mounted Police

The RCMP is unique among the world's police forces and is organized into 16 divisions, 14 of which are operational divisions. The RCMP Act provides the framework for the operations of the RCMP. As the federal police force in all provinces and territories, the RCMP enforces most federal statutes, the Controlled Drugs and Substances Act, the Securities Act, and the lesser-known statutes such as the Canada Shipping Act and the Student Loans Act. Under the RCMP Act, RCMP officers have the powers of peace officers as well as the powers of customs and excise officers for the entire country. This makes RCMP members unique among Canada's police officers.

Although the RCMP is a federal police force, roughly 60% of RCMP personnel are involved in contract policing, serving as provincial and municipal police officers under agreements between the RCMP and the provinces/territories to provide policing services under contract; the RCMP, through the Government of Canada, negotiates municipal policing agreements with individual municipalities. The RCMP's reach extends to the international level: there are RCMP liaison officers in a number of countries in the Asia Pacific region, Europe, and the Americas. RCMP liaison officers provide a bridge between foreign police forces and their Canadian counterparts; they also assist in cross-national investigations.

Provincial Police Services

There are currently three provincial police forces in Canada: the OPP, the SQ, and the Royal Newfoundland Constabulary. Provincial police forces police rural areas and areas outside municipalities. They enforce provincial laws as well as the Criminal Code. Some municipalities in Ontario are policed under contract by the OPP. Except in Ontario and Quebec and certain parts of Newfoundland and Labrador, the RCMP provides provincial policing under contract with provincial governments. When the RCMP acts as a provincial police force, it has full jurisdiction over the Criminal Code as well as provincial laws. Similar to the RCMP, provincial police officers may be rotated between detachments.

Regional Police Services

Especially in the eastern regions of the country, regional police services are a key feature of Canadian policing. Most of these services have been formed through the amalgamation of several independent police departments into one large organization. Regional police services have been a feature of policing in Ontario for many years. Today, a number of regional police services, including the Peel Regional Police (the largest regional police force in Canada) and the Durham Regional Police, provide policing services to more than half of Ontarians. In Quebec, the SPVM provides policing services to the city of Montreal and several surrounding municipalities.

Municipal Police Services

Municipal police services have jurisdiction within a city's boundaries. Municipal police officers constitute two-thirds of the police personnel in the country and enforce the Criminal Code, provincial statutes, municipal bylaws, and certain federal statutes such as the Controlled Drugs and Substances Act. Most of the police work is carried out by services operating at this level.

Municipalities can provide police services in one of three ways: (1) by creating their own independent police service, (2) by joining with another municipality's existing police force, which often means becoming involved with a regional police force, or (3) by contracting with a provincial police force—the OPP in Ontario, and the RCMP in the rest of Canada except Quebec where there is no provision under provincial law for the SQ to contract out municipal policing services.

First Nations Police Services

Aboriginal peoples have become increasingly involved in the administration of justice, especially in the area of policing. This is perhaps appropriate, given the conflicts that have arisen between the police and the Aboriginal peoples both today and in the past. There are autonomous Aboriginal police services in all of the provinces except Prince Edward Island (PEI) and Newfoundland/Labrador, although there are none in the territories. Among the larger Aboriginal police forces that are involved in policing multiple reserve communities are the Ontario First Nations Constable Program, the Six Nations Tribal Police and the Nishnawbe-Aski Police Service in Ontario, the Amerindian Police in Quebec, and the Dakota Ojibway Police Service in Manitoba. There are smaller Aboriginal police forces in Alberta and British Columbia (BC).

Aboriginal police officers generally have full powers to enforce the Criminal Code, federal and provincial statutes, and in some circumstances, off reserve as well. There are also band constables, appointed under provisions of the Indian Act, who are responsible for enforcing band bylaws. Band constables are not fully sworn police officers, and their powers are limited.

The interview with Deputy Chief Constable LePard was conducted in Vancouver, BC, which was one and a half hours long. Deputy Chief Constable LePard responded to all of the questions that were posed to him and answered in a forthright and candid manner. With the exception of a few introductory comments and some editing, the following comments are those of Deputy Chief Constable LePard.

Career

DL: I was very motivated to become a police officer by the time I was around age 12. I had started to think about it. It seemed like it was an appealing career because it offered variety, excitement, and opportunity and also an element of altruism. So in a nutshell, all of those things combined. By age 16, I had already decided and I heard a presentation at my high school from a parole officer who taught at a local community college. He talked about the criminal justice system and law enforcement. That convinced me to begin my studies first at a community college and then to continue in Criminology at Simon Fraser University. However, I was hired by the Vancouver Police Department in 1981 after one year in the Douglas College program. I subsequently completed my BA in Criminology at Simon Fraser University in 2000.

When I was hired in I started out in the patrol division and spent seven years there. I did undercover work for the Vice unit and the Drug unit, and two years with the Strike Force, a covert surveillance and undercover unit. Then 18 months in the Communication Centre. I was then promoted to Corporal and transferred to our Planning and Research Section for a year, and acted as Staff Sgt. in my 2nd year there. I was recruited to planning and research by a Staff Sgt. I had worked for who thought I would do well there. I was surprised by this assignment having been a very operational police officer. I found out that I really did enjoy it; it was really developmental for me. I left planning and research for the Major Crime Section and was there for a number of years. I was a Detective and a Sergeant in the Sex Crime unit; the Sergeant in charge of the Home Invasion Task Force, and the Sergeant in charge of the Domestic Violence and Criminal Harassment Unit, which I created in 1996/1997. In the year 2000, I was promoted to Inspector and was sent back to the Planning and Research Section. I spent three years there as the Officer in Charge. I was then placed in charge of a new policing model in the Downtown Eastside of Vancouver (often described as the "poorest postal code in Canada" and with many crime and social problems). In 2003, I was promoted to Deputy Chief Constable. I began as the DCC in charge of the

Investigation Division, and in 2008, was placed in charge of the Operations Division, which is our front-line policing.

I've had a very varied career. I think to succeed at my level you have to have had a varied career. The more varied career you have, the more you can learn to allow you to excel in different areas. You demonstrate your adaptability. The more knowledge you have, the more value you can bring value to the organization.

CG: Has the Vancouver Police Department (VPD) provided you with opportunities during your career?

DL: Yes. It's all about how hard you are willing to work. What your attitude is and your natural aptitude is. You really can be the author of your history and success in our organization. You bring your ability and work hard and learn as much as you can, add value to the organization every day and try to add value every day; to coach and teach others. It doesn't make any difference what family you came from, what school you went to. There isn't a caste system. It really is a place where your work ethic and your ability will dictate your success, however you define that.

There is so much opportunity to do different things. I tell people that you can decide whether you are successful or not; whether you characterize success as being at the line level or being a detective or becoming a supervisor or being in management. It's about having that choice.

When I came into the police service, I really wanted to be a Corporal because you had to be a Corporal to be a detective. And my aspiration was to be a detective. I did that for a while and enjoyed that. But after that, there was a lot of pressure to go for promotion and my boss who was a great Sergeant provided a high level of support to me to go for promotion. And others did as well. I felt that if you have something to contribute to make the organization better, then there is a sense of obligation. As one of my bosses said when I told him that I enjoyed what I was doing, he said, "It's not about you. It's about the organization."

CG: Your career spans over three decades. Do you think that the VPD is unique in that way? That nurturing environment where officers are encouraged to be the best that they can be? And be the best at what they want to do?

DL: Obviously, my in depth experience is with the VPD. I have talked to police officers from other police services who have come to the VPD and who said that in their former organization, rather than the focus being on doing really good work, the focus was on getting promoted, period, as opposed to doing really good work and getting promoted as a consequence of that. I would say that some of the opportunities that I have had haven't been because of a master plan. It's just that things come up and people encourage you and you take advantage of the opportunity.

I think that in recent years, we have been very focused on trying to develop people to their best potential. Teaching them early on to be successful, however they frame that. Providing them with mentors. Our promotion process is built around developing very well-rounded officers. Our tenure plan sets out that we don't want you to get too entrenched early in your career in one particular area. We want you to experience some variety. And when you are able to make a more mature decision and you decide to do that, that's fine. But we have seen officers who, too early in their careers, made a choice that they thought was a good one and then regretted it. If they had returned to Patrol from whatever specialty assignment they were on and got more patrol experience, they would have been better suited down the road when they decided they wanted to be a supervisor, but they didn't have the experience necessary to do that. I think that we do a pretty good job of paying attention to that and delivering mentorship to our officers.

We have a quarterly meeting with the police board where we talk about succession planning right down to the Constable level: "Who are the officers who look like they are going to be high achievers? What are we doing to give them the best chance at success? At the middle management level, we actually assign people to keep an eye on these officers to make certain they are getting mentorship. This includes supporting them when they are applying for specific positions. We really do pay attention to that.

We hire bright, educated people who bring so much to the organization. It's our job that if they are lacking certain skills, we can provide the opportunity for them to develop.

Changes Experienced

CG: Over the three decades you have been in the organization, how have things changed in terms of the organization's philosophy and priorities? How have gender issues been addressed?

DL: There are so many things that have changed. Part of the change is due to the natural evolution that occurs in society. With respect to the Lesbian/Gay/Bisexual/Transsexual/Queer (LGBT) community, for example, there have been significant changes. If one thinks back to New York and other cities in the 1980s, the police were raiding bathhouses and there was hostility toward the police in the LGBT community. In Vancouver, we certainly had our challenges with that as well. An example of how far we have come: last Saturday, I was at the funeral of a prominent activist in the LGBT community. Here, we are at his funeral and in his honour, there was a VPD piper and Honour Guard. The number one speaker that his partner wanted to speak was the Chief Constable of the VPD. He was the co-owner of a bookstore dating back to the 1970s. They were importing materials that were very controversial and were seized by the Canadian Border Services. He fought that seizure and the case went all the way to the Supreme Court of Canada which recognized their right to have LGBT materials in their bookstore, which the Canadian Border Services Agency had deemed obscene. I think this example speaks volumes about the strong relationship with the LGBT community that they want us at events like this.

Another factor in developing relationships with the LGBT community is pro-actively recruiting officers from that community. It's about being a modern, forward-thinking police agency that is focused on providing safety, not promoting an ideology. I would like to think that most police departments have evolved and understand those issues, although we see on the news instances in which police agencies have not developed relationships with their communities and the problems that this can cause.

There have been many other changes in policing. Technology is a major one. We are moving into predictive policing, a program that provides patrol officers with real-time crime information in the patrol car, and to actually predict when and where crime is most likely to occur so we can take steps to prevent it. The technology is cutting edge and designed to get the best information out to the patrol officers.

CG: How has the whole discussion of the economics of policing played out in terms of VPD and you as a senior police leader?

DL: I think there is a fair amount of rhetoric and a bit of hysteria around the notion of the sustainability of policing. The reality is that policing costs, on a per-officer basis, have increased because police unions in Canada have been very successful in getting increases that are higher than the Consumer Price Index and that are higher than the rate of inflation and higher than other unions are getting in the municipalities. That can't go on forever. Those lines are going to have to come closer together.

The other thing that is going on is that police agencies need to work on becoming more efficient. If your per-unit costs are higher, we have to find ways to deliver more. Actually, our percentage of the $1 billion plus municipal budget has averaged around 20% for decades. And the reason is that even though our costs per officer have gone up compared to other employers in the city, our overall costs have not gone up because we have found ways to do more with less. And now we have taken that to the next level and are looking at what else can we do in order to reduce the overall costs of policing and still deliver a high level of service. The Community Safety Officer program and tiered policing is one way to do that as is taking advantage of technology, whether it's CCTV, car license plate scanners, body-worn videos which may make us more efficient in some areas.

CG: In terms of the economics of policing, how do you reverse the down-
       loading onto the police that has been occurring?
DL: That's a hard one. We've advocated at different levels right up to the level of
       health minister that the government needs to put more money into
       the area of mental health. That there should be more resources. We're
       collaborating with the regional health authority to be proactive to
       make certain persons with mental illness are taking their medica-
       tions and receiving the resources they need to avoid being victimized
       and coming in conflict with the justice system. And it's had a major
       impact on their contact with the police. We have so many mentally
       ill people. The government has put new resources into new beds at
       the hospital and in several new residential facilities. We're trying
       to prevent these people from being in crisis. By working with the
       local health authority to go out where they are and to make certain
       that they are taking their medications so they don't get into a cri-
       sis situation. So far, the results from the study cohort of 82 mentally
       ill persons have been promising. There has been a 50% reduction in
       negative contacts with the police and a 60% reduction in Emergency
       Room visits. We've shown that at that level we can have a big impact.

Farther upstream, the police shouldn't be dealing with this group of people; we have so many mentally ill people. You can't go from 4,400 beds in
Riverview (a now-closed mental health facility) to zero beds and not have
an impact when those beds aren't replaced in the community. The government and many people need to get their heads around the fact that there are
people who need to be institutionalized. Not all of them, but hundreds who
require a safe, secure, and humane environment; and not be out wandering
around in the community. We've gone from the 1980s where there were lots
of complaints about how persons with mental illness were treated in institutions and the abuses that occurred to a situation where it was decided to get
rid of those facilities and put them in the community where they would be
supported. But they were not supported in the community. Now, instead of
places that were designed for the mentally ill, they are in places that were
not designed for the mentally ill—prisons. We have way more people who

are mentally ill in prisons than we have in hospitals. They are victimized there; they are victimized out on the street; they victimize others. You have paranoid schizophrenics who are attacking innocent persons on the street. Mentally ill persons are 23 times more likely to be the victim of a crime themselves. We have been clear as a police service in saying that the government needs to do much more to address the needs of persons with mental illness.

And we'll do our part in training our members to deal with persons with mental illness and working with others to ensure that they don't get into a state of crisis where we are going to have to use, in the most extreme cases, deadly force. When you look at the number of police-involved shootings that involve the mentally ill, including suicide by cop; it's a tragedy. There's lots of work going on in that realm but we think that the government needs to do more in dealing with the mentally ill, the homeless, addiction, poverty; those things that drive street-level crime.

CG: What are some of the other sources of challenges for police that challenge your efficiency and the resources in your police service?

DL: Court scheduling was historically a big issue that took up a lot of our officer's time. In recent years, not so much. There are fewer cases going to court, due to the decrease in the crime rate. Also, there are pressures on Crown (the state prosecution) to deal with cases by a plea, which doesn't require our officers to be there.

Competing pressures are new emerging crime trends, including the Internet; from selling stolen bicycles to fraud and cyber-bulling. The legal tools have not kept up with this.

And there have been a series of decisions from the Supreme Court of Canada that present new challenges for the police resource-wise. Those strategies get bumped up in terms of the seriousness of cases in which we will use them. It will have to be a more serious crime because of the resource impacts, whether it's "one party consents," tracking devices, undercover operations, etc.

Those are things that we are going to have to adapt to and the courts will interpret what the acceptable community standards are. We always prefer to have the mind-set of being proactive so that we can control things rather than just reacting; so that we are preventing the worst crimes from happening in the first place. We have a model in which we have high resource intensive projects that are 90 days or so in length; rather than lengthy investigations that drag on for years and that may not result in arrests and convictions, yet which tie up resources. You can spend a lot of time and resources and you have to have a high likelihood of a successful outcome. These days, it's important to look at the return on investment in terms of public safety.

That said, there is a place for long-term organized crime investigations. The question is whether a municipal police department like us should take these on. Perhaps, perhaps not. There is an organized crime agency that has funding and human resources. The question for us is: "where can we have the greatest impact on public safety?" In terms of violence on our streets where we can get the "biggest bang" from those short and medium-term investigations? And to get the word out that Vancouver is not a good place to do crime.

Personal Policing Philosophy

DL: We have really focused on what kind of police department do we really want to be. In terms of our philosophies surrounding policing; some police departments characterize themselves as "Kick Ass, Take Names" organization. Others are "No call too small." We have really focused on our values, including proportionality and being the least intrusive that we can be to achieve our purpose. Real respect for people's rights. You'll see that reflected in our sex worker enforcement guidelines; in our public demonstration guidelines. Saying, as in the case of public protests that we could go in there with sticks flying or we can develop relationships with those people and down the road getting an injunction if we need to. And because of the respect that has been developed, when an injunction comes, there is generally no push-back. Or we could be like some police departments that we've seen that wade in with tear gas and sticks flying and then get mired down in law suits and they have laid the groundwork for even more disputes.

We tried to develop excellence in terms of our actual police work, our technical skills around police work while at the same time building relationships and reducing friction with those who have traditionally been critical of the police. The objective is not to be too defensive; not to get our backs up about it, and to recognize that these people have a voice no matter how uncomfortable it gets. The irony is that when we are criticized, if we actually open our ears and listen, we ask "can we do better?" If you're willing to listen, it can make you a better police agency.

CG: Do you think that over the years the community has come to expect too much of the police or do you think that the community now has a pretty good idea of what your limitations are since you've been so proactive in developing relationships? And in raising red flags on issues such as persons with mental illness? And drawing attention to the fact that it's not just a problem for the police.

DL: I think that there are big portions of the community that are somewhat shocked that most of what our officers spend doing on the front lines is not dealing with crimes or criminal offences; that it's about 25% and the other 75% is social order issues. It's A to Z. People with mental illness, for example. We're not only the agency of last resort, in many instances we're the agency of first resort. I think that the public has an understanding that the police shouldn't necessarily be the agency dealing with all of those issues. But the question is, then "who"?

What the public wants to know is that they are safe and that they are served by a professional, accountable police agency. That we are responsive. Some people have unrealistic demands while others should perhaps have more. When critical events happen, we can either turtle and not accept responsibility; or we can be open and honest and learn what we can and take our lumps; and not wait for someone else to tell us how to do that. It's been mentioned that it's unusual for a police department to do so many internal audits on themselves in order to learn how to be better. There is a price to pay for that because you give people ammunition to criticize you but you have to accept that if you want to be better.

Right now, we think we are doing well with the community, but we don't want to rest on our laurels. Right now, I'm heading up a project to explore the ways in which we can perpetuate our core values and philosophy. How we can institutionalize them at all levels of the organization. Not just me or the Chief Constable. How can we ingrain them? If we care about the organization and want to entrench these values going forward, how do we do that? So we are looking at different entry points, for example, in training members; the promotion process; in management meetings. What are the different entry points and access points for our people that we can constantly reinforce those views? We don't want them to be just words on a piece of paper in a Strategic Plan that gathers dust on the shelf. We are continually reinforcing it in real and practical ways. Even things like training for our Public Safety members for policing demonstrations; changing the name of our Vice Unit, which was a moralistic term, to Counter-Exploitation Unit; and re-focusing their work on viewing sex workers as victims, especially the women who are at the street level and at the highest risk.

There may be resistance to change. When I started the Domestic Violence Unit, I invited the community in to help select the detectives and people were saying, "you are letting other people have a say in who gets selected to this unit?" And I said, "yes." We started that in 1996 and it's been in operation for nearly 20 years and it's totally normalized that we partner with a social service agency, Family Services of Greater Vancouver. And there was a steering committee that involves persons from the community. It's the way we are. We have the same model with Vancouver Coastal Health around our Community Treatment Teams; outreach teams to deal with the mentally ill. It's just normal.

Problems and Successes Experienced

DL: I think a lot of government institutions, including police agencies, are afraid to try big change. The easiest thing to do is to maintain the status quo. We've tried for a number of years to be looking at what else is out there; what is cutting edge. Let's try things and not be afraid to fail. If they don't work, it's better that we tried. Then we'll try something else. It's a more business-oriented model that you can't stand still. You have to be trying different things.

One of the key reasons for our success in crime-fighting in recent years has been the analytic capacity. Back then, we didn't know what we didn't know. We didn't know how much better we could be by having that level of capacity in our analytics. And now it drives so much in our organization, especially around crime-reduction strategies. You've got to have good information. So analytics really underpin our operations.

CG: How much of how the VPD has evolved over the past several decades been the result of external demands on it from the community, legislation, and other drivers; and how much has come from the organization itself in an attempt to stay ahead of the proverbial curve?

DL: That's a good question. It is definitely both of those things. I think that what we have tried to do is to develop sufficient capacities so we can deal with the things we have to respond to, but also get ahead of the curve and be proactive so that we are not just reacting. Police agencies generally have been so 911-oriented (which was a direct result of technology) and call-driven. We tried to stay on top of that and say, "What can we do to stay on top of our crime issues and public safety issues and what can we do differently to be more proactive?" In 2008–2009, we had a gang war on the streets of Vancouver. We had headlines in the paper proclaiming, "9th Shooting in 11 Days." It was terrible. But that was also the point at which we developed the expertise and the capacity and said, "We're not going to solve this problem by solving 35% of the gang murders," which is where the clearance rates were for these crimes because gang murders are so difficult to solve. We're going to be proactive and have our analysts give us the best information they can about who is most likely to go out there and do the shootings and the murders. And we're going to proactively target those people with undercover operations to get them for serious offenses such as firearms and drug trafficking, extortions, and so on, so we can put them in jail for a significant period of time.

Firearms trafficking, extortion, kidnapping, these gang-bangers are doing all of these things. We charged 28 gangsters who were involved in the gang warfare. Nearly all of them were detained prior to trial and nearly all of them either pleaded guilty or were found guilty at trial. And all of a sudden we virtually eliminated gang homicides in Vancouver. We've continued with other projects. In 2012, we had the lowest number of murders in recorded history, with eight. In 2013, it was even lower at six. On my first full year on the job in 1982 we had 41 murders and in 1991 we had 41 murders. We often averaged in the high 20s or low 30s. In other comparable cities, the murder rates are much higher. That is one of the benefits of having the capacity in analytics and well-trained people who have developed expertise in doing very proactive investigations. These are complemented by other units such as our Firearms Interdiction Team and programs like BarWatch and RestaurantWatch, which focus on known gang members who may be in Vancouver. This program is a collaborative effort of the Vancouver Police Department and business owners, wherein persons who are known to police as gang-involved can be removed from premises by police officers. This program has resulted in a significant reduction in gang-related shootings in the city. All of these initiatives are focused on making it uncomfortable as possible to be a gangster in the city of Vancouver.

Theory and Practice

CG: What should be the relationship between theory and practice and the relationship between the "theory builders," that is, academics and police practitioners?

DL: When those theories are evidence-based and have a practical application, we would not be meeting our obligations as professionals if we didn't inform ourselves and take advantage of quality research. So we certainly pay attention to theories around crime causation and effective strategies, whether it's hot spot policing, the importance of police legitimacy and community engagement, or evaluation of educational programs. We have partnered with academics on many issues to develop best practices, including dealing with mental health issues, deployment regimes, predictive analysis, and many others. So in my view, the relationship between theory and practice should be a two-way process in which we benefit from quality research, but research benefits from the extraordinary access we can provide to data and experiences that academics otherwise wouldn't be able to take advantage of.

For example, right now we are in a research partnership with academics looking at the relationship between welfare cheque distribution patterns and crime and disorder. We have a common hypothesis that the once-a-month cheque distribution results in increased victimization of marginalized welfare recipients and increased disorder created by the frenzy of the "Mardi Gras" drug buying frenzy that occurs. We want to know whether certain crime types can be reduced by spreading welfare cheque distribution dates across the month, thereby confounding the drug dealers who hover around ATMs waiting at 12:01 a.m. for marginalized welfare recipients to withdraw their automatically deposited cheques, among other undesirable impacts. Sometimes research suffers from not being informed by the real world experiences of policing, so there is a mutual benefit for police to collaborate with academics on matters of mutual interests. Most police agencies don't have the capacity to do rigorous research and so partnering with academics creates a win-win.

CG: Is there any one theoretical perspective that has informed your view of policing and your role as a police leader?

DL: I would say that it is a combination of theoretical perspectives that collectively add up to the knowledge that crime and criminals are the product of a highly complex set of factors and that people don't get involved in crime in a vacuum. Family dysfunction, abuse, addiction, alcohol abuse, a lack of good role models, mental health issues, and many other are all in the mix. As police, we need to deal with both the downstream and, to the extent we can, the upstream drivers of crime, remembering always what Peel said about effective policing, that is, that it is measured not by our activity but by the absence of crime.

CG: What kind of research do you find most useful for practice?

DL: One example is evaluation of various policing programs. For example, we are experimenting with "tiered policing" and we are working collaboratively with academics and our police union to evaluate the impact across a variety of factors of deploying uniformed "community safety officers" with lesser training and responsibility than fully trained and equipped police officers. Our theory is that we can provide a better service to the public around low priority/low risk incidents and better support for our police officers in delivering a high-quality service in a more economically sustainable fashion than requiring an expensive, highly trained police officer to attend to every incident or duty. Carefully designed research will deliver the answer and it would be difficult and less credible without the involvement of external, independent researchers from the academic world.

So that's an example of research that has a very practical application: Should we continue with this pilot program in terms of value for money or not, rather than relying on anecdotal information? Another example is the cutting edge research on predictive policing. Because of the analytical capacity we've developed in the VPD—at the urging of independent consultants from academia—and the relationships we have with those doing policing research, we are at the forefront of implementing predictive policing technology that has the potential to help us make significant strides in reducing property crime within existing resources.

CG: What could theory builders do to make their "products" more useful to you as a police leader?

DL: The best thing they could do is develop their research and "products" in an iterative fashion, with theories being informed by practice and developed incrementally drawing on our experience and data so that the best, most practical products can be developed, whether it is policing strategies, new technology, or new uses for existing technology. Body worn cameras are part of the next wave of technology in policing and some of the challenges aren't the actual technology, it is the myriad of social, legal, and privacy issues that are implicated, requiring a systematic approach to developing policies and practices to guide HOW the technology can best be used to improve policing, improve police accountability, and do it in a way that is respectful of privacy rights and in a way that enhances good policing, rather than discourage it.

Transnational Relations

CG: How does your police service respond to transnational crime? And how does it decide how to allocate your resources, given that there are federal agencies with mandates in this area and other specialty units outside of the VPD?

DL: We have tried to address these challenges in a number of ways. We participate in organizations that have a broader mandate. We have investigators, for example, who have recently been in Belgium and South Africa; they are seconded officers working within a provincial and federal policing framework. We provide the officers and they provide the funding. We do pay a price in that we give away good officers for a few years. But then we get them and their expertise and experience back in the department. We also have an organized crime unit in the department that serves as the conduit for information that comes from the front-line officers. There is a lot of original informant information that comes to officers at the street level that would never make it directly to specialized units. It's important to have mechanisms and processes in place to make certain we can receive and process this information. To make certain that that information is cultivated and routed to the right places by the right people.

Democratic Policing

CG: How do you view the role of the police in a democratic society? How do you view the potential conflicts that might exist between the need to ensure public safety and security while at the same time ensuring the rights of citizens?

DL: There are often situations where different rights collide. For example, the Canadian Charter of Rights and Freedoms protects free speech and the right of assembly, but not without limits, as set out in s.1. of this Chapter. In Vancouver, we regularly deal with demonstrations and protests, ranging from "Critical Mass," which is a large number of cyclists who obstruct traffic on their route to advance a certain agenda once a month, to various groups that protest on the grounds of the Vancouver Art Gallery because of its prominent location. With respect to Critical Mass, many citizens whose commute is interfered with have a first reaction that we ought to be strictly enforcing the law. Well, we are dealing with relatively minor traffic offences but to actually enforce the law when hundreds of cyclists are involved would require a massive and expensive police response and might very well require the use of force. In that situation, we would generally manage it by making the ride as safe as possible and prevent conflicts. The exercise of free speech will trump the traffic laws requiring certain behavior, particularly given the disproportional police response that would be required to safely intervene.

We take the same approach with a yearly "marihuana smoke-in" on April 11 in the grounds of the Vancouver Art Gallery. If we were to try to enforce the law against simple possession of marihuana on an international day of protest, we would likely create a situation far worse than we had in the first place, particularly considering community values and attitudes towards possession of small amounts of marihuana (in Canada the majority believe it should be legalized or at least decriminalized). What guides us is the law, our values as an organization, which include responding proportionately with the least intrusive measures necessary to provide public safety, and our Public Demonstration Guidelines, which we put for all to see on our website—that's a tool to educate the public about why we do what we do.

When the Occupy movement was in full swing several years ago, we were criticized—especially because there was a mayoral race going on—for not taking more aggressive enforcement action. In the end, we encouraged the City to obtain an injunction which the protesters respected and we safely resolved and defused the protest without arrests or violence. The public paid a price in terms of essentially the inconvenience of traffic being blocked sometimes and the protest site not being available for others—we think that was a reasonable price in the context. We prefer our philosophy, as opposed to some American jurisdictions who are still today mired in lawsuits because they took a very heavy-handed approach to Occupy demonstrations. We all need to learn from the lessons of the past and respond proportionately where rights collide unless there is violence involved—then we must act immediately.

CG: How does a police service resolve those potential conflicts? How does a police service attempt to balance these two, often competing demands?

DL: We focus on our priority, which is to provide public safety. We have clear policies in place, which we communicate. We attempt to build relationships—to make friends before we need them—so that we're able to attempt to defuse conflicts, and to be seen as neutral. In our system of policing inherited from the UK, where the Chief is only beholden to the law when it comes to operational matters, that is, he does not report to the mayor or city manager and has operational independence, we are able to make decisions that in other systems might not be possible.

CG: As a police leader, how do you view the challenges of policing in a democratic society?

DL: Well, as Churchill said, "Democracy is the worst form of government, except for all those other forms that have been tried from time to time." Democracy can be messy. In Canada, we are among the luckiest people in the world to live in a safe, democratic country where we are relatively safe from both criminals and the oppressive types of government we see in so many other places in the world. So I consider myself unbelievably fortunate to have the challenges of policing in a democratic society, and to navigate between legitimate but competing interests where rights sometimes collide. It's a challenge but a privilege.

Looking Ahead

DL: There will always be issues with violent crime and we have to stay on top of that. But if we are going to make any significant improvements in property crime, which has always been a big challenge for us due to our high addiction population, then we'll need to continue to exert pressure upstream: to deal with mental illness, homelessness, and poverty. We are not going to make any headway in dealing with stolen property unless we deal with the underlying factors.

Predictive policing is designed to help address our high property crime rates, although it won't address the underlying driver of addiction. This will tell us where the crimes are going to happen so we can either prevent them or capture the person and have a higher solve rate. However, we know that we are part of a system and that, no matter how well we do, if there aren't others who are pulling their weight—whether it is the courts or Crown—or those responsible for mentally ill or drug addicted, we're not going to be successful. Judges sometimes need to impose sentences that are long enough for the person to get detoxed, to deal with their addictions, and to learn some skills and get their life together. We all need to be way more creative about that.

I am really interested to see how we use technology to address these issues. The technology genie is out of the bottle. The sky is the limit as to what we can do. There are all sorts of ways that technology can be used that we probably haven't yet thought about. There are so many more things that we could use technology for; but we need to find the right balance between privacy issues and the need for public safety. Technology is far more cost-effective than deploying officers in some instances. It's been used to such great effect.

So much has changed in policing but one thing that has not changed in my 33 years in this field is that when I go out with patrol officers not only are the scenarios the same, but some of the people are the same! They say, "I remember you." Human pathology has not changed. People get drunk and do drugs and engage in domestic disputes and fights. It's the human condition. And that has not changed. They have found new ways to harass each other by using texting and the Internet. You still require that human interaction and problem-solving to address these issues.

The officers I learned from were such good communicators. They did not feel the need to resort to tools often. Now we have Tasers and pepper spray and computers and handhelds. We have a generation where it is natural for them to resort to technology. When I hear younger officers say they are glad to have the Taser to deal with a person on transit, I wonder "how did we manage before we had those tools"? When I was hired, officers generally had only a baton and a revolver and they didn't often use them. They knew that their most powerful weapon was their voice—communication.

Now, in policing generally, there is sometimes a tendency to resort to the tools. There are definitely officers out there who "get it," but I would say that we have more officers who are inclined to rely on their technology. On the other hand, they do use their technology in effective ways. They have iPhones and share photos of suspects. When I was in patrol many years ago, we kept the picture of a suspect in our hat—now this information is available on their in-car laptops they're sharing it with their iPhones. So they are using technology to solve crimes.

Conclusion

Deputy Chief Constable Doug LePard brought three decades of policing experience in the Vancouver Police Department to the interview. His philosophy of policing and his commitment to best practice, evidence-based service is reflected in his responses to the interviewer's questions. Among the themes of his responses was an organizational commitment to developing officers to be the best they can be, establishing strong relationships with the various communities in Vancouver, and collaborating with other agencies in addressing issues of mental illness, homelessness, addiction and poverty, the "upstream" drivers of crime.

The examples that were provided illustrate the innovative approach to policing a dynamic, growing Pacific Rim city. Notable in his responses were a focus on community safety and a willingness to listen to criticism and to learn from less than positive experiences. Deputy Chief Constable LePard's responses captured the challenges facing police services in the early twenty-first century while providing insights into how one police service strive to engrain and sustain core values that will contribute to a high quality of life in the city.

In January 2016, Deputy Chief Constable LePard was appointed as the Chief Officer, South Coast British Columbia Transportation Authority Police Service, the regional police service for the transit system in the Greater Vancouver area.

Horacio Alberto Gimenez, Buenos Aires City Chief of the Metropolitan Police, Argentina

2

INTERVIEWED BY
SEBASTIÁN SAL

Contents

Introduction

The Argentine Republic suffered many changes in its political map between 1930 and 1983, going from democratic governments to dictatorial ones. These political changes affected not only people's human rights but also the scope of police activities.

The last dictatorial government—commonly known as "Junta Militar"— was in power from 1976 to 1983, after which the government switched to a democratic one. The "Junta Militar" consisted of members of the Argentine Army, Navy, and Air Force. Many civil rights were suppressed during that time in order to control the population. The Police Forces were one of the most important national institutions which collaborated with the dictatorial government. No matter how many years of democratic governments Argentina has had since that time, people still associate Police Forces with military control and repression.

Sadly, even in times of democracy, many police agents have been involved in police brutality and corruption. Moreover, it is widely held that drug dealers and "pimps" are protected by police officers; or worse, that the Police Chief is or was in charge of illicit acts. As a consequence, almost nobody today really trusts, likes, or relies on the police. Nevertheless, feelings and attitudes change when people are in need of protection from crime. Obviously in these cases people look for police help and really appreciate and are thankful when police officers perform their duties. There is, then, a kind of schizophrenic relationship with the police. On the one hand people do not want to be controlled by them. On the other hand, they often ask for more protection and control of crime on the streets and in public areas.

Argentina is a Federal State. That means that each province has its own Police Department. In addition, it has a Federal Police, which is commanded by the National Administration, in other words, it works at national level.

The City of Buenos Aires is a Federal Territory and it was protected by the Federal Police until 1996, when the City became an "Autonomous City" with similar rights to the provinces. Due to that, the City of Buenos Aires was, after some time, allowed to have its own Police Department: the "Metropolitan Police." It was created in 2009 by the current Mayor of the City of Buenos Aires, Mauricio Macri. Currently, Mayor Macri is the leader of a political party, which is part of the "opposition" to the National Administration. It is because of this situation, among others, that there are certain tensions between the Metropolitan Police and the Federal Police.

At the beginning, the staff of the Metropolitan Police was recruited from the Federal Police. Officers decided to become part of the Metropolitan force because it offered better salaries and better opportunities. Nowadays, the City of Buenos Aires is protected by two different forces: the Metropolitan Police and the Federal Police. Outside the City—in the suburban area—there is another jurisdiction, with yet another Police Department (The Buenos Aires Province Police). That means that within a small territory there are three different Police Forces, that sometimes work together with the same objectives and sometimes they do not—for different reasons.

The current Chief of the Metropolitan Police is Horacio Alberto Gimenez. He started his career at the Federal Police Department in 1972, resigning in 2011 to work for the Metropolitan Police. His first assignment in this force was as a Liaison between the Ministry of Security of the City of Buenos Aires and the Judiciary Power of the City. During his almost 40 years of service at the Federal Police he had worked in several police units: the Infantry Corps, the Department of Vehicles Control, as Chief of Bodyguards of the Senate President, as Advisor on security matters at the Ministry of Internal Affairs, as Chief of the Security Department of National Institutions, as General Director of Internal Security Office (from 2005 to 2007), and as

Superintendent of the Complex Crimes Office (from 2008 to 2010). He was appointed Chief of the Metropolitan Police on December 2011.

The interview took place in the Chief's office on May 20, 2013 at the Headquarters of the Metropolitan Police. The Headquarters are located in the southern part of the City (close to the Boca Juniors Stadium).

Career

SS: Why did you choose to be a police officer? What was your motivation when you were a teenager for being a cop?

HG: There were many things. To start with, it is important to take into account that it was a family thing, because my father was a Police Officer too. He worked as Chief Inspector for the Federal Police. For me, it was something common to be surrounded by police matters. Besides, I looked up on him.

SS: That is a good reason for choosing your career…

HG: Yes, but it was not the only one. When I was a teenager I watched many TV shows in which police officers were heroes. Being a police officer could be a life of adventure. It seemed to me that to be a police officer would be spectacular and that you could always be solving problems and catching criminals. You know, the good people always defeat the bad guys. For this reason I wanted to be a police officer; and I still do. I am proud of that.

SS: No matter that real life is not like the movies?

HG: Real life is harder and good people do not always win, but it is great to be there when it happens.

SS: As far as I know, you started to work for the Metropolitan Police on May 2011, and in December 2011 you were appointed Chief of the Metropolitan Police.

HG: That is right. December 14, 2011.

SS: The Metropolitan Police is still quite a small Police Department isn't it?

HG: We started with 500 agents in 2009, and nowadays we are 3800 police officers and six hundred 600 civilians.

Changes Experienced

SS: What do you think have been the most important changes that have occurred in the Metropolitan Police since you were appointed Chief?

HG: Well, in my opinion it is that the citizens of the City are starting to realize that the Metropolitan Police are on the streets, that they can be seen. At the beginning, in 2009, we had very few officers for a population of more than two million people. Most of them came from other forces, such as the Federal Police, the "Prefectura" or "Gendarmería." Nowadays we have our "own-made" police officers, who have received a degree from our Metropolitan Police School (Instituto de Formación de la Policía). At the beginning, we focused our duties on just one neighborhood, but little by little we are spreading our range. We started to work in the City center, but our objective is to be close to all the citizens in order to get their trust and confidence.

SS: Do you think that people trust the Metropolitan Police more than on the Federal Police?

HG: Yes, because we are a different and a new police force. We had a fresh start. Besides, to get the trust of the common citizen is one of our most important aims. We are working on that, investing time and resources, and emphasizing this to our new officers. Trust and confidence are a round trip and should be earned. It is not a one way thing. That is why we are focusing our duties on community work, on helping the citizens in their everyday issues. We are trying to gain back the confidence and respect of the people. The main idea for doing that is that citizens should know and trust their "corner police officer" as it was many years ago. When I was a child, everybody knew the police officer who was in charge of the block, by his name. That makes a police officer not just a person in uniform that controls and helps you, but a person, or better, a friend. And a person is close to the people because he or she is one of them. Police officers are ordinary people who live, breathe, and eat as everybody else in the city. We have to listen to the people.

Personal Policing Philosophy

SS: What do you think is/should be the role and functions of the police?

HG: In my opinion, the mission of any police force is to prevent crimes, to protect people, and property. Besides in our role, we are auxiliaries of the judicial system, in my case, of the City of Buenos Aires. Moreover, we have to be close to the people in order to hear them and know their needs.

SS: What should be done about un-policed areas?

HG: In the Buenos Aires City Areas there are no un-policed areas. The city is divided in areas that are in control of the Metropolitan Police or the Federal Police. In the areas in which our force is in charge, we count on the help of the residents who are involved in security forums. We are currently working in different neighborhoods such as Saavedra, Villa Pueyrredon, Coghlan, Villa Urquiza, Agronomy, Paternal, Parque Chas, Chacarita, Villa Ortuzar, Villa Crespo, Pompeii, Parque Patricios, Barracas, La Boca, and in the Bank Area, commonly known as "the City" or "downtown."

SS: What facilitates/hinders good relations with the community, with government, with other criminal justice organizations, with non-state security providers such as community groups, and commercial enterprises?

HG: We work with the Judiciary Power of the City of Buenos Aires helping in any procedure and in full cooperation. To facilitate the investigations our department is divided in different offices or areas depending on the type of crime. We have security cameras in the district and offices to care for victims of gender violence. We allow full access to prosecutors to these areas. In addition, we have an auditorium with capacity for a hundred people, available for the use of residents of the district. In each police station we have a "panic button system" receiver to help victims of domestic violence as soon as it is required. We are also aware of the social problems that some people face. In this way, we have done social work, helping with the "Cold Program" which provided food and shelter to the homeless during wintertime. This was done by working together with other government agencies such as the Ministry of Public Space and the Social Development and Health Department. For business protection we have regular meetings with the members of the Chamber of Commerce of the City in order to listen to their ideas and suggestions for improvements in safety.

SS: What should be the priorities of the police service?

HG: Right now our priority is to be present on the streets in order to prevent crimes and to do special services such as ambulance escorts, tourist assistance, and control of the public transport such as the new Metrobus and underground lines.

Problems and Successes

SS: What are the problems that people most often complain about? What are the most common crimes in the city?

HG: The huge problem nowadays is violence, the violence that takes place after crimes. Twenty years ago the situation was very different. You could be robbed, but the thieves only got, for example, your sneakers, and then they fled. You were not afraid of suffering any physical damage. Nowadays, that has changed. Thieves not only rob you. After doing that they may shoot you. Many times these thieves or burglars are acting under the influence of drugs or alcohol. Crimes are much more violent.

SS: Is it very difficult to keep criminals in jail during the judicial process?

HG: This is part of the problem. When we arrest people the Judiciary Power releases the criminals almost the same day, no matter what kind of evidence we have. To our understanding, we have provided the Judiciary Power with enough evidence for keeping criminals in jail. But this is not a simple issue. I mean, it is not a fault of Judges or Prosecutors. Maybe some laws should be changed. Anyway, and as a consequence, criminals do not take the possibility of being in jail seriously. They do not care about it because they consider this as something almost impossible. The judicial system allows them to think that way. It seems that the only punishment that they receive is the criminal (judicial) process itself. Nothing else. That means no punishment at all. It is difficult for us to work without the help of the Judges. It seems that we cannot do anything about that, but this is not an accurate diagnosis. We have worked hard in order to help the Judiciary Power. Prosecutors' offices are located in the same building that as the "Comunas." The idea is to speed up the prosecution process by working together in order to achieve our goals. In my opinion, the judiciary system needs new tools for reforming many situations that hinder the process. It is known that punitive rules are passed after new crimes have emerged. That is why criminal organizations change their *modus operandi* with incredible speed.

SS: What about public places?

HG: Another common issue for people is security in public places. We suffer from it every day in the City. The "okupas" is a serious problem, too. Everybody knows and has seen what happened at the San Martin Theater. The "okupas" kicked, insulted, hurled rocks at the police and tried to put the theater on fire. They destroyed many expensive and unique art sculptures. Some police officers were hurt. But police officers were not allowed to react to this entire situation, because if the police had reacted, using force, some media organizations would have said that the police were using repressive power without any reason or cause. But if we do not do anything, the same press would say that we are useless.

SS: Is it difficult to win the support of the public when it appears that criminals have more rights than ordinary people and that they are not being punished.

HG: Yes, sometimes it is difficult, but anyway, we are trying our best no matter what the politicians or media say. Besides, through our own press department and social networks we are trying to keep the people informed, showing them the full story, not a fragmented and partial version of the situation.

SS: What personal achievements are you most proud of?

HG: I am especially proud of the way we handle gender crimes. We have developed a very good policy and response as regards gender violence crimes. Currently, we have under our control about five hundred cases of women that have suffered these kinds of crimes. We have provided them with "panic buttons" that are similar to a small cell phone. They carry it in their purses or their pockets and, if something happens, they just need to press a button. We are able to track the "panic devices" with a GPS. We recognize every device by its own number, and we can be at the place in which the victim is in a very short time. Further, the victim can talk using the device, explaining to us what is happening. If she cannot speak, we are still able to hear what is going on. When the victim presses the button, a microphone on the device is activated and we can listen to what is going on. That allows us to assess how urgent our intervention should be.

SS: How do you decide on the allocation of the "panic button device"?

HG: It is not our decision. The decision is made at the Prosecutor's office. The Prosecutor studies the case and if he considers it appropriate to provide someone with a panic button for protection, he contacts us in order to inform us about the case and gives us the instructions to deliver the device and to do the surveillance.

SS: The City has many surveillance cameras in the street. Do the Metropolitan Police control all of them?

HG: Almost all the street cameras belong to the Metropolitan Police, and I am very proud of that. It is a huge achievement for us to have two thousand surveillance cameras around the City. We have a very good system that allows us to detect any suspicious situation.

SS: Do the cameras allow you to prevent crime?

HG: The cameras have multiple purposes. First, they serve for prevention. When criminals realize that a camera is there, they avoid the place because they know that they are recorded. Second, they serve for protection. Cameras are live, that means that if we see a crime we can inform immediately the units that are close to where the crime is taking place. We share this kind of information with the Federal Police in order to ensure that there is always someone close to the place where the action is happening. Third, if we are late, and the crime was committed, the records of the cameras allow us to identify criminals and to provide evidence to the Prosecutors.

SS: Many people also complain about Drugs and Illegal Prostitution. Are the Metropolitan Police doing something in these areas?

HG: Yes. We have jurisdiction over all kinds of crimes that take place in the City of Buenos Aires. Regarding illegal prostitution, we have done a very good job in dismantling a net of pedophiles which operated using the Internet. It was a national job, because the net has widely spread across the entire country. Our cybercrime department is one of the best in the area. It is a small department with few agents, but highly specialized.

SS: And drug crimes?

HG: We have helped many Federal Courts in drug smuggling cases. Sometimes the cases start in the City but their branches extend all over the country and also abroad. We collaborate not only with our cybercrime department but also with our police officers in the field. Many Federal Courts are asking us for our help in doing search warrants on drug related crimes. It seems that they are recognizing our professionalism and expertise. I am happy about that.

SS: Do you collaborate with many other police forces around the world?

HG: I have been very lucky and I have attended many international seminars and worked with other Police forces. For example, on July 2006 I was appointed Chief of the "Operativo Comando Unificado" of the Mercosur. I worked as a Chief of Security at many international political summits in South America. Besides, in 2008 I worked as Liaison Officer between the Argentinean Ministry of Justice and the American Embassy in relation to the Anti-Terrorism Program. I have had the privilege of studying in Paris and Lyon, France, about the new systems for recognizing and identifying people through facial, fingerprint or tattoo recognizing methods—a new science called biometrics. I was also invited by the New York Police Department and the Washington Police to study systems for reading car plates in movement. I also attended the Senior Crisis Management Seminar at the American University in Washington, DC.

Theory and Practice

SS: Would you say that theory is an important part in your job?

HG: Of course. It is not only important but necessary. I have learnt a lot from those seminars and exchanges. I expect that the people who are working at the Metropolitan Police to have the same opportunities, because theory helps decisions at the moment of the practice. They are complementary.

SS: Do you consider that the police officers of the Metropolitan Police know enough theory?

HG: At the Metropolitan Police School we give our students many lectures on both theory and practice. We have to provide them with the necessary tools for facing the current problems that affect society. Criminals evolve every day and crimes get more complex.

SS: Do you evaluate your staff?

HG: At the Metropolitan Police School we evaluate them not only about theory—law, human rights, and psychology—but also regarding their physical and psychological health. We do so twice a year. Police officers need to be in good shape and with an adequate state of mind. They have to go through a physical and psychological test for being on duty. We have to train them for taking action in critical situations and staying "cool."

SS: It is pretty difficult to keep calm in some situations...

HG: Yes, you can see how people react in the street. For instance, when two cars crash, the drivers usually get out of their vehicles and start to complain, to argue, and even sometimes, to fight. For sure, both drivers have their insurance policy that will cover the damages, so why are they mad? It is human nature. Police agents sometimes are under incredible pressure and they have to learn how to react.

Transnational and Inter-Agency Relations

SS: When you were at the seminar or working with other police forces, you exchanged points of view with your international colleagues. What do you envy most about other police departments?

HG: (Laughter). Many things... I think I envy most the technology. Some countries invest huge amounts of money on technology, and that investment is really important for providing internal and external security to and for a jurisdiction. Sometimes, I also envy how, in some countries, prosecutors and police officers work together in order to achieve a common goal. In Buenos Aires City, we work closely with the Prosecutors but, in my opinion, not as much as in others countries. We have to work in those fields a little more. Besides, we have to learn more about how to work with the police in different jurisdictions or countries. In the end, we all have the same purpose: to provide more security to the people, to prevent crimes and to arrest criminals.

SS: What technological tools do you need most?

HG: Sometimes simple things are needed. For example, we do not have a criminal record unified national database. We have access to the National Registry of Criminal Records, but sometimes the system does not provide the full information. The National Registry only informs about the criminal records that happened during the last ten years, and if more is needed a Judge's authorization is necessary.

SS: What about communication with other Police Forces?

HG: Well, we share the same radio frequency—in almost all the situations— with the Federal Police and the Police of the Province of Buenos Aires. This is really useful, because many crimes committed in the Buenos Aires City were performed by people who live in the suburban area, where we do not have jurisdiction. This system has allowed the Police of the Province of Buenos Aires to catch many criminals when they were running away from the City. Working well and together increases the confidence, trust, and reliability among police forces.

SS: What do you think that other Police Departments might envy the Metropolitan Police for?

HG: (Laughter)...It is difficult to say...I think that, since we are a very new police force, we have the possibility to be very meticulous in choosing people for our Metropolitan Police School. We evaluate each application very carefully, and we prepare these students very well before giving them a degree and sending them onto the streets...

SS: And what happens when they are in the streets?

HG: When they are on the streets we continue controlling them, maybe even more closely. We are still a small Police Force. I know personally almost all the police agents of the Metropolitan Police. Besides, we are really interested in knowing every one of them in order to bring them any personal support that might be necessary.

SS: Could you give me an example?

HG: We are aware that many of our police officers live in the suburbs of the Buenos Aires City. We do not like that. We would prefer our police officers to live in the City for many reasons, but mainly because, if they live here, they will feel the City as their own home, creating in this way a deeper bond with their duties. If it is your home you will take more care about everything. To accomplish the moving of our police officers from the suburbs to the City, we have made some agreements with the Bank of the City of Buenos Aires in order to get cheap home loans for them.

Democratic Policing

SS: What do you see as the key elements of democratic policing?

HG: I think that working with the community is the best way to democratize the police power. Dialogue is the key. In addition, we have to work as mediators in some conflicts between neighbors. We realize that we have to impose our authority without showing weakness, but without being rude or violent. I emphasize the use of dialogue and mediation. A key element is to exert the minimum force necessary to halt the misconduct that was causing the commission of a crime or misdemeanor.

SS: Is corruption or brutality an issue in the Metropolitan Police?

HG: We have received different types of complaints involving Metropolitan Police officers, but fortunately very few ones. Some of them are related to alleged crimes, others with administrative issues. If one our officers is accused of committing a crime, we seek immediate intervention by the Criminal Justice. We are not allowed to deal with it internally, and I think that this kind of procedure creates transparency in the force, sending a clear message to our officers and to the population. If the complaint is a serious one, we order a preventive suspension of duties for the officer involved until the situation is clarified. If the officer is considered guilty, we remove him from the Metropolitan Police. We spend a lot of time instructing our officers on Ethics and Human Rights in order to avoid this disgusting situation.

SS. Do you have an internal accountability office?

HG: We do not have an internal accountability office. We are controlled by an external accountability office that is managed by the City of Buenos Aires Ministry of Justice. If one of our officers commits an administrative fault, we have to inform this external office. The external accountability office is also controlled by an NGO. As you can see, we have many eyes over us. But I think it is better that way.

SS: Are the mass media and politicians very critical of the Metropolitan Police? Are they always looking for something that could stain your office?

HG: I prefer not to mix political issues or what the media say with the Metropolitan Police. We pay attention to every opinion and different points of view that can help us to improve our work.

SS: Some mass media and some politicians from political parties opposed to the current Mayor of the City say that the Metropolitan Police are the Mayor's police department. Is there any truth in that?

HG: Yes, I am aware of that charge. But we are the police of all the citizens of Buenos Aires, not the police of any political party, no matter who is or will be the Mayor of Buenos Aires. The purpose of the Metropolitan Police is to provide the population of the city with its own police department that is controlled by the same population by means of the City Courts and the Ministry of Justice of the City.

SS: Do criticisms—made by citizens, politicians, or mass media—affect the perception of the people about the police force?

HG: It depends on the complaints, if they are true or false ones. If the grounds of the complaints are true, it helps us to improve the quality of our service. But if the complaints are false, or were made in "bad faith," they can create confusion. We are doing our best. We have had some corruption cases, but they affect a minimum proportion of our officers. It is our duty to show the people that corrupt officers are only a small proportion of our police force. It is not our policy to hide officer misconduct. If we want to get back the confidence of the city population we have to be transparent.

SS: Could you give me some examples of actions taken by the Metropolitan Police that people support?

HG: As you know, a few months ago, the City suffered an incredible and rare flood because of an extraordinary storm. The climate is changing, no doubt about it. Our officers collaborated with "Defensa Civil" in order to help people to leave their houses to avoid the flood and to save some of their properties. We also transported many people to hospitals and shelters. We were there where the people needed us most, on the same side of the people.

SS: What levels of public support does the police service have?

HG: I think that we have support from the community. Besides we are fortunate to have administrative and legislative support in order to carry our duties in the City of Buenos Aires.

SS: And do the people show you their recognition?

HG: Yes, that is the most rewarding thing. We are here to work for the people and we really like it when people show their appreciation. It is a good thing and sometimes needed. Besides, it helps us to improve our feedback to the people. Everybody likes to do things that could help people and be recognized for that. It is in our nature, and when it happens we reaffirm that we are doing a good job. I read an article that reported a recent survey which showed that the most rewarding jobs, the ones that provide most satisfaction for people are Firemen and Parish Priests. Firemen and Parish Priests feel a real gratification in doing their jobs, and I think it is because people recognize their work immediately. But the police field is different. Investigations usually take time and in many cases the success only shows in the long term.

SS: How do you convey that to your police officers?

HG: I try every day to instill in every officer of the Metropolitan Police that we have to do our best, and that in this way, professional and personal recognition in our work will follow. We are not looking for it, but it is gratifying when someone recognizes the work we are doing and the efforts that we are making. And it is starting to happen. We think that it will take time, but if we continue in this way, we will finally change the perception that most people have about the Police Forces. Police officers should be happy and proud for being police officers. We have a long road to walk ahead, but I consider that this is the only way to strengthen the police institution. We have to take care of our officers, stay close to them, and help them when they have any problems.

SS: Positive perceptions about police officers will presumably increase application to the Metropolitan Police School. How many new police officers do you expect to have at the end of the year?

HG: We expect 600 new officers to get their degrees from the Metropolitan School.

SS: And will they be assigned to work in a street patrol?

HG: Possibly. People need to see more police agents on the street. That helps to prevent crimes. Prevention is one of the most important things for getting a safer City. Citizens need to feel safe. We have to make Buenos Aires a safe city again. Some areas are pretty safe, but others are not. We have to be there, collaborating with the Federal Police and other police forces. Little by little we are getting more presence on the streets.

Looking Ahead

SS: What are the most likely developments you see happening?

HG: We will have new police stations in the new neighborhoods in which we will work in a near future. The total coverage of the City by the Metropolitan Police is something that will happen for sure. And we will have to incorporate the Underground Police Department. Our Police Department will grow with new police agents, some of them "new ones," from our Police Institute and some others that will come from other similar forces such as Federal Police and the Gendarmerie. The last ones will also have to receive specific training at our Police Institute, no matter how experienced they would be.

SS: What would you like to see happening?

HG: I would like to see a coordinated action, with no disputes, with the National Government who control the Federal Police. It is my desire that the Metropolitan Police will finally have enough police to cover all the areas of Buenos Aires City, making the City a very safe place, as it once was.

SS: Thank you for your time.

Conclusion

I was surprised during the interview. I was accustomed to dealing with Chief Police Officers when I worked at a criminal court. That is why I expected to find a "hard cop." Instead I found not only a trained man but also an instructed man, one who seems more like the CEO of an international corporation than a Police Chief. Horacio Gimenez knows how to express his ideas and clearly he seems equipped for his job. He has experience on the streets and concerning theoretical issues, plus an international background. Further, it seems that he understands politicians and has an accurate idea of what his role is. Maybe, finally, Police Forces are starting to change in Argentina.

Glossary

Prefectura: a Naval prefecture for controlling river and marine traffic. It is similar to the Coast Guard in the United States of America.
Gendarmería: a National Border Police Department.
Metrobus: an exclusive express lane for buses that cross the city from North to South.
Comunas: the Guildhall offices.
Okupas: People who occupy public places or abandoned places illegally.
Defensa civil: a Civil Institution that coordinates different forces; for example, firemen, MDs, ambulances, in emergency situations. It could be translated as an Emergency Squadron Civil Defense Brigade.

Jon Murphy, Chief Constable of Merseyside Police, UK

INTERVIEWED BY DAVID LOWE

Contents

Introduction

Provincial policing in England and Wales was formed in the 1830s with numerous local police forces, but from 1948, there have been a series of restructuring programs of the provincial forces where the number of forces in the country has been reduced. The last restructuring of provincial policing took place in 1974, when Merseyside Police was created after merging Liverpool and Bootle Constabulary, part of Lancashire Constabulary and Cheshire Constabulary. Serving a population of 1.4 million people, Merseyside Police is one of the UK's largest police forces. The force area consists mainly of the urban areas of the city of Liverpool together with Bootle, St. Helens, Southport, Kirkby, Huyton, Birkenhead, Wallasey, and New Brighton. Sitting on the banks of the River Mersey, Liverpool has been and is one of the UK's major ports. Its capacity and importance as a port grew during the Industrial Revolution (1780s–1830s) especially due to the textile industry in the north of England. With it being a long established port, Liverpool has one of the oldest Chinese communities in the United Kingdom, along with other established ethnic and national communities. For example, during the Irish Potato Famine in 1847, a large number of Irish citizens came over to Liverpool so as to emigrate to North America. In fact, many stayed in Liverpool, settling in the north of the city and forming one of the largest Irish Catholic communities in Britain. During the interview, Jon Murphy discusses how the residents of Merseyside have a village mentality, which is one of the insularity from the rest of the United Kingdom. It is seen in the residents' pride in displaying Merseyside's uniqueness and individuality, especially within England.

A structured form of policing in the United Kingdom can be traced to the former Home Secretary, Sir Robert Peel, who created the Metropolitan Police force to serve the greater London area in 1825. Based on a local policing model, where the police were seen as local citizens in uniform serving their own community, thereby policing with the consent of the public it policed, this is also referred to as the Anglo-Saxon model of policing. This is the model of policing which Jon Murphy is discussing in the interview when he introduces Peel's principles of policing. This model of policing was rolled out across England and Wales from the late 1820s into the 1830s. In the area that now forms Merseyside Police, there were a number of small police forces. For example, Liverpool City Police, St Helens Borough Police, Bootle Borough Police, and Birkenhead Borough Police, among many others. All of these forces had a rank structure similar to what we see today, all headed by a Chief Constable. As mentioned above, following World War II (1939–1945), the UK Government introduced police reform through Acts of Parliament that included restructuring the number of police forces in order to increase efficiency and to make them more economic. Except for London's Metropolitan Police, which was under the governance of the Home Secretary, the other forces in England and Wales were under the governance of their local government's police authority that then was constituted by a selection of local councilors. At that time and up to the 1990s, the Chief Constable was solely responsible, without any central government interference, for the running of the operational policing within the designated force area.

Since the 1990s, the UK central government has introduced widespread reform of policing in England and Wales. Following the *Police and Magistrates Court Act* 1994, there came the change of the makeup of police authorities. From now on, they were to consist of local councilors, magistrates, and those appointed by the Home Secretary due to their success in business. In 2012, the police authorities were abolished with the introduction of a directly elected Police and Crime Commissioner who took over the role and duties of the police authority. Also, from the 1990s into the first decade of the twenty-first century, there were further police reforms that effectively saw control of the provincial police forces shift from local authority governance to governance by the UK central government. As a result, national policing plans were introduced that includes policing objectives for all 42 provincial police forces, requirements regarding the forces' budgets, and powers for the Home Secretary to dismiss a Chief Constable, should they not be performing effectively and efficiently in their role. This shift from local government to central government control is discussed below by Jon Murphy.

There has also been reform in the policing of terrorism and organized crime at national level in the United Kingdom. In 1999, the National Crime Squad (NCS) was formed alongside the National Criminal Intelligence Section, both led by a director appointed by the UK government's Home Secretary. Following the *Serious Organised Crime and Police Act* 2005, both of these agencies were merged to form the Serious Organised Crime Agency in 2006 that also included officers from Customs, Inland Revenue Investigation, and the Border Agency, which in turn was reformed in 2013 to become the National Crime Agency (NCA). In its various forms, this agency has worked in cooperation with policing agencies across Europe and North America, investigating drug trafficking, firearms trafficking, human trafficking, counterfeiting and money laundering, and other organized criminal activity. As covered in his interview, Jon Murphy was one of the original senior officers posted to the NCS.

The interview was conducted in October 2013 in the Chief Constable's personal office at Merseyside Police Headquarters in Liverpool city center.

Career

The son of a former Liverpool City and Merseyside Police officer, Jon Murphy joined Merseyside Police as a cadet in January 1975, shortly after Merseyside Police was created from the amalgamation of Liverpool and Bootle Constabulary, Lancashire Constabulary, and Cheshire Constabulary. The police cadet scheme, that then ran, allowed those aged 16–18 to join the police service where they received education and training, carrying out nonpublic contact roles to familiarize themselves with the police service. It was only toward the end of the cadet service when they reached the age of 18 that cadets went out with a police officer on patrol. In 1976, Jon joined Merseyside Police. After serving his probationary period in uniform duties in Liverpool city center, in 1980 Jon joined the force's uniform Operational Support Department (OSD). OSD officers were trained in public order tactics and supported police divisions by adding extra uniform officers to focus on criminal activity. In 1982, he was posted as a detective to the Criminal Investigation Department (CID) where, other than a brief 12-month spell as a uniform sergeant, he served for the next 20 years in various CID departments at force, regional, and national level. During this time, he was promoted up through the ranks.

In 2001, after completing the Strategic Command Course, Jon was posted as Head of Operations in the NCS in the rank of Assistant Chief Constable. In this post, he held overall responsibility for all NCS-organized crime national and international investigations. Operations covered drug trafficking, firearms trafficking, kidnap, extortion, and human trafficking. These investigations led to working in cooperation with policing agencies throughout Europe and North America. The NCS was the forerunner of the UK's current NCA that was formerly known as the Serious Organised Crime Agency. He returned to Merseyside Police in 2004 when he was promoted to Deputy Chief Constable. After just over 3 years in that post, Jon spent 6 months working directly with the then Home Secretary, Jackie Smith, when he set up the national Tackling Gangs Action Programme (TGAP). He was then appointed the National Coordinator for Serious and Organised Crime within the Association of Chief Police Officers (ACPO). In 2010, Jon once more returned to Merseyside Police on promotion to Chief Constable, the position he currently holds. In such a varied career, he has experience of working with other UK police forces as a well as other global policing agencies, including using the services of the European Union's policing agency Europol and US' Federal Bureau of Investigation (FBI). In 1995, he was awarded a Fulbright Fellowship for his work researching undercover policing and informant handling with the FBI in the United States. For his services to policing, he was awarded the Queen's Police Medal in 2007. During his service, Jon graduated with an LLB (Hons) in Law from Liverpool University, and in 2001, he graduated from Cambridge University with a postgraduate diploma in Applied Criminology.

Changes in Policing Experienced

JM: Organizationally, the make-up of the police is far more diverse as regards female and ethnic representations. The service is more reflective of the communities we police. It's still not as good as we would like it to be, but it is a lot better. The basic philosophies of policing have not changed. I have tried to take the force back to its real traditional values that had been lost since the time I joined. When I joined, the police were out of touch with communities. Individual officers were able to get on with communities when they walked the beat, but it was never part of their training, it was never part of the ideology of the force as we were engaged almost exclusively in reactive policing. There was little or no proactive behavior either in terms of investigation, problem solving in communities, or in community relations. Then the phone rang when someone called for the police and we did the best we could, but during that period, at times, it wasn't very good. I think that we have improved immeasurably.

In terms of seminal moments, the introduction of PACE (*Police Criminal Evidence Act*), the recording of (suspect) interviews, the HRA (*Human Rights Act* 1998), all of these events have been watersheds in the way we do our job. Mobile phones (cell phones) have made a huge difference to how we deliver our services as demand has grown exponentially.

Austerity has brought huge budget cuts. The Merseyside Police budget has been cut by £61.4 million, to be realized by 2015. Initially, there was a feeling of unfairness because the cuts only applied to the central grant. Merseyside Police's budget is 85% reliant on government funding, whereas some other forces have central grants as low as 49%. Since 20% of the 85% was cut, we were disproportionately affected. At the time, we felt a sense of unfairness. We don't like what's gone on, but we've got to get on with our job and accept our share of the pain.

The cuts have forced us to look at everything we do, the way we deliver our services, our business processes, the terms and conditions of our staff, and the grading of our support staff. There have been some positive aspects of the cuts. First of all, we are more efficient than when I took over because we have had to be. Second, we have always been told that we were, comparatively, a well-funded force and actually we were. Like housekeeping, whatever you've got you spend. Looking at what we have managed to do in re-engineering the force whilst losing, to this point, 1,200 people, we're doing OK. In fact, remarkably well, even though we have suffered a larger percentage cut than nearly every other force.

There is a political and public obsession with visibility and reassurance. Everybody likes to see a "bobby" (police officer) in their street and the neighborhood policing model is consequently extremely popular with the public. At the same time, we have to manage our risks and threats to communities— local communities and minority/vulnerable groups. As resources diminish, the decisions around where to put them become more acute. Do we give way to the obsession with visibility when we know that what many of our more affluent communities' need is less than those that are more challenged and where the public do need that physical presence? There are significantly sized areas where if citizens call the police twice in their lives that will be a surprise, some may never call us at all, but we have this one size fits all model. Yet, in other parts of the organization, we are struggling to identify and manage our risks. In July 2013, we learned of a further 4.9% cut to our budget, this is on top of the £91.4 million cut we have already suffered. Taking into account pay awards and other pressures, we will have to fund, there are some really difficult decisions ahead.

There's intelligence led policing, using intelligence to identify risk and to solve problems before they occur. It is clear, increasingly (and this is what I meant about returning to traditional values), that Robert Peel was spot on: the test of the police is the absence of crime. Prevention is better than cure and that's what we're about in this organization. For me, the fundamental issue is determining what is meant by neighborhood policing (NHP). I made this observation in a speech I gave at the National Superintendents' Association Conference and was subsequently misquoted in the media. They reported that the Chief Constable of Merseyside Police does not believe there is a future for NHP. I absolutely do believe in NHP, though I don't think it's necessarily the same as what other people believe it is. It's not about having groups of "bobbies" wearing big hats and green jackets performing in a numbers game—"how many times you can spot a bobby in your street?" NHP is about the relationship we have with the public, how we talk to them, how effectively we listen, and do we deliver on our promises? Ultimately, what it comes down to is, do they trust us, do they have confidence in us? Will they turn to us when they need help? It doesn't matter whether you have the label neighborhood officer, response office, a detective, a dog handler. Whatever role you have in this organization, you have a responsibility to be part of NHP. That is based on the relationship we have with the public.

The problem we've had previously is that we had NHP with some "bobbies" who did it and those that didn't, and my point is that you had a neighborhood policing section and they were NHP. That's wrong. I'm saying they're all neighborhood policing, not just those with the label, and that's the difference.

Personal Policing Philosophy

JM: Before I became Chief, my experience as a citizen was spending a Saturday morning shopping with my wife and having a coffee. I would see a "bobby" and a Police Community Support Officer (PCSO) walking along talking to each and wearing body armor. I wanted to go out and rip off their body armor and tell them not to be so stupid (subject to location of course) and say "*you* walk that way, *you* go the other way and talk to the public not each other." If we don't talk to the public, the public won't talk to us. Here's the problem—when I was a young "bobby," you were given a radio and told to make a nuisance of yourself and "do process, process, process" (A Merseyside Police phrase for reporting persons for summons or issuing affixed penalty notice). Does it help community relations? Absolutely not! Yet, that's what we used to do, but we did talk to people. If we didn't, we were bored. Today my officers attend up to one and half million calls a year. They are bounced from job to job to job. There are no canteens to come into for refreshment, they have sandwiches in the back of the car and they do their job in a goldfish bowl and work much harder than we ever did. They would say "we haven't time to just talk to the public."

Immediately on appointment as Chief, I introduced a campaign called "Just Talk." It is simple and straightforward, doing exactly what it says on the tin. Officers are told to talk to the public whenever they can, wherever they can, and about whatever they can. Don't wait until they're victims or when they're a witness, or when you're locking them up. Just talk to people. And that has been phenomenally successful. I know that from the letters I receive into my office, from public feedback and what I get from the officers themselves. For me, the relationship with the public is founded on two fundamental things. One, listening to them and two, talking to them; then beyond that, solving their problems and delivering on promises. That is what builds a relationship with the public.

Merseyside Police is a great police force. Our satisfaction levels are high compared to the other forces. When the Labour Government of 1997–2010 introduced public confidence surveys as the single measure of success applied to policing, this force, even though it polices some of the most challenging and deprived communities in the country, was never lower than sixth out of forty-three. On one occasion we came top. Now when you get that level of confidence from the public that is a massive testimony to the people of this organization.

Another perspective is that Liverpool is a village. Merseyside Police, despite being a metropolitan force, is geographically one of the two smallest forces in the country and that's why it's like a village. If you go back to the often quoted Peel principle, "the police are the public and the public are the police," that is epitomized here. The vast majority of our officers are drawn from these communities. Their parents are here, their children go to school here, they live here. We are as much a part of the community as those we police. I think the human touch is important as we are all in this together.

There is a paradox in this. In the days when I joined, there were still police houses. Those police houses were in some challenging estates and the police was very much a working class profession. The majority of officers came from and still lived in the more challenging communities, more than they tend to now. Policing has become relatively well paid and even though police officers have moved to the middle-class suburbs of Mossley Hill, Formby or the Wirral, it is still Merseyside, it is still part of the community. They've not forgotten their roots and they care about their communities—this is a fundamental philosophy of the force and something I constantly refer to when addressing officers and staff.

Problems and Successes

Working with Other Agencies

JM: I think we have a much better working relationship with other agencies than in the past. The strength of those relationships is evident
in the fact that we are able to continue to work together in a time
of austerity when people are almost being forced to shrink to
core business. Often partnership work is done in the margins and
is the first to give in times of financial difficulty. The Probation
Service, as an example, has a core service to deliver that does
not necessarily involve any joint partnership with the police.
As discretionary spend diminishes, the temptation is to reduce
back to core business. Despite all of us being "under the cosh"
(struggling) for resources, we have been able to continue to work
with local authorities, social services, residents' associations, and
social landlords. With all the people we work with, the relationships have been strong enough to be able to continue with the
good work we have done. At the end of the day, 30% of what we
do is social service work. We are a social service whether we like
it or not. Talking about change, I would argue strongly that of all
the public services, it is the police whose operating paradigm has
shifted the most. For example, I have almost forty officers whose
full time job is to work in schools. I don't see other agencies having had that kind of culture shift. I want this Force to have a
hard edge, but also the human touch, compassion, with humility.
Enforcement isn't a solution to anything, it is a response. It brings
respite to communities, but it is a short to medium term solution
at best. In the long term, you've got to get everyone around the
table and give young people in particular an opportunity in life,
an alternative lifestyle. At the moment that is becoming increasingly difficult.

Regulation of Investigatory Powers Act 2000

JM: Whilst bureaucratic, I regard RIPA (*Regulation of Investigatory Powers
Act* 2000) as a significant step forward in the successful investigation of serious organized crime. Prior to RIPA, things were very
uncertain. There was no regulation and evidence obtained during
an investigation would be subject of lengthy pre-trial hearings.
You may or may not get your evidence passed in a pre-trial hear-
ing and you may or may not get someone convicted. With RIPA,
it's made the requirement of article 8 (the right to privacy in the

European Convention of Human Rights) in particular clear and RIPA provides a framework whereby we know if we follow a particular process and fulfil the requirements of lawfulness, justification, and proportionality, then generally legal argument as to admissibility will be kept to a minimum. The regime is also subject to the governance of the Office of the Surveillance Commissioner. RIPA has given us clear guidelines and legislation and something to "hang our hat on" (utilize). It's bureaucratic, it takes time, but in the context of an investigation that takes a couple of years, you've got the security that if you have operated within RIPA, you haven't wasted those two years. As a force, we have significant resource dedicated to dealing with organized crime groups. Authorization of covert and intrusive surveillance takes up a significant amount of my time, for most of the RIPA authorizations can only be signed by me. I don't just sign them, I ensure that I am properly briefed and take the time to read the detail.

Working with the Judiciary

JM: I think we've got much better relationships with the Crown Prosecution Service and the Judiciary than when I was a young detective. Chief and senior officers meet regularly with the Recorder of Liverpool (Senior District Court judge who usually sits in the Crown Court presiding over criminal trials) and the head of the Crown Prosecution Service. On occasions, the Recorder will ask me or one of the chief officers to go and talk through a particular issue. For example, I've talked about cannabis farms, how cannabis farms are established and operated and the profits are made. That context helps judges when sentencing. On occasions, we go over and give presentations to the judges and say this is the business, this is how it operates, and help them. Not in the context of individual cases, but the professional relationship we share has led to a situation where they are able to come to us and ask for that context. At the same time, the Recorder will make clear when we have not come up to his expectations. The other good thing is, not infrequently, a judge will approach me and ask if they can go out on patrol with my officers. A number of judges have done this and they have always commented afterwards on the benefit to them in their role. They always come back to me and say they had no idea of the complexity of the job the police do, the challenges they face, and the difficult "in the heat of the moment" judgments they have to make.

Theory and Practice

JM: The force conducts research guided by necessity—a desire to develop
or improve the manner in which we deliver a particular service to
the public. And in the MSc in Police Leadership, students conduct,
as part of their course, research projects considered of potential
value to the force. But for myself, I would say that rather than being
guided by theories about policing, I am guided by particular philosophical questions. Namely, what is meant by legitimacy and policing by consent?; what is the police mission?; is what we think of as
the police mission the same as what the public think?; and how far
should the police intrude into the lives of individuals in order to
protect the wider public?. The answers to these questions are fundamental to how I lead the force.

Transnational Relations

JM: The level of intelligence sharing and co-operation is largely dependent
on which country you are dealing with. Some are very much easier to deal with than others; you would expect that. It can be a
consequence of the political regime at the time, there can also be
huge cultural differences. The level of integrity and honesty that
exists in the UK is not universal across the globe. Sometimes you
have to work with countries with poor human rights records. For
example, when I was Head of Operations in the National Crime
Squad, we were looking to establish a joint intelligence unit in a
source country of illicit commodities to the UK. They were having trouble getting local officers to work in it. You would think
officers would be clambering to secure a post. The truth is, when
posted inside you can't take cash bribes on the street. Despite this,
you have to adapt and still have to work with these agencies if you
want to get the job done.

In terms of international serious organized crime, there is a continuum of
harm that stretches from source countries producing illicit commodities, be it
heroin, firearms, or people. There is a chain of interactions and criminal relationships stretching across the globe, but ultimately, the harm plays out in our
communities. The challenge is how you get your response to match the scope
of the challenge at every point on the continuum. I don't think at this point
we are particularly brilliant at that, but things are getting better and I expect
to see a step change as the new National Crime Agency (NCA) settles down.

In the past, I have worked through Europol and with Eurojust. Both are invaluable agencies in delivering that end to end response in their facilitation of international investigations. The UK is one of the biggest contributors of intelligence into Europol, and on the occasions, I needed Europol's services, they always delivered for me. Europol serves a similar purpose but is a much more developed capability than Interpol for the EU. Accessed via our own national systems, Europol acts as a conduit for connecting law enforcement agencies, whilst Eurojust ensures all legal requirements are satisfied and any evidence secured can be adduced in the English courts. That said, once you've got a bilateral relationship with another agency you don't necessarily need somebody in the middle to get things done. It depends which country it is. Some need to work through Europol, others don't. For example, Merseyside Police work regularly with the Dutch police. You've got Liverpool criminals resident in Amsterdam. We've had several operations involving the Dutch, so we work directly with the Dutch police. Europol knew what we were doing. The international desk at SOCA (UK's Serious Organised Crime Agency) knew what we were doing, but we can do things easily. There are protocols to go through. Some other countries are more challenging and you would have to be far more reliant on Europol. I did a lot of work (in the NCS) with the Spanish police. The requirements for the Spanish courts are different from the requirements of our courts. Sometimes, the Spanish would pursue a prosecution that our legal system would not allow. So if you did an operation with another country you would come to an agreement, which is the most appropriate jurisdiction to deal with the prosecution.

Democratic Policing

JM: The key element of democratic policing is policing by consent—but what does that mean? The police have always been good at training its people in law, procedure, codes of practice, and tactics. What we are not so good at is teaching young officers about what policing actually is, about legitimacy, and where it comes from. We are, I am pleased to say, getting better and talking again about Robert Peel and his principles. My view is that legitimacy comes less from what we do and more from how we do it, and our relationship with communities. The public give us powers to exercise on their behalf. That's why we're here. That is why it's important that we listen to them, talk to them, and give them the policing service they want. All of that comes back to Liverpool's Toxteth Riots of 1981. You ask yourself why the riots happened; where was policing by consent in 1981? I was there. I was in the Support Group. No one had ever even spoken to me about policing by consent or legitimacy. I didn't know what it was. It's different now. I talk to my officers about it all the time, but there's still more work to do.

The other thing that is different now is that when I was a young officer nobody said to me, you're a leader. I was a follower. I was there to do as I was told. There is a massive difference between rank and leadership. Rank is what happens in the police station. When officers go out, the public do not see age, experience, or rank, they see a uniform and they expect the police to be there for them. As Chief, I make decisions with other chief officers about purchasing equipment, what IT systems to buy, how the cuts will be made, and who we might collaborate with. But the important decisions involving life or death and certainly some individual's personal crisis, are made by constables and PCSOs (Police Community Support Officer). The most junior rank in the police service is the one which is the most critical and I don't think they get that. They develop leadership skills without even knowing they are doing so.

I can give a fantastic example. I gave a policewoman a commendation a few weeks ago. This officer, very young in age and service, was sent to a house where a woman had been drinking and fallen asleep leaving her three year old toddler and baby twins in the house unsupervised. The toddler decided he would bath the babies and tragically he drowned them both. The policewoman turned up and there are two apparently dead babies on the bathroom floor with a three year old toddler running around shouting that the babies are dead. The decisions she then had to make (and she's younger than my kids) required leadership skills of the highest order. She decided to give one of the babies CPR (Cardiopulmonary resuscitation) and then has to decide which baby to save. That's not an easy decision, is it? Also, she had to try and calm the mother down and try to protect the three year old while giving the baby CPR. All this is going on while one baby is having to lie there, apparently dead. A short time later, another officer turns up and he's got an equally difficult decision, as the three year old is still having a bad time. He sees the policewoman giving CPR to one of the babies and looks at the other baby. He determined this baby was beyond help, so focused on protecting the three year old. The leadership qualities those two officers displayed were phenomenal. That kind of leadership goes on day in, day out, and all at the front end of the organization. If you ask them who the leaders are in the service, they'll say the Chief or one of the Assistant Chief Constables or a chief superintendent. It never occurs to them that they themselves are leaders. It is *them*. The most junior rank in the service is the one that deals with most carnage. That ability to prioritize what's the most important thing in the protection of life and property is often leadership of the highest order.

We live in a democracy. People have the right to legitimate protest. There is a legal framework in which this can take place as regards routes, designated areas, and various orders that can be signed by various people. The job of the police is to maintain law and order, to allow people to peaceably demonstrate, and to protect the larger section of the public from what goes on within that framework. That's pretty straightforward for me. It's not the job of the police to engage in the politics. Of course, proportionality is important in the middle of that. That's less straightforward.

Looking Ahead

JM: I'll tell you one likely development, it is fragmentation. We have a police service that despite us being "under the cosh" at the moment—and there is a parallel world here that I will come back to—is the envy of the world. That is as a consequence of our liberal democracy—because we police by consent. At a more tactical level, we wear the same uniforms, we get the same training, we get the same pay, we have got inter-operability that gives the same, consistent policing approach right across the UK that does not exist anywhere else in the world. Local interests at heart, with a commitment to mutual support in times of crisis, and dealing with cross border and national issues. At the moment, in the name of savings and less on efficiency, we are being pushed down the road of privatization and collaboration. In my view, there will be circumstances when those things are right, but they're not ends in themselves. At the moment, there is a tendency for them to become an end in themselves, and what it's doing is systematically unpicking that consistency of approach. I'm being encouraged to collaborate with Cheshire Police, with other forces in the region of the northwest of England and beyond the region, to collaborate with local authorities, to outsource to commercial security companies like G4S or whoever it may be. All of that is fragmenting the service. I don't think that's going to help us in the long run.

I would like to see a police service that recognizes the need for change. That said, I don't see any evidence that it doesn't and I'd like to see the government put their arm around the police service and say "we love you really." In all of the thirty nine years, I've been part of it, I've never seen the service so consistently under siege. That's partly because of austerity, it's partly because of the reform agenda, and it's partly because the service hasn't helped itself. There have been too many officers who have let us down. The consequence is that we've got no moral high ground to cling to. We find it very difficult to influence change for the better both for the public and the service itself. The parallel world I was talking about was the paradox in this. The police service as a national body is in a really difficult place, but locally we're doing all right. The public have confidence in us. There's high satisfaction levels, crime's down, the (local) papers aren't on our back. We're doing all right. If you went to most chiefs in the country, they will most probably tell you the same thing. So you've got this parallel world of what the national media is reporting about the police, the difficulties between the Federation (Police Union of the ranks constable to chief inspector) and the government, between ACPO (The Association of Chief Police Officers) and the Government, but locally I genuinely believe the relationship between the police, the public, the media, and the local authorities is better than at any time in my police service, which is at complete odds with what we read nationally. That's because our attitude changed and it needed to.

The worry for the force, the big worry for society itself, is increasingly less opportunity for an increasing number of young people with less chance of taking advantage of what opportunities there are. So if you go back to when I was a Detective Sergeant in the mid-1980s, you'd get a fingerprint identity for a burglary and go to the "dole office" (public unemployment office). Then when they sign on we'd go and "lock them up" (arrest them) on that fingerprint identity. They would be there with the girlfriend with their child in a buggy (push-chair) and their idea of parenting was to shove a Macdonald's (burger) in its mouth and put some clothes on its back. The notion of values, of standards of behavior have been non-existent in that generation and those children in the buggies are now parents of current teenagers who think nothing, in some communities, of pulling a sawn-off shotgun from underneath their hoodie (hooded coat) and blowing someone's head off. There's never been a positive role model in the family. They're with their mothers. There's been no man on the scene, no positive male influence in their lives. That's the big worry for the future.

The police mentality of going out and locking everyone up doing anything wrong doesn't work. It doesn't secure the support of the law-abiding members of society. They don't want to see young people criminalized when there is another way of dealing with it. Powers need to be used for the right reason, not because we can, which is what we were encouraged to do in the past—go out and get some jobs to prove your worth. If we are genuinely policing by consent, we should be using our powers for the right reason because it's the thing to do in the right circumstances. Let me be clear, enforcement is not a dirty word. I want to see bad people locked up and put in prison. Actually, what I don't want to see is young people being criminalized and ruining whatever small chance of employment they may get in the future.

Conclusion

Leading one of the UK's busiest police forces, there is a constant demand for Jon's time, and it is greatly appreciated that in agreeing to be interviewed for this book, he gave up an hour and a half of his time. Throughout his service, Jon has always had a reputation for being open, honest, and not afraid to be forthright with his views on policing. In the interview, he was very open and honest in his assessment of what occurred in policing in the past that formed the foundations of problems the police have to deal with today. During his interview, he acknowledges that his early police service was part of that policing period that brought about political and social issues the police have to face up to today. His honesty and passion for the police doing the right thing comes across in his ideas of how the police should develop and progress. What came out of the interview is that for Jon Murphy policing is not just a job, for him, it is still a vocation in which protecting and providing an excellent service to the public that he and his colleagues serve is of paramount importance.

The interview for me had two outstanding themes, one being Jon Murphy's opinions on the philosophical aspects of policing and, importantly, how he is addressing this to enhance the quality of policing provided by Merseyside Police. What came out strongly was Jon's commitment to policing by consent. It is seen in how it underpins his approach to developing neighborhood policing, his "Just Talk" initiative, his policing protests, and in his initiatives in working with other criminal justice agencies. For Jon, this will work towards gaining legitimacy from those the police serve. An original concept of policing that Jon is developing is how the junior police ranks are the real leaders in the police as it is they, not senior ranking officers, who have to make the important decisions affecting life and death, and security of the person and their property. Another important theme was how not just UK police forces should cooperate when investigating serious and organized crime, but how this has to be carried out at international level.

For most of his police service, Jon had been an operational officer, even as a senior investigating officer his operational experience permeates into his decision making. Operational policing is something he has never eschewed as he has risen through the ranks, as seen in his posting to the National Crime Squad where he was operationally hands-on during investigations into transnational organized crime. In the UK many chief officers are career managers first and a "bobby" second, whereas it is the other way round with Jon. As a result, he may be one of the last of his generation of senior police officers where their own policing experience not only allows a genuine knowledge and appreciation of the pressure operational junior police ranks are under, but how that operational experience can shape managerial policies implemented in his police force.

Glossary

Crown prosecution service: created in 1986, it is a public service department that contains English lawyers (both barristers and solicitors) that prosecute criminal cases on behalf of the Crown and assist police forces in the charging and collation of evidence in serious criminal investigations as well deciding whether or not to proceed with a prosecution. A role similar to that of a US District attorney or European examining magistrate.

Dole office: Dole is a colloquialism for unemployment benefit that is given by the UK Benefits Agency.

Eurojust: the agency of the European Union dealing with judicial cooperation in criminal matters.

Europol: the European Union's policing agency. While it does not have operational powers of investigation, it is an intelligence service and assists the European Union's Member States' policing agencies in coordinating joint investigations.

HRA: the *Human Rights Act* 1998—a UK statute that incorporated the jurisprudence and articles of the European Convention on Human Rights into the English legal system.

Job: a British police colloquialism for an investigation, a crime, or a call from the public requesting the police.

Lock up/locked up: Merseyside Police colloquialism for arrest.

PACE: *Police and Criminal Evidence Act* 1984—a statute that governs most police powers for officers in forces in England and Wales.

Recorder: Senior District Court judge who usually sits in the Crown Court presiding over criminal trials.

SOCA: the Serious Organised Crime Agency that existed from 2006–2013 to deal with organized crime at national and transnational level and as replaced by the NCA in October 2013.

Alberto Melis, Douglas Police Department, Arizona, USA

4

INTERVIEWED BY
SCOTT W. PHILLIPS

Contents

Introduction

Criminal justice administrators who manage local-level agencies face many challenges. They have to manage their agencies, including developing policies or programs that guide the decision-making of their workers. Administrators must deal with citizens, stakeholders, and politicians in their local environment. They must adjust to changes in their working environment that impact their role in the society. Contemporary criminal justice leaders, even those at the local level, must also consider international and global issues, and the impact those issues may have upon the administration of their agencies.

How does national or international level policy impact a municipal criminal justice agency that is located far from higher-level power structures? First, some policies or programs that are enacted in one location are diffused to other locations. For example, community policing, arguably developed by police agencies in the United States in the late 1970s, has been adopted by police departments in many other countries. More recently, intelligence-led policing that originated in the United Kingdom has been recently integrated into many police agencies in the United States. Therefore, municipal law enforcement organizations are often impacted by seemingly disconnected governmental agencies is subtle and unique ways.

This chapter explores the views of a former police chief from the United States. Alberto Melis retired from the Douglas, Arizona Police Department in 2012. He discussed a variety of policing topics, including discretion, politics, and technology. During the interview, Alberto discussed changes in policing philosophies and priorities. He scrutinized shifts in the legal powers of the police and the impact of state legislation and federal anticrime programs. Alberto provided an enlightening view of how a small, local police agency is impacted by its location on an international border. It should also be noted that Alberto has a somewhat dry but healthy sense of humor, which was evident at several points during the interview. This personality trait gives his comments and observations a stronger sense of honesty and candor.

Career

In 1973, Alberto Melis started his law enforcement career as a police officer in Delray Beach, Florida, a seaside city roughly 60 miles north of Miami. At the time the city of Delray Beach had a population of about 50,000 that was mostly Caucasian, roughly 25% African-Americans, and a small population of Haitian immigrants (5,000–6,000). He spent 24 years in Delray Beach, retiring from the police department as a Captain, and having spent time working in every division in the agency. When Alberto left Del Ray Beach he became the police chief of Lauderhill, Florida, located about 25 miles north of Miami. In the late 1990s, Lauderhill had a population of roughly 50,000 that was mostly retired persons. About 50% of the citizens were Caucasian, and most of the others were of Caribbean ancestry, such as Jamaican or Trinidad and Tobago. He described the people of Lauderhill as, not so much soup, rather a salad: "everything stands out."

In 2000, Chief Melis moved to Waco, Texas, a move that meant a substantial change of scenery. Delray Beach and Lauderhill are surrounded by other cities and municipalities in the Miami Metropolitan Statistical Area (MSA), and the Miami MSA had a population just over 5.5 million in 2010. Waco, on the other hand, is located in Central Texas, is surrounded by an extensive open space. The city is at a midway point between Dallas and Austin; about 100 miles from either city. The city of Waco had a population of about 110,000 in 2000, and the Waco MSA was 213,000. The population of Waco was mostly Caucasian with about 25% Hispanic and 16% African-Americans.

After spending 7 years in Waco, in 2007 Alberto moved to Douglas, Arizona, where he was the chief of police for 5 years. Douglas is located on the United States—Mexican border, adjacent to Agua Prieta, Mexico, about

15 miles from the state of New Mexico. In 2010, Douglas had a population of roughly 17,000; over 82% were classified as Hispanic, and the African-American population was less than 3%.

Alberto retired from Douglas in 2012. There were several reasons for his decision. First, he had been in law enforcement for 40 years, and simply felt it was time. Second, he recalled a medical emergency incident he assisted with just after finishing his academy training in the early 1970s. In sum, an elderly person who had just retired had died, so Alberto "didn't want to wait until (he) was ready to die to retire." Finally, the area had become fairly depressed economically. As he "could afford to retire," and felt a calling for the Christian ministry, he decided it was time to go.

In addition to his practical experience in policing and administrative experience as a chief, Alberto attended the Southern Police Institute at the University of Louisville, as well as extensive training in many areas of law enforcement. He earned a bachelor's degree and master's degree, and is currently attending seminary school.

Changes Experienced

When I spoke with Alberto, I first asked him about the most important philosophical changes in law enforcement. He was asked to consider the question based on his overall career and his time as an administrator. Alberto first addressed policing changes from a practical perspective, suggesting that the improvements in communication are an obvious change in policing. He recalled the time when technological changes allowed him to "carry a radio in (his) pocket, not a monster of a walkie-talkie. Forty years later we carry cell phones to communicate." Later in our conversation, the issue of cell phones would be revisited in a way that demonstrates efficiency in how different law enforcement agencies work together.

If improved communications was a practical shift in law enforcement, Alberto identified community policing as the obvious philosophical change in policing over the past forty years. He suggested that various community policing programs have contributed to positive relationships between the police and the public. These programs improve the police–public relationships even if there is limited evidence that the program contributes to a reduction in crime. "Try and get rid of DARE (Drug Awareness Resistance Education) from the schools and see what happens" he stated. He believes community policing is an "evolving" approach to policing. "The pure community policing that Trojanowitz, Wilson, and others envisioned, I think, has changed."

At this early point in our conversation, Alberto shifted his focus a bit and provided what amounted to a brief history lesson of policing, illuminating his overall thinking of why policing has changed over the past 50 years. He mentioned the 1967 Kerner Commission, which examined the police and the state of civil rights in the United States. The Commission report led to the Law Enforcement Assistance Administration (LEAA), a federal agency providing funding to professionalize the police through higher education, advanced training, and some specialized units. To Alberto, this example explains changes in law enforcement: "policing follows where the money is." He stated that during the late 1980s and in the 1990s, thanks to the COPS Office (the Department of Justice's Office of Community Oriented Policing Services), and until fairly recently, "the money was … in CP, and we have a whole generation (of police officers and administrators) trained in that area." Over the past decade, however, that generation of community policing "is now trying to adapt to the next wave of money, which is Homeland Security." (The issue of Homeland Security would be discussed at other points in our conversation.) Despite the funding shift, Alberto believes that if the police have a Homeland Security focus they still cannot abandon "some form of CP."

AM: When you study some of the terrorist groups of the past, the Baader Meinhof (in Germany), the IRA (in Northern Ireland), ETA in Spain, the main reason they were able to survive is that they had a lot of "fellow travelers" that they could get shelter with, they could get funds, they could get protected from "the man," so to speak. That has not been the case in the United States, except in isolated examples, such as the Aryan groups. None of these (terrorist) groups in the United States can afford to maintain a major insurrection.

He suggested that one of the reasons that terrorist groups outside the United States can maintain connections and stability is that "by and large, in most places outside the United States, the police have not been a popular group. There is an old joke in Spain that you shouldn't stand next to a cop because you might get your picture taken. The meaning being that a police officer may actually get bombed because he was a target of ETA." Basically, some terrorist groups would identify police officers, take their pictures as part of their intelligence collection, and target the officers; hence, don't stand next to a cop. Targeting police officers in the United States, despite what might be said by some Militia groups, just doesn't happen. "But the police in the United States have the best relationship with the public, better than in most of the world." He suspects that most street officers may not see or feel this positive relationship with the public. He discussed this a bit later in the conversation.

I then asked Alberto to consider the changes in policing priorities over the past forty years, as opposed to overall philosophical changes in policing.

He observed that while the police are now focused on Homeland Security, the police still have fundamental priorities.

AM: Nobody wants other crimes, nobody wants to be a victim; by and large people want to feel safe. You have to remember that police officers are conservers of the status quo; that's our job, to insure nobody's status quo changes. Back in the heyday of the start of Community Policing … it was a quality of life issue. Under Community Policing people wanted to return back to a gentler period, let the kids play in the yard.

He suggested that because of the Homeland Security mindset, contemporary priorities have changed nationwide. It is no longer neighborhood status quo, but national status quo.

AM: Now, when you ask people, they will say they want to feel safe, but they are talking about keeping our borders secure. None of them can explain exactly what border security means, but it is obviously good because everyone else is saying it. I usually ask "will a ditch do it? Maybe put alligators in the ditch?"

Alberto's comments suggest that "groupthink" is occurring at a national as well as local level, and this thinking impacts policing. He returned to the issue of funding and the recent federal programs to support Homeland Security. "Back in the 1960s, the money was intended to professionalize the police. That money dried up in the late 1970s. Then we had funding for Community Policing. Now, the Homeland Security money is flowing." In fact, while Alberto was Chief of Police in Douglas, Arizona, his agency received funding through Operation Stonegarden, a federally funded grant program to support a coordinated effort between local, state, and federal law enforcement agencies. Operation Stonegarden is described as "a joint mission to secure the United States' borders along routes of ingress from international borders to include travel corridors in States bordering Mexico and Canada, as well as states and territories with international water borders" (FEMA website). The Douglas police routinely spent over half million dollars a year to pay the overtime expenses of police officers. Alberto's interpretation of the funding was

AM: to have my police officers work traffic to see if there were illegal immigrants or "undesirables" that looked like one of, what, 19 different terrorists? And I don't know a chief who would pass up the opportunity to have more officers on the road, even if it were on overtime, on the federal government's penny.

He returned to the subject of Operation Stonegarden a little later in our conversation, but it should be noted that taking the federal funding to pay for overtime did not seem to shift his view on the veracity or utility of this program. When the funding is appropriated and police agencies spend the money some "people could then make the statement that 'Bush kept us safe'. But safe is such a relative term."

Personal Policing Philosophy

Alberto was asked about his personal view of the fundamental role and function of the police. He provided, first, a retrospective view of recent policing history. He argued that the advent of community policing was thought to include a triad: officers who answer calls for service, a social work component, and a paramilitary element to handle the most serious problems. Even after the events of September 11, 2001, policing still contains this triad. While the bulk of policing is traditional—answering calls for service and dealing with crime—the police deal with other problems along the lines of "social work." Officers solve problems and escort social workers who deal with youths and the elderly in problem areas. And while many officers lament that social work is not part of the job, Alberto suggests that this approach is important for police when "dealing with different aspects of the hydra."

In addition, the paramilitary element is expanding in policing, even into smaller police agencies. He suggests that a move to paramilitary policing on a local level is illogical, and a regional paramilitary approach is more economical and rational for homeland security and defense. Overall, however, he believes that the fundamental role of the police, while a political decision that is commonly made by internal and external administrators who control the police, must include aspects of traditional policing, social work, and a more rational paramilitary model.

I then asked about the parts of policing that should be dropped or left to other agencies or organizations.

AM: Caring for mentally ill patients should be provided by other social services. Often the police serve as nothing more than transport vehicles, but this can tie up officers for extensive periods of time. Officers may be needed to deal with the immediate problems of a patient, but other entities should take over.

When asked about the police role in "un-policed areas," he took a different approach than expected. While "the police" may be spread thin in some locations, everyone can get the police to respond. Thus, Alberto's perspective focused on civil matters, particularly Internet transactions. The police can do little to deal with Internet fraud—the un-policed area—and it is the responsibility of legislatures to deal with this new criminal paradigm.

As part of Alberto's policing philosophy I asked about the things that facilitate or hinder a good working relationship with the community, the government, other criminal justice organizations, or others that make up the police working world. He focused on two issues, the first being communications. While most people would suspect that police agencies at all levels would be able to talk to each other, most cannot. In fact, many police agencies can't even talk to neighboring agencies. The second hindrance to a good working relationship is politics. Police agencies consistently respond, directly or indirectly, to elected officials. For example, legislators "pander to their party's base with social touchstone issues like illegal immigration, illegal workers, securing borders, (and) refusing to enforce existing gun laws ... (they) use the police as pawns." Further, laws may expose the police to legal action if they are accused of not doing what the public expects. These issues can "polarize the populace and the community groups." All this being said, Alberto's personal views of policing include two priorities: to protect the public, and to address, as best they can, quality of life issues.

Problems and Successes Experienced

The fact that Alberto worked in Douglas Arizona, a small, and fairly isolated, border community situated across from Mexico, provides an excellent opportunity to understand the challenges facing an administrator when dealing with issues and changes coming from different directions outside the agency. His position also allows an examination of democratic policing, the demands of the state and federal government, and the executive and legislative issues that flow in the direction of a local law enforcement agency. It must be remembered that Alberto worked in Douglas when there was a confluence of national and international events related to the economy, immigration, drugs, and politics. I asked him about the legal powers of policing and how the events of the time, and the location of Douglas, were impacted by the law or changes in the law. He stated that when there were changes in the law "most of these were posturing ... everyone wanted to outdo everyone else at border security."

AM: Phoenix, in particular, would pass various and sundry laws. For example, if there were a group of people gathered on the side of the road waiting to be picked up for a job—which was common practice—companies that were using these "day laborers" were now expected to check their citizenship. The state passed an awful lot of laws ... to control what they saw as unchecked illegal immigration. And of course, everybody in the United States read about headless bodies being found in the desert and waves of brown people coming over the border. But we were actually seeing a decrease in the number of undocumented aliens. If there was reasonable cause, we were expected to check on the provenance; where did this person come from? Is he legal or illegal? This is what they were calling the "Papers Please" law. But in reality these laws did not have a material effect on us.

Essentially, the police in Douglas behaved in a way that reflected precedent: they enforced the law the way they had always enforced the law. If a police officer had probable cause to stop a vehicle, and there were a few people in the car, the officer would check the license of the driver, write a ticket (or not), and send the people on their way. "What the government was hoping is that we would check everyone." From a Constitutional perspective, there was no cause to check the identity of all the people in the car.

AM: Now, if that same car were carrying 17 people, they damn well better be a college fraternity. If not, everyone in the car is going to get carded, because that would fit a pattern that we've seen and that would be probable cause. But, by and large we were not going to stop and ID people for no particular reason.

There were also practical considerations with checking the identity or nationality of everyone stopped by a police officer. First, if a person was arrested it was irrelevant to Alberto if the officer checked the person's status; once booked into jail, it was the county's responsibility to determine the person's nationality. But "if we release a person after a momentary detention that results in a citation, if the person was brown or talked with an accent, it doesn't matter. We would issue a ticket and say have a good day. We're not going to check." Furthermore,

AM: how were we going to check? We didn't have the equipment, so we'd have to call ICE (Immigration and Customs Enforcement) or Border Patrol, who had to come in from distant locations to look at the person and go through the whole process. It's fine if you're sitting in an air conditioned building when its 105°F, but the reality is different.

Overall, these comments indicate that the actions of the state legislature in passing new laws are not always implemented at the local level because of local considerations. The leader of the police agency believed the laws to be potential Constitutional violations, there was a "mental model" that drove street officer behavior, and there were practical limitations to full application of the law. It is, therefore, interesting that the state seemed to ignore these issues, or they were simply "posturing" more when they qualified the law. Alberto stated that the means of proving nationality required "a driver's license issued after a certain date to prove the provenance of the person. At that point I don't have the time to do much more. The person will likely get a ticket and move on."

State legislation was not the only venue for the development of legal considerations. Alberto again mentioned the federal legislation that provided funding for Operation Stonegarden. The federal funding covered primarily overtime for police officers, thus the only practical way he could apply officers to satisfy the goal of the program (i.e., "secure the United States' borders along routes of ingress from international borders") was to assign them to road patrol. Road patrol officers would, not surprisingly, focus on traffic stops. But as Alberto pointed out, stopping a vehicle for a legitimate traffic violation would likely lead to a short detention and possible citation. Checking the citizenship of people in the vehicle would only occur if the stop fitted the pattern of behavior associated with illegal immigration.

There was also a practical problem with the assumptions associated with Operation Stonegarden. The program funded only those jurisdictions located on the border with Canada, Mexico, or those located on international waters. Yet, "most of the undocumented aliens were not coming to Douglas, or any other border town. They were heading north to work; they don't want to stay on the border." Alberto explained that most border towns don't have sufficient work for undocumented aliens. This was certainly true in Douglas. Also, "the border" is where everyone expects the aliens to be located, but they rarely stayed in a border community. Thus, Operation Stonegarden was based on faulty assumptions.

At this point in our discussion, Alberto sought to clarify several aspects he felt were associated with much of the political posturing that he associated with the legal changes at the federal and state levels of government. First, the issue of national security is commonly associated with international borders. However, as he suggested, undocumented aliens, most commonly Mexican, were passing through and heading north to work. There was a small percentage of "OTM's" (other than Mexican) who were occasionally caught crossing the border, but with few exceptions these people were Guatemalan. In both cases these were not the illegal aliens that most people associate with national security issues. Alberto also stated there were reports of "middle-easterners in the area based on prayer rugs being found everywhere." He stated these reports were complete fabrications. "Not once in the five years I was in Douglas, did we see prayer rugs. It just did not happen."

Second, he suggested that beyond the "national security" component of some of these laws, there was an assumption that illegal aliens were strongly associated with crime. "I kept getting asked about the crime: 'what about the crime?' The crime rate in Douglas was low. In the 5 years in Douglas, I had one homicide and that was a murder—suicide case." He mentioned there was an occasional gang beating, but undocumented aliens were not staying in Douglas; they were heading north.

Alberto's time in Douglas also exposed him to other aspects associated with national-level politics and the realities of living on a border town. "The relationship between both sides now is very cloudy. City officials from Agua Prieta, Mexico, lived" on the American side of the border.

AM: Everybody on the border was related to everyone on the other side. The people who have lived in Douglas for a long time remember when there was no fence. You could literally walk across the border, but there may have been some barbed wire to keep the cattle from wandering off. There would be horse races between people along either side of the fence. Kids could cross over to play ball, and we've lost that.

Still, the way Alberto described conditions in the area, it seems as if the lives of the people living in Douglas and Agua Prieta are, mostly, inconvenienced by the new laws and increased scrutiny when crossing the border. For example, children from Mexico cross the border to go to school. Because the children cross both in the morning and afternoon, border protection agencies "have to put extra people on the border." This is called "school OT." Thus, it appears some traditional aspects of border life still exist, even if accompanied with symbolic enforcement efforts.

Alberto's observation illustrates that the local-level practitioner's working world is disconnected from the views of those at the higher levels of government. Some local criminal justice administrators existed in an internationally interconnected world, and simple legislative changes are unlikely to severely impact that relationship. The organizational structures of these local-level agencies retain their role in their immediate environment. This suggests that an organizational and societal culture exists, leading to continuity of behavior not easily changed.

To this point in our conversation, Alberto had provided information specifically related to local law enforcement and its connection to national and international issues. Local-level police agencies also deal with issues or problems that occur on a local level, but then evolve into subjects that draw national attention for all police agencies. With respect to overall changes in policing, Alberto was asked about the positive and negative issues that have developed in U.S. law enforcement during his forty years of experience. "As far as the 40 years I've been in law enforcement, there has certainly been a steady flow of laws coming from the 'Supremes' affecting search and seizure." He was referring to the United States Supreme Court. Interestingly, he suggested that individual cases that reach the court don't commonly reflect what actually occurs at the street level. He stated that the Miranda decision (the right to remain silent) and the Escobedo case (the right to counsel during an investigation) were typically considered "the big ones" in policing. "They taught us in the academy that we were concerned about these decisions, but the reality was we had to shut people up in order to read them their rights. It still works the same way." Essentially, he was arguing that while fundamental rights are just that, the reality is that suspects are often willing to cooperate. Further, it is not the police typically who violate Constitutional procedures, rather it is almost necessary to "gag them" so that Constitutional procedures are not accidentally disrupted by the suspect.

Further, Alberto seems to agree with a reasonable approach to policing that is articulated by the Supreme Court. He discussed a recent Court ruling regarding the use of drug-sniffing dogs (Florida v. Jardines). In sum, the police were walking drug-sniffing dogs up to the front door of a house "and when the dog alerts, the officers use that as an excuse to search the house. Come on! That works for a car but a house isn't going anywhere." Alberto argued that the police should not take the easy way when dealing with crime prevention and investigations. A car is mobile and detaining a person for a period of time in order to allow a dog to check the vehicle seems reasonable. As he stated, however, the house is static, and if people are using the home to grow marijuana or manufacture larger quantities of narcotics, the police should put effort into collecting evidence and producing a solid case.

Alberto again turned to the influence and impact of politics on local policing. He reiterated the various state and federal laws and policies that influenced not only what was expected from the police but what community members believed the police would do.

AM: Arizona lost Napolitano as governor and had a very, very conservative governor come in. That's when we saw all the passing of the laws. There was a sharp increase of mistrust with not only the community but across the line. I continuously had to meet with the [Mexican] Consulate to reassure them that we're not going head hunting.

He cited motor vehicle laws and some soft pressure from above that wanted the police to focus on "out of state tags" or license plates from Mexico. The result was concern from the local public that they were the focus of increased enforcement efforts. The public's belief in increased enforcement "escalated with McCain acting out, trying to run for office (the Presidency 2008).

Everyone way trying to out macho each other as far as their border protection, seeing how tough they were on border protection." The political reality of national level presidential elections and state level political posturing forced Alberto into a state of "continual fence mending and extinguishing fires."

Theory and Practice

I asked Alberto about the use of research to support his decision making as a chief. He stated that he didn't have his police department in Douglas engage in research because there were resource limitations resulting from the local economic conditions. "But when I was in Waco I used Baylor University quite bit in doing surveys, analyzing surveys, and demographic research." He explained that public-opinion surveys would be included in residential water bills, and questions often asked about the police-public relations. "In every survey that I've done . . . the popularity of the police has been from 80%–89%. It is only when a major case is in the paper that you may drop, but by and large, people like seeing a cop driving down the street." The positive relationship between the police and the public in the United States can be seen in the policies he mentioned earlier, such as DARE.

Inter-Agency Relations

Alberto's comments about border agencies prompted me to ask about working with federal agencies while he was the chief in Douglas. Alberto stated, "One of the things I noticed when I first came to Douglas is that so many of the cars in town have something to do with law enforcement. We probably had between 500–600 border and customs people living in town." He then joked that this may explain the lack of burglary crimes in Douglas, as it was very likely a burglar would be introduced to the business end of a gun.

I then inquired about conditions or issues that facilitated or hindered the local police agency's relationship with other state or federal law enforcement agencies in the area. "There is a saying that 'it's amazing how much you can get done if nobody cares who gets the credit.'" As he was not an elected official, Alberto did not need credit for law enforcement successes that involved other agencies. Further, most of the officers who worked in Douglas were from the town. The area was small enough that their involvement in any multi-agency success would be known to citizens. "Whenever possible I would let the feds get the credit. If we'd stop a car full of dope, let the feds take the credit. Let us have the car because we can auction it and use the money."

Another factor that facilitated a positive relationship between the local police and federal law enforcement was Alberto's actions as Chief. First, he obtained a top-secret security clearance so the federal agencies could trust him. Second, because he knew there would be a close working relationship between the officers in his agency and the federal agencies, he informed the federal agencies they "did not have to come to me if they needed my people. Call them directly, call their cell phones." As suggested earlier in this chapter, the improved communications made possible through cell phones helps improve the efficiency of the different agencies.

The informal relationship between Alberto and some of the federal agents was demonstrated when he related a story about three Guatemalans, he found hiding in his car-port on Thanksgiving morning. After determining their origins and the fact that they really had nowhere to go, Alberto called the Border Patrol. When the border agents arrived and ascertained the situation, they advised him they would do a "voluntary repatriation," a process where illegal aliens are simply taken to the border and sent back across. Simply stated, in this case, the agents would treat the three Guatemalans as if they were Mexican.

AM: I recall telling the Border Patrol "they are not Mexican" as they were short in stature and in native clothing, thus they are "OTM" or other than Mexican. The Border Patrol agents said "no, *they are Mexican*." Then I recalled it was Thanksgiving Day, and voluntary repatriation of Mexicans would save about 4 hours of paperwork. Voluntary repatriation, however, has been eliminated because they got too much political feedback.

This example illustrates a federal level sample of what Alberto discussed earlier. That is, the behavior of Border Patrol workers with respect to the legal changes; the border agents, as best they could, adjusted to the new federal laws and policies.

Working in venues such as Florida and along the Mexican border, Alberto's experiences with the federal government were also examined in a discussion regarding the "war on drugs." I asked about working in Florida during the days of "Miami Vice," and in Douglas with the rumors about "headless bodies" being found in the desert (as he mentioned earlier in our conversation). He briefly mentioned his time in Florida, stating that the police did have to deal with the Drug Enforcement Administration and their efforts to focus on drugs coming from the Caribbean basin. While this fits the picture that most people think about, when they hear about the drug war and Florida, the police also had dealings with the Russian Mafia, the Israeli Mafia, the Jamaican Posies, and Columbians.

Alberto shifted his attention to an illuminating discussion of the drug cartels, particularly in the Douglas area, that painted a picture both predictable and paradoxical. At first he described drug cartels in a graphic but predictable way: members of drug cartels are "less than human; they are the devil incarnate." The behavior of cartel members in Florida was "brutal." He then, however, provided a description of the cartels that truly provides a better understanding of their behavior. "I'm not praising them in any form, but they are, first and last, businessmen. This is what they do—drugs. They do it for the money." In fact, Alberto stated without hesitation that the cartels would avoid behavior that was "bad for business." This is where paradoxical examples were uncovered. Crime inside Mexico "did not blow over" into the United States. Further, his position as a police chief in an American city carried over into Mexico. "It's bad business to whack an American police chief." A police chief from Mexico had no such protection because they were trying to stop the cartels from doing business. In the event a Mexican police chief was corrupt, they were now considered part of the competition because they had taken sides.

AM: But as long as you're not selling yourself—you're not crossing that line between law enforcement and being crooked—you're safe. The last thing the cartels want to do is attract massive attention. That doesn't mean, however, that you might not accidentally walk into the path of a bullet.

Alberto's description of the cartel leaders as businessmen also leads to examples of paradoxical behavior. For example, he described the cartel leaders as "problem solvers." They demonstrated innovative thinking and activity that advanced their business. Alberto had reports from phone company workers who found communications equipment on cellphone towers that did not belong to the phone company. It seems the drug dealers put repeaters in the towers on the American side of the border so their phones would work in the United States. It was also discovered that drug cartels would put solid metal wheels inside standard pneumatic tires; if law enforcement were able to "spike" the tire it would continue to roll sufficiently to escape the police.

Another example of problem solving was the use of "rescue trucks" on the Mexican side of the border to help fleeing drug smugglers escaping from the American side and avoid the police on the Mexican side of the border.

AM: If a drug truck was spotted on the United States side, they would drive back to the border and dump the drug truck, cross back into Mexico, and get into the rescue truck. The drugs they could afford to lose, but they didn't want to lose the men because someone could talk.

Typically, the drug truck carried only drugs; there were no guns or weapons. One time, however, a border patrol agent fired at a drug truck because he thought the truck was going to run him down. While this was not the case, the drug traffickers were not too offended; there were "no repercussions for that, as it's the cost of doing business."

Alberto provided another "war story" that illustrated the paradox of cartel behavior.

AM: I had one incident, almost unbelievable, shortly after I got to Douglas. My guys working narcotics had information that (drugs) were going to come over the border, crossing the fence with a car-carrier, (the type pulled by trucks to deliver cars to dealerships). They put the ramps over the fence to drive a vehicle with drugs into the United States, and my guys announced (identified themselves to the drug couriers). One of the drug dealers opened fire on my guys, who promptly buried themselves in the dirt. There is actually a good video of this from Border Patrol cameras and you can see the "star effect" from the muzzle of a gun. My guys shot back and the dealers ended up setting fire to the vehicle and ran back south. About a week later, I got a message through an informant from the other side that basically said "we apologize; we had an overzealous employee; we did not mean to shoot at you; please forgive us; the person has been disciplined." I imagine they put a letter in his file. But that just shocked me.

"War stories" are heuristic devices, and this example of unexpected behavior from the drug cartel provides more than an interesting yarn. It supports Alberto's point that they are businessmen, and the fact that one of their "employees" fired upon American law enforcement officers was "bad for business." Alberto stated that this was the only episode during his time in Douglas that someone from the drug gangs fired at the American police. "We shot at them several times, and actually shot one of them. But that's what can happen. Now, if they shoot at us initially, things escalate," which is exactly what the cartels don't want to happen. They know that if they escalate their bad behavior, American law enforcement, particularly at the federal level, will intensify their response. "They're going to see the military, they'll see airplanes. All of that is bad for business."

Alberto's experience in local law enforcement, particularly in Douglas, provides a better understanding of the interactions that local agencies have in relation to federal law enforcement. Thus, the police in Douglas, working in an environment that includes federal issues of immigration, national security, and national drug policy, are heavily influenced by the role that the federal agencies play in relation to these issues. This can also be seen in the fact that Alberto told the federal agency to call his people directly; there was no need to seek his permission for the officers to work with the federal agents.

In addition, as Alberto described, Douglas is a small town and the officers live close to the federal agents. Overall, the context of the situation leads the local police to work very closely with federal law enforcement.

Democratic Policing

I asked Alberto, "what do you see as the key elements of democratic policing?" He stated that civilian controls and fragmentation are key parts of democratic policing. While he mentioned that people may question the existence of some types of police agencies (i.e., pharmacist police, the Smithsonian Police, and the Capital and National Archives Police), "it is scary to think of an all reaching national police" force. Second, the police must remain, if not improve, transparency.

The discussion moved into the area of the police maintaining law and order as a way of maintaining the existing social order and power structures. Alberto's candor indicated that one's perspective on "law and order" plays a role in this issue.

AM: By nature, design, and definition what the police do is maintain the status quo ante. By definition the status quo ante favors maintaining the social order and all its props and life support systems. Police function is well described by Egon Bittner's "something is happening that ought not to be happening and about which someone had better do something now."

Alberto stated that Bittner's view does work well, but it may likely fail in some contexts, as it did in the 1960s during civil rights protests in southern states, such as marches at the Edmund Pettus Bridge in Selma, Alabama. During a peaceful march protesting for civil rights, sheriff's deputies and state troopers fired teargas into the crowd and beat protesters with nightsticks. Even now, the police response to some protests is not stellar. For example, "Occupy Wall Street" was a movement started in New York City protesting the social and economic inequality in society and the presumed corruption between the government and financial services organizations.

I then asked if the police can "resist demands from the government to crack down on opposition and protest?" Alberto admitted that he was using "a weasel word" when he said "well, it depends." Interruptions, protests, or vocal picketing during town meetings that are legally convened is unacceptable, and the police should help maintain order during the meeting. However, if a person is "expressing a contrary opinion" during the meeting, then civil discourse should not be interrupted by un-civil behavior by either side. If a protest is held outside a town meeting that would be fine. Essentially, Alberto believes that if a protest is held in a legal manner that is acceptable. When a protest crosses over into illegal activity, the police should take action.

Finally, while the police must maintain a balance in a democratic society between the rights of an individual and the collective needs of society, I asked Alberto's thoughts on the level of public support for the police. He stated that the police receive average high approval from the public. "People like the police, except when they are being ticketed."

Looking Ahead

Alberto's experience in policing also exposed him to issues and concerns that influence how policing deals with changes in technology. "The biggest single change—and I think you're going to see this take off on a steep curve—is what we can do with DNA." He briefly reviewed the 20-year history of DNA and its relationship to policing. Originally, a relatively large sample of body fluid was needed to conduct a DNA test, and testing could take months. Now policing has the ability to do "touch DNA" testing. For example, where a person may leave a fingerprint on an envelope, now a DNA test can be done on the residue that resulted in the fingerprint. Further, "we are at a point where we can almost do DNA matching on the spot." The same technological advancements assist in breathalyzer testing. At one time chemicals were needed to conduct a breathalyzer text, but now people can blow into a tube during a traffic stop and the tube includes alcohol sensors that can determine the blood alcohol content of the person. Also, the mobile data terminals that were available in the 1980s allowed officers to enter names, license numbers, or plate numbers, but otherwise they were quite limited in their street-level utility. "But now an officer in a patrol car can get pictures, or roll a person's fingers on a glass plate and get an instant ID and criminal history check. At one time it was science fiction, now it's not." He also discussed the positive benefits of mounting cameras in patrol cars and in some cases on the officers. "Cameras in cars have gotten more officers OUT of trouble than into trouble." Officers who use offensive language while knowingly wearing a microphone, or who beat a suspect in full view of the camera, deserve what they get. But many officers wear a microphone that is linked to the in-car camera. The sound recording is often enough to refute false accusations from citizens.

Alberto closed our conversation with a discussion of the policies that are intended to improve the appearance of the police, but there is no evidence to demonstrate that the police reduce crime or solve a problem. Specifically, he mentioned popular programs such as DARE and McGruff the Crime Dog (a cartoon used to promote crime prevention to children). Essentially, these programs are symbolic gestures enacted to satisfy the general public, but there is no evidence of long-term success. "DARE fails on many grounds, excepting perhaps in having kids see officers, and vice versa. But we can get that contact better, cheaper, in other ways." He stated that most fire departments are very good at "selling themselves." "Put on my hat. Sit in the truck. Pull the string and make the siren wale. Let's go play with the hoses. They know how to sell themselves." The police, however, do a poor job at these types of positive public relations. "We take ourselves for granted. 'Look at me, I'm a hero, I'm putting my life on the line every day. Love me.' We think selling ourselves is below us." He even mentioned the United States Marines. These are Uncle Sam's great big green killing machine. "But every Christmas they have everyone in dress blues out there collecting toys. How could they hurt anyone? You just want to hug them. We don't know how to sell ourselves and we don't teach it either."

Conclusion

It is hard to imagine that the chief of a relatively small local law enforcement agency would contribute new knowledge to an understanding of the issues faced by criminal justice leaders. Most local police will deal with several of the issues identified by Alberto, such as the use of modern technology or issues related to community policing. Yet, the experiences of working in a smaller police agency located on an international border demonstrated how interconnected these agencies are with many different constituents in their external environment. While there is an inherent disconnect from the upper level administrators or legislators at the state and federal levels of the government, the local police must still work with the agents who implement policies from these other levels of government. Alberto demonstrated an organizational structure that is open to an informal relationship with other agencies. This is seen in his willingness to allow the federal agents to contact the police officers without having to negotiate the communication channels of the local agency.

It is also clear that this type of local law enforcement agency must directly consider the political environment. Federal and state legislators enact new laws that impact the local police, develop public policies to fund programs at the local level, and executives will present a "posture" to satisfy the general public. Yet, each of these political considerations impacts the organizational structure, leadership, and public expectations at the local level. While studies of police organizations have exposed some of these issues, the information provided by Alberto provides the "practitioner's eye view" of how these issues and considerations directly impact local level police agencies.

Reference

FEMA web site: http://www.fema.gov/fy-2012-homeland-security-grant-program.

Dominic Staltari APM, Assistant Commissioner, Professional Standards, Western Australian Police

5

INTERVIEWED BY
ANN-CLAIRE LARSEN

Contents

Introduction

Early policing in Western Australia (WA) was modeled on the British system of policing. Consequently, colonial Australia "established a militaristic style of command" (Findlay, 2004: 21) that the "professional method" and managerialism later replaced (Holdaway, 1983: 158–159; Findlay, 2004: 136–140). The Commissioner of Police, Dr. Karl O'Callaghan, stated in the WA Police Strategic Plan (2010–2013) that WA Police "will move towards a more business-orientated model over the coming years."

In terms of organizational priorities, the focus of the WA Police is to the frontline and in delivering policing services. The services are guided by the Agency's "Service Delivery Standards" and these, inter alia, make clear Agency and community expectations. In the metropolitan area, services are delivered by seven police districts and in regional WA by another seven police districts. Supporting the districts are a number of divisions in various portfolios delivering specialist and support services. The State is also serviced by a State Crime Command which principally investigates serious and organized crime. Aside from front end policing, the districts engage local stakeholders (local government, state government agency representatives, and community groups) in creating local emergency management arrangements and in attempting to secure investment and support in responding to local social issues that impact on community safety, crime, and antisocial behavior.

In his message in the WA Police Strategic Plan (2010–2013), the Commissioner acknowledges that legislative reforms have granted Police increasing powers, which he said, must be exercised with caution. The overrepresentation of Aboriginal people in the justice system also concerns the Commissioner. Addressing the community's needs and expectations, he continues, requires Police to work collaboratively with other agencies and stakeholders. In 2002, the Kennedy Royal Commission examined WA Police culture. In 2003, the Corruption and Crime Commission was established as a police oversight agency.

The Perth metropolitan region covers 7,272 square kilometers. The number of police officers is 2,433 for a population of 1,781,870 (Annual Report, 2011: 7). Regional WA is spread over 2,524,302 square kilometers. Over 1,000 police officers (1,352) service 511,631 people as of June 30, 2010 (Annual Report, 2011: 8).

WA Police is independent of police services in other states of Australia. This means that a WA police officer cannot work in that capacity in any other state. The Australian Federal Police work under Commonwealth laws such as terrorism laws and their jurisdiction extends to WA. But WA police officers work within the bounds of the *Police Act* 1892 (WA) that regulates areas such as the appointment of officers as well as their duties and responsibilities which are specifically provisioned for under the Police Force Regulations 1979. WA Police apply the provisions of State Legislation and have in some cases, the legislative authority to apply Federal Legislation.

The interview with Dominic Staltari, Assistant Commissioner of Western Australian Police, was held in his 10th floor office in Perth's central business district early one Wednesday morning in August 2012. The view from wide office windows of the Swan River and city landscape was spectacular.

Career

ACL: What motivated you to enter police work?
DS: After successfully completing the high school leaving certificate, I wasn't sure what I wanted to do. My father was a laborer and a market gardener, an Italian immigrant, as was my mother. My mother was a

"stay at home" mum, who worked in the family operated market garden, as I had to after school, on weekends and during school holidays. Although I didn't realize at the time, my parents provided me the right personal grounding and values to be a police officer. After some six years in manual work with a number of employers and clerical work in government, I applied for and was successful in being accepted into the police academy.

What attracted me to policing was the opportunity to make a difference—make a contribution to humanity. It was an exciting work; it provided the opportunity to work in and travel to different locations within Western Australia and indeed Australia. It was a secure employment with the real opportunity for advancement and promotion. And being a police officer was a highly recognized and respected position to hold.

Since joining, I have not looked back and I stand appreciative of what my career has given me and my family and the opportunities it has presented to me. Absolutely no regrets and reflecting on my career, I wouldn't change any part of it. Has it been tough at times? Yes it has. Has it been rewarding? Extremely. Would I do it all again? Yes I would. Some officers I have worked with in the past had the unfortunate attitude that the job owed them something because of their commitment to it and their length of service. I am not of that attitude. The job does not owe me. I owe it plenty.

ACL: How long have you worked for the Western Australian police service?
DS: I have been in the police service coming up to 35 years. I joined in January 1978 and after academy training I spent three months at the central police station. At that time, most graduates from the police academy were assigned to either of Perth's then two major police stations, those being the Central (Perth) and Fremantle police stations. I remained at central police station for three months before being transferred to a plain clothes squad then commonly known as the "bodgie" squad, the primary role of which was to clean up and rid the streets of Perth of petty crime and antisocial behavior.

I remained with the central plain clothes squad for twelve months before being transferred to the Wanneroo police station, working general duties in uniform. Three years later I transferred to 79 Division, named so because it commenced in 1979. My primary role there was working in uniform with a detective providing the primary response to serious incidents of crime. Twelve months later in 1983, I joined the ranks of Detectives and between 1983 and 1994 I worked in various suburban locations and specialized squads, including the armed robbery squad for four years. In 1994, I was appointed the officer in charge of what was then the Nollamara CIB (Criminal Investigation

Branch) office, my first position as an officer in charge of an organizational unit. At this time, being a detective was what was important to me, being firmly entrenched in that kind of work as it was what I enjoyed doing most and it was my intention to progress through the detective ranks as was then possible.

In the mid-1990s, WA Police underwent significant organizational and cultural reform under a program named "Delta Reform." At the time Bob Falconer (Robert Falconer, Commissioner: 1994–1999) had just been appointed the Commissioner of Police and it was his strong and influential leadership that led to the reform program and the significant positive changes that resulted. As part of the reform program and to create a break from the existing culture, officer redundancies were offered (many were taken up); the promotional policy was modified and opened up to ensure a wide pool of applicants for commissioned officer positions, (then and still considered critical to deliver organizational and cultural change); and promotional systems were modified to ensure greater scrutiny and examination of applicants.

In spite of my then attraction to the detective ranks, I sought to be challenged. I engaged in the selection process and after an exhaustive effort I, along with others, was promoted to the rank of inspector; in my case, from the rank and designation of detective sergeant. Effectively, I bypassed the rank of Senior Sergeant, something which was not a norm in the Agency at that time and given the Agency's long history of promotion by seniority, it proved difficult for many in the Agency to accept.

Three years after my promotion to inspector (1997), I was promoted to the rank of superintendent (2000) and eight years later, I was promoted to the rank of assistant commissioner (2008), having for two years acted as an assisting commissioner (a period I sometimes jokingly refer as being my apprenticeship).

As a superintendent and assistant commissioner, my career was directed and focused on district and regional policing, positions I practiced in with the confidence to get the job done, delivering on core functional and organizational priorities. Prior to being promoted to the rank of assistant commissioner, I had been the district superintendent over three metropolitan police districts and had been acting in the position of assistant commissioner, north metropolitan region, for almost two years. In 2008, I was appointed the assistant commissioner over the corruption, prevention, and investigation portfolio, later renamed the professional standards portfolio on my recommendation. I remain in that position, one that I thoroughly enjoy, albeit it is not one that many of my peers would pursue. That is a summary of my policing career with WA Police.

My current role is one that I enjoy and it often places me in the position of protecting the Agency and the Agency "brand" by ensuring the Agency not only is best equipped to deal with unprofessional conduct, but to do so decisively in accordance with legislative provisions and the expectations of government, the community, and various oversight agencies.

I recently took the decision to make a submission to the government's Joint Standing Committee on the Corruption and Crime Commission, to their inquiry on how the Corruption and Crime Commission deals with police misconduct. The end product, which was acclaimed by the Committee, was a comprehensive document detailing the structural and functional profile of the Professional Standards portfolio. The document, with minor amendments, will now be used to promote the portfolio and to serve as a primary reference document for new inductees to the portfolio.

My team and I work closely with the Corruption and Crime Commission of Western Australia and it is fair to say the relationship is often robust, but firmly premised on honesty and openness. We do not place ourselves as subservient to the Corruption and Crime Commission and both organizations often challenge each other on various aspects of business. To be honest, my leadership and direction is to get the job done because it needs to be done and I am not driven by the fear that we may be exposed by one of a number of oversight agencies. If we get it right, as an Agency, we will be well protected—we will have achieved corruption resistance—that's what counts and that is what drives my primary effort.

What we as an Agency are required to do is exemplified by our mission statement which reads: "To enhance the quality of life and well-being of all people in Western Australia by contributing to making our State a safe and secure place." How well we deliver on this mission is characterized by the ethical health of the Agency and in the way our people behave and conduct themselves. That of course is simply put and not representative of the complexities of policing. However, we must never forget policing is a people business and to be successful, we need to make service delivery as simple as possible.

ACL: Is there anything in how your career developed that surprised you?
DS: If you had asked me whether I would achieve the rank of assistant commissioner either at the start of my career or well into it, I would have said no. It was the opportunity for promotion to senior ranks, premised only by skill, ability, and experience alone that surprised me, as was the reality that my achievements had been recognized. In reflection, what I have said here confirms what I have always believed—get the job done honestly and fairly, producing real and measurable outcomes and you will be recognized and rewarded. It is not just about the talking—it is all about the doing.
ACL: Have there been any failures over the years?
DS: On a personal, professional, and organizational level, there have not been any failures as such. Things went wrong from time to time;

they will always go wrong. No failures though. Organizationally, history will document the last twenty years as a period of significant change and in building Agency resilience and sustainability in all business and service delivery levels. Organizationally, we have been very lucky in Western Australia to have had three successive visionary police commissioners, all of whom confronted issues and led profound change.

Bob Falconer kicked the change process off in the early to mid-nineties. Love or hate the man, and I say that in the context that some people play the man and not the ball, he did an exceptional job in creating profound change and achieving business and cultural changes, as well as building sustainability in business and service delivery, all in just five years under the auspices of the Delta change program. Barry Matthews (Commissioner from 1999 to 2004) took over from Bob Falconer and entrenched the changes into normal business, building on sustainability and resilience, and bringing a period of stability. Following Barry Mathews' tenure, the Agency was exceptionally lucky to secure Dr. Karl O'Callaghan as Commissioner (2004 to the present). Karl O'Callaghan is a local officer, whilst Bob Falconer came from Victoria and returned there and Barry Matthews was from New Zealand and returned there. Karl O'Callaghan led the Agency into the twenty-first century, employing significant technology solutions to make the Agency more effective and efficient, and refocusing business and service delivery to the frontline.

So, looking back on history and comparing us to other policing agencies in Australia, my view is that we've done exceptionally well. So, there's not much that I could call failures. Things could have been done better, gone smoother, but no failures as such. Having said that though, let me say that with significant change comes internal turmoil and resistance. Yet, though these were stumbling blocks, they were easily overcome through resilience in and by strong leadership.

ACL: Has anything made you anxious?

DS: There isn't anything now that makes me anxious. Time will tell whether some of what I have witnessed and had to experience in doing the job, will have an adverse effect on my health going forward. So far, I have been able to keep it all in perspective and balance. Generally, not much makes me anxious. Do I get excited at times? Well, yes I do, but that is more about the passion than the anxiety.

ACL: Why do you keep coming to work every day?

DS: Policing is a consuming occupation, one that doesn't stop when you finish work. Like it or not, when you are a police officer, in Western Australia at least, you are *on* seven days a week, 24 hours a day. You might not be on duty all of the time, but you are a police officer all of the time. That demands dedication and discipline, and that is how it becomes entrenched in lifestyle. What keeps me coming to work every day?—put simply, policing has become a big part of my life and it is what I do best. What attracted me to policing has remained constant to this day. As I alluded to previously, if you asked me twenty years ago would I be an Assistant Commissioner today, I would have said, "not in your wildest dreams." This is, however, demonstrative of the opportunities a career in policing will afford you.

Changes Experienced

ACL: What do you see as the most important changes which have happened within your organization over the course of your career?

DS: As a police officer, in delivering policing services, there have been many changes over the years, mostly technology based, not only to make it easier for us to get the job done, but to also make us more effective and efficient. Has it done that? Well, yes it has, but I have to say it has also increased our work load because computers and technology dramatically improve capacity and because information and communications are readily available and accessible in real time; officers are easily distracted and diverted from assigned tasks. The net effect is that grades of service are adversely impacted. The Agency then led to remedy this by putting more police on the front line, which exponentially increases the cost of policing for government.

In my view, improvements in doing business and improved technologies need to be employed, but continuously tempered against delivering core functionality and core services. Sounds simple, however, it's more difficult to do as technology is a strong driver and it is consuming. Policing is about dealing with people, so the focus should be the people, not the technology. An example to explain my point here is that these days an investigator will primarily rely on intelligence holdings, technology deliverables, and forensics to obtain evidence to solve a crime, when in the past, we had to get out and talk to a lot of people to do so. The sad reality is the latter is now not often done for less serious offences.

Organizationally, the most significant change was the Delta Reform Program led by Bob Falconer. It challenged who and what we were as an Agency to reform and to drive a new future. It also not only challenged the Agency's culture and the professionalism of those within it, but the ethical health of the Agency. It created profound change, one that established purpose and direction, entrenched responsibility and accountability, and created a new future for the Agency. The simple message was, "get on board or disembark." Delta created a new organizational culture premised on integrity and professionalism, and decentralized structure and service delivery.

New regions and districts were created and the focus was local solutions to local problems. Was the reform necessary? Most definitely. Did it work? Most definitely. Was it exciting? Extremely. Was the pressure on to perform and get the job done? The expectations and the consequences were very clear. Was it rewarding? Yes it was and the achievement was premised and demonstrated by the results—reduced crime/improved crime clearances. The new Agency made those within both responsible and accountable for the results of their decisions and actions. Was there resistance to change? Most definitely. Was that overcome? Yes it was. Was it easy to do so? No, but tenacity and determination always win. Having said all of that, it was not all about business and service delivery. Development of our people was also foremost during this time and Bob Falconer's vision of creating a purpose built and best practice police training and development institution was realized with the opening of the new Police Academy at Joondalup in 2002.

Personal Policing Philosophy

ACL: What is the role of the police as regards security?
DS: Security is only one part of the policing effort and it is when it is operationally premised that police have a primary responsibility. Ordinarily, it is fair to say that security is everyone's responsibility and all in the community need to make an investment in their own security and that of the communities generally. WA Police, like any other Western world policing jurisdiction, have sophisticated and practiced plans in place to deal with any natural or man-made disasters and to this end, is well placed to protect and serve the community in times of need and emergency. With the plans come a leadership structure and operational facilities to roll out the response and recovery effort. Community members will always look to the police for leadership and for security when disaster strikes and it is for these reasons policing agencies need to have a well-established capacity and proven skills to deliver. Police will always be the first point of call for the community; and why not? —we are out there seven days a week, 24 hours a day.
ACL: Should the police focus on the causes of crime rather than the effects?
DS: The better long term investment by government and the community would be to treat the cause. Some 35 years policing experience demonstrates to me you can't deal with crime by dealing with it

at the effects end of the offending cycle. The difficulty of course is that increasing penalties, longer jail terms, being "tough on crime," and funding more police officers, make for good politics and all these attract votes. Unfortunately, initiatives and strategies are confined to the election cycle. The variables and social influences that impact on crime and which lead people to the offending cycle, are many, varied and they are almost always complex. The reality is that when investment by government is harmonized across all government agencies, to target and tackle crime, the causal effects may be better understood, so therefore better targeted. And the harmonized approach of itself, will deliver not only effectiveness and efficiency gains for government, but a sound investment to prevent crime into the future—not one or two years out, but 10 to 15 years out.

Premier Gallop (Geoff Gallop, Western Australian Premier 2001–2006, Australian Labor Party) attempted to harmonize the social agenda, creating a structural model for a joined up effort across government at a leadership level to deal with all aspects of social disadvantage generally. Unfortunately, for reasons not entirely known by me, the structure did not survive and the deliverables not achieved. My assumption is that CEOs and Director Generals of government agencies did not sufficiently commit to the model and accordingly, with a change in political leadership, it was dispensed with.

Unfortunately, organizations and governments react to statistics alone and therefore look for a quick fix to manage community concern and reaction. It is the quick fix that drives attention to the effect rather than the cause, because dealing with the cause takes a lot longer, years longer in fact.

In a policing environment, the focus is on statistics to demonstrate performance, for example, a reduction in crime or an increase in crime. In my view, though, the true performance measure is whether the level of offending has decreased or in fact increased. The reality is that this statistic is not as attractive generally to that of a significant increase or significant decrease in crime. Policing in modern times has increasingly become more reactive, for example, doing an operation to target an increase in burglary offences, then on completion, showcasing the numbers of offenders arrested and the number of charges preferred. No doubt such a result may seem impressive and the operation will cause an immediate decrease in the number of burglary offences. However, the outcome is not sustainable as it is in response to the effect not the cause. Has the level of offending stopped for good?—I dare say not. The worst that can happen to a policing agency is being accused of taking credit when a reduction in crime and antisocial behavior occurs and in response to an increase in both, being accused of attempting to shift responsibility to others or attributing it to social/financial disadvantage.

The truth is that crime and antisocial behavior is the responsibility of all in the community and police have the added responsibility to apply the law in response to offending. That is not to say that police should not make a contribution, indeed an investment to the cause. They need to, in my firm view, as police are a part of the community and jointly own the problem whatever it might be. Traditionally, police have made a contribution through working with youth and by actively engaging in community policing/crime prevention type strategies. Unfortunately, the previous level of investment in this regard is no longer considered a priority.

Our investment in technology has caused greater effort at the effects end. Gone are the days when you had to be in a building to access a computer. It can now all be done in a car and all our front line response and tasking vehicles are significantly equipped with technology. The technology allows police to access information and intelligence in real time, thus having the effect of focusing police effort on the effects end. It also causes our response times to suffer, as often, police vehicles on route to a job, are diverted to another task by reason of the technology. For instance, responding to an automated vehicle registration number plate alert, or checking a vehicle registration number and finding the owner is wanted for questioning. Response times are important to ensure the community maintains confidence in police and to reassure the community we have the capacity to achieve community safety and security. At the end of the day, both the community and the government will judge us on our grades of service.

ACL: Do you want to say something about causal factors?
DS: It doesn't take very long in this job before it becomes clear that you need to make an investment in the causal factors of crime and antisocial behavior. As a detective I found myself dealing with the same people, the same types of people, the same people locked into that social demographic of and in society. You soon ask yourself, "is this ever going to change?" Unless there is or you create a break in the cycle, nothing will change. Criminally charging people and relying on the justice system to get the job done, will not always work. Whilst the justice system causes a break in the offending cycle, by reason of the social disadvantage and other related influences, the break is often not sustainable. For instance, the adverse effects of alcohol and drugs on society and the community generally are well known and well understood. Unfortunately, we attempt to deal with these issues as policing problems and look to the justice system for the ultimate solution. The causal effects are principally health issues and greater focus and investment in this regard will achieve better and more sustainable outcomes.

To get the best value, to get the best outcome, the social agenda of government needs to be owned and harmonized across all government agencies as well as across all related community groups. I remain frustrated at the lack of investment in this regard, born principally by financial stresses. Make the investment and the revolving door of crime will slow—I'm absolutely certain about that.

ACL: From where do you get ideas for leadership?

DS: I personally learn best from actual experience and from observing. You not only learn from those leaders that excel but also from those that are poor leaders. Poor leaders demonstrate what not to do and the consequences of poor leadership. My ideas come from every day experiences and influences whether they are work related or otherwise. The reality is, from my experience at least, not all people can become leaders. Although not generally accepted, some people are natural leaders, with such skills being entrenched in character and in a natural skill base. To me, being a leader is about standing up to issues and problems, making things happen, making clear concise decisions, providing purpose and direction, accepting responsibility and accountability, and having a presence of ethical and professional standing.

ACL: So, information and experience are required for successful changes?

DS: Information is important in every aspect of leadership. Information and experience inspire confidence. Confidence is what then inspires leadership. Some people do not have the confidence to be an effective leader no matter what the extent of training and development. Good decision making relies heavily on the information being right at the time. It is not always going to be right, but that of itself should not deter a decision. A leader has to have the courage to make decisions, more so in critical situations. Our current Commissioner will say to graduating recruits, "I expect you to make decisions in difficult situations; you are not always going to get it right, but because I expect you to make them, you deserve my support." That in my view says it all.

ACL: How do you go about evaluating your processes?

DS: By being my own worst critic. I have to say that I am really tough on myself and quite frankly, as a leader, you have to be. I know when I have done it right; achieved the intended result; done a good job. I don't need someone else to tell me that. I don't crave and expect recognition. Let's face it, you don't always get it. Put simply, I question and evaluate everything I do and the decisions I make and take cognizance of the effects of my actions and decisions on others and on the business generally. Being open minded as I am and prepared to accept feedback and the views of others, no matter their rank or status, also greatly helps me to evaluate and learn.

ACL: What is your view on the police using guns?

DS: WA Police officers carrying guns as a use of force option was introduced in the late 1980s when we were confronted with a spate of serious armed robberies on banks. Given the propensity for some offenders to use violence against police officers and given the psychotic episodes some offenders suffer, for instance following illicit drug taking, the Police were issued with firearms. Like all use of force options, they have become necessary to ensure the safety of the police officer as well as the safety of the community generally. Although I understand in the UK police officers do not ordinarily carry firearms and rely on special squads of armed police to respond to such incidents, such an arrangement anywhere in Australia could not be supported, given the geographic demographics and sprawling police beats. Additionally, and I have to say with some disappointment, violence now touches many people in society and police are often challenged to deal with the perpetrators of such violence. Incidents of violence are usually dynamic in nature and circumstance requiring an immediate response by police.

ACL: And what is your position on the use of Tasers?

DS: Again, like firearms and for the same reason, Tasers now are a necessary use of force option when lethal force cannot be justified. The use of Tasers has been the subject of substantial review by both the Agency and by the Corruption and Crime Commission that oversees WA Police. There are also substantial policy and guidelines around the use of Tasers and with all use of force options. Operational police officers are required to engage in regular and periodic training. There is a high expectation placed on officers on the use of force options and should an officer engage in any unprofessional conduct with respect to its use or application, responsibility, and accountability are applied and an officer may face criminal prosecution and or managerial intervention to correct behavior.

Problems and Successes Experienced

ACL: What were the most challenging areas that you worked in?

DS: Investigating serious crimes against the person was and I suspect remains challenging, not because of the investigation process, but because of having to personally and professionally deal with abhorrent crime scenes and with the victims of such crimes. Dealing with human behavior is usually difficult, but more so when there is conflict and when there is distress. Solving the crime is usually not the difficult bit. Dealing with and managing the people and victims involved, managing emotions, expectations and grief, takes a lot of effort, patience, and empathy.

Going forward, the challenges for policing will be added to by some of the things that will fall out of declining global and financial markets and indeed climate change. Increased social disadvantage and increasing unemployment are variables that significantly influence the commission of crime and correspondingly, place greater pressure on policing resources. Policing agencies will need to become more resilient in doing more with less, focusing more on leadership and perhaps less on management to get the job done. I say this in the context of something I read some years back which went as follows: "Managers merely work in an agency and rely on fear and desperation, whilst leaders work on an agency and rely on hope and inspiration." Leadership is what will guide policing agencies through the tough and challenging times. When people turn to police for assistance, they expect leadership, not management.

ACL: Has the increase in the number of women in police service changed the service?

DS: Most definitely and for the better! Putting aside the obvious benefits on an operational level, women bring a new and different perspective to leadership and to the corporate table. The benefits here are well documented. Did I harbor an old school prejudice? The truth is, yes, but many years ago and my experience in working with many women over the years quickly changed my views in this regard. Bottom line, women have been great for policing and as an Agency, we need to do more to attract more women to policing generally and to senior and corporate roles in policing.

ACL: Would you like to say something about working with Australia's various ethnic groups?

DS: Over my career, I made an investment of time and effort, from a community policing perspective, to assist people from Cultural and Linguistically Diverse (CALD) communities. The need for this investment became clear to me as far back as 1994 when I was the officer in charge of the (then) Nollamara CIB. At that time, we were confronted with the difficulty of dealing with and in investigating serious crimes arising out of domestic violence occurring within CALD communities. It soon became obvious to us that we needed to make an investment in understanding the different cultures, to best position ourselves to positively influence those cultures to protect vulnerable members and to ensure breaches of the peace and of the law did not occur. This could only be achieved by taking the time to meet and to influence people in an attempt to gain the trust and respect of the various communities. We employed a whole range of initiatives and strategies to achieve this, from simple "meet and greet" sessions to arranging social soccer matches between police teams and teams from the various CALD communities.

The strategy was successful because at that time, through a federally funded project titled "Community Policing in a Multicultural Society," a full time multicultural community liaison officer was assigned to manage the project and worked to establish and entrench the relationship between the police and the various communities. Following the conclusion of the project, as recommended by the project evaluation, WA Police employed a full time multicultural liaison officer to continue the work as a part of normal business. As it turned out, the officer employed was the project officer.

As a District Superintendent and to further empower such community groups I, on advice, caused the establishment of a "Multicultural Safer WA Group" to complement the (then) Safer WA strategy that existed to engage the community generally. The intention was to give members, indeed leaders from CALD communities, a say on community crime prevention matters and so empower them to make a contribution and to make a difference in this regard. The approach was successful to the point where CALD community members actively engaged with police on a range of issues and in assisting police.

Unfortunately, with a change in Government, the Safer WA program was dispensed with and accordingly, the direct connection between police and various communities, created by the strategy, diminished. Additionally, for reasons not fully known by me, WA Police no longer employs a dedicated multicultural liaison officer, although a number of other community engagement strategies have been implemented to attempt to achieve the same outcome.

ACL: Are they teaching police recruits at the academy about multicultural issues?

DS: Yes. I do not know the extent or type of training in this regard other than to say that importance is placed on such training, given that it is key to achieving service delivery standards—knowing and understanding the community you serve.

ACL: Is the police service employing more police from various ethnic backgrounds?

DS: We try to and as an agency we have made significant investment and have tried hard in the past to attempt to attract recruits from CALD communities. However, language and education barriers present the greatest difficulty in this regard. The same could be said of the Agency's effort to attract and retain officers from the Indigenous community. Despite the barriers though, the effort by the Agency in this regard will not waiver and nor should it. A policing agency should reflect the people it serves.

ACL: Is the police service employing Indigenous police officers?

DS: We try very hard to. Again, over the years the Agency has made a significant investment to employ more Indigenous officers, albeit education skills and social disadvantage present as the greatest barriers in this regard. Going to history, the Agency under an act of parliament employed Aboriginal liaison officers in an attempt to connect local Indigenous communities to police. As I understand it, the intention was to place these officers in the various communities and for them to liaise with local police. Unfortunately, in my view at least, we put these officers in uniform, placed them in a police station and they become part of the policing effort which in effect served to extinguish the liaison function.

In recent years, the Agency stopped employing Aboriginal liaison officers and attempted to transition these officers into fully operational police officers. Many have transitioned, albeit the skill and education level in some cases was marginal. Some Aboriginal liaison officers remain and will be retained until such time as the officers decide to separate. The approach now is to replace Aboriginal police liaison officers with cultural competent officers, a status achieved through knowledge and experience of local Indigenous customs and culture. Some years back, I did some work with a former Member of Parliament and prominent Indigenous community leader, Ernie Bridge, to attract more Indigenous people into policing through a number of training and development programs. Unfortunately and sadly, education and social disadvantage remain as barriers to that effort.

ACL: How serious is police corruption in Western Australia?

DS: There is no overt corruption as such in WA Police. However, that is not to say corruption does not exist or is unlikely to occur at any time. When it comes to achieving corruption resistance, the reality is that the job is never done and it is never done because we employ human beings and human beings, even those that are police officers, by reason of unfortunate social disadvantage and consequences; failed relationships; greed; gambling and drug addictions; misguided ambition—to mention but a few influences and motivations, may or will engage in unprofessional conduct at some point in their lives and careers.

WA Police makes a significant investment in a number of proactive activities and programs to both improve and enhance the ethical and professional culture of the Agency. These include an early intervention program; a confidential reporting mechanism; a supported internal witness program; alcohol and drug testing; personnel security vetting; an audit program; and a declarable associations policy. The intent is to identify unprofessional conduct, adverse behavior, and potential risks at the earliest possible opportunity to prevent escalation.

Theory and Practice

ACL: What kind of research, in what form, on what issues do you find most useful for practice?

DS: The WA Police does invest in research on topic specific issues; however, the extent of this investment is reserved given the resource focus is to the front line. Research that is done is shared to avoid duplication. In terms of practice, I have not found general type research particularly useful and, to be honest, I place more weight and reliance on the outcomes of subject/issue specific reviews and assessments. To be honest, it hasn't helped me over the years, although I do appreciate the value of research and the benefits it may deliver. Although policing might be the same around the world, the way policing services are delivered in terms of style and structure is different and needs to be unique to local communities and local demographics to achieve best effect and efficiency. The benefits of research in policing are more about what and how an issue and trend should be policed, as opposed to the actual delivery of services. Statistics and statistical research are important as indicators of performance and ethical health. Research also helps all policing agencies to remain contemporary by being both nationally and globally informed.

Transnational Relations

ACL: What about WA Police's relationship with what's happening globally. Is your work informed by what's happening internationally?

DS: It is critically important for policing agencies to be informed on a global and national level, not only to ensure best practice is being employed in terms of community safety and security but to learn from policing and community security issues and trends. World events like 9/11, for example, and then the London bombings, significantly shook the world into reality and remind us to be always vigilant and ready and prepared to respond. Policing is very similar throughout the Western world and to that end, the lessons learnt, the issues and the trends in one country, are relevant to all. Terrorism is real, as is the capacity for a pandemic to occur. With both, a global response is necessary and for that to occur, the planning, the prevention, the response, and the recovery effort in any one policing jurisdiction needs to be well understood and well practiced so as to complement the overall global effort to ensure the best possible outcome is achieved.

Democratic Policing

ACL: What does democratic policing mean to you?

DS: Idealism is the greatest enemy of reality and to that end, theory has a place in policing, but experience has an even greater place. I am not well read on democratic policing, but from what I have read I consider it largely just another academic title. Democracy and its principles are all well understood across the world. In policing terms, it is about good governance, fairness, equity, compassion, transparency, and about being open and accountable. It is also about fairly and equitably representing, serving, and protecting the community.

ACL: Does maintaining law and order mean that policing is involved in maintaining the existing social order and power structures or can it allow serious protests against the government and laws and powerful elites?

DS: Maintaining law and order is about improving and maintaining social order, but not specifically power structures as such. Police apply the law and the Courts enforce the law. As in any other democracy, protest action is permitted as long as it is within the bounds of the law and not in contravention of it. It is relatively common for the community to peacefully and publicly protest the decisions and actions of Government, other government instrumentalities, major corporate entities, and major community groups. As long as the protests are within the boundary of the law, they are permitted. Police will in many cases monitor such protests and will act to maintain the peace and if necessary, apply the law to do so.

ACL: Can the police resist demands from the government to crack down on opposition and protest?

DS: Yes. There is clear separation of powers between the Government, the
        Courts, the Judiciary and the Police. Police in WA are appointed
        under the provisions of the *Police Act* 1892 and all police officers
        are autonomous and personally liable in applying the law. For
        example, a police officer cannot instruct another police officer to
        arrest and charge a person. Additionally, the Government cannot
        instruct the Police Commissioner on an operational issue. Police
        may only act and respond within the boundaries of the law and
        in response to a core function issue. Police have a responsibility to
        Government to deliver policing services and to meet agreed key
        performance indicators in this regard.

ACL: What levels of public support does the WA Police service have?

DS: In Western Australia and from my experience and feedback, there is
        high public support for police. The current Commissioner of Police
        has a high media profile and will engage on all social/community
        issues that touch policing. This of itself has contributed to the high
        levels of public support as has the practice by the Agency to be
        open and honest with the community and to publicly accept both
        responsibility and accountability when things go wrong.

Looking Ahead

ACL: How do you see the future of policing a decade or so from now? Is
        there much that you'd change?

DS: Change is the only constant in life and the capacity to change together
        with creating the flexibility to change is what will premise and
        drive our capacity to deliver on business and service delivery out-
        comes into the future. Without change, you can't improve. To that
        end then and as an Agency, the government and the community
        place a responsibility on us to deliver and to do so effectively and
        within financial means. To achieve all of that, we need to continu-
        ously improve on how we run our business and that requires con-
        tinuous change.

As I said previously, technology is consuming and it has the capacity to drive
business and service delivery away from core functionality. Policing has to
embrace all technologies that contribute to achieving efficiency gains, however, not at the expense of becoming less effective. We are in the business of
policing, not technology development. Foremost is being effective and delivering value in service delivery. Simply put, we need to be efficient in the way
we do business so that we are effective in the services we deliver.

In terms of the way we conduct business and deliver policing, there are some fundamentals of policing that in my view should not change. I see policing as having five distinct core functions. They are the prevention and control of crime; maintenance of the peace; traffic management and enforcement; emergency management and coordination; and assisting members of the community in times of emergency and need. These core functions are primary and should remain the focus of the policing effort. The frontline first strategy initiated by Karl O'Callaghan demonstrates this focus is being employed. I reiterate—we should remain in the business of policing and not deviate to other roles and functions. Police should always be the first point of contact in times of need or emergency. If we can't help, then we should be able to point people in the right direction for assistance. For all policing services, the one contact should be on the basis of a one stop shop. Police are usually the only government agency that can be relied on to be around 24 hours per day, 7 days a week. That level of investment by government demands a return. The demand for policing services has caused the Agency to divert police officer effort away from crime prevention work to focus on front end service delivery. This diversion of effort is unfortunately a stark reality of the times. However, given funding levels and resources, together with a better strategy, an investment in crime prevention is undoubtedly sound given it targets the causal factors of crime.

In my opinion, policing as service will not change significantly going forward. The primary role and functionality of policing will also change little. What will change is what police will be required to respond to and deal with. Organized crime, criminal organizations, and criminals generally are becoming more sophisticated and organized, utilizing technologies that are now common to all in the community. Law makers will need to respond to ensure police retain the capacity to police effectively. Style, systems, processes, practices, and structures of policing may change going forward. What will not change is the reliance on police to set and maintain community standards of behavior, ordinarily achieved by police applying the law, supported by the courts in executing and enforcing the law.

Conclusion

Dominic Staltari has dedicated his working life to policing in WA. His firm convictions shine through in his approach to leadership, decision-making, and practical accomplishments. For him, external agencies have a part to play in assisting the police to deal with pockets of offending behavior. Overall, as Dominic Staltari's orientation is predominately practical, theoretical concerns do not feature highly. Research may have a place at high-end policing, but not on the beat. For him, policing must remain focused on people who expect police officers to show leadership and exercise high integrity. Over his 35 years, policing has experienced many changes, including the introduction of firearms, Glock 22 in the 1980s, and more recently the X-26 Taser Electronic Control Device, and other technologies. The Police Academy was completed in 2002. All recent developments, together with managerial changes that the last two Commissioners have implemented, according to Dominic Staltari, have been for the better.

References

Findlay, M. 2004. *Introducing Policing Challenges for Police and Australian Communities.* Melbourne, Australia: Oxford University Press.

Holdaway, S. 1983. *Inside the British Police A Force at Work.* Oxford: Basil Blackwell.

Western Australia Police. 2010. *WA Police Strategic Plan 2010–2013.* Perth: Western Australia Police, http://www.police.wa.gov.au/LinkClick.aspx?fileticket=9Ua UQEvo%2bdo%3d&tabid=1029. Accessed October 4, 2012.

Western Australia Police. 2011. *WA Police Annual Report 2011.* Perth: Western Australia Police, http://www.police.wa.gov.au/Aboutus/Annualreport/tabid/935/Default. aspx. Accessed October 4, 2012.

Peter Marshall, Commissioner, New Zealand Police

INTERVIEWED BY
GARTH DEN HEYER

Contents

Introduction

In April 2011, Peter Marshall was appointed Commissioner of the New Zealand Police, a police service of approximately 9,500 sworn officers and 2,500 civilian staff. He joined the New Zealand Police in 1972 as a 19-year-old, and after 26 weeks of recruit training at the Police College in Trentham, an industrial city approximately 40 km from Wellington, the capital city, he was posted to Auckland, New Zealand's largest city.

Peter Marshall has completed approximately 42 years of continuous service with the New Zealand Police, and although most of his career has been with the Criminal Investigation Branch, there have been lengthy periods within the Uniform Branch at various ranks.

Commissioner Marshall leads a national police service that is responsible for the full range of law enforcement services and investigations from minor criminal offending and traffic enforcement to major and organized crimes. The organization comprises approximately 8,500 sworn officers and 2,000 civilian employees and is structured to include National Headquarters, the Royal New Zealand Police Training College, and 12 districts. The 12 districts are made up of 50 policing areas, which encompass more than 400 police stations.

During early colonization, New Zealand had no organized national police force. Law and order was managed by local magistrates and then by provincial authorities. In 1846, the centralized Armed Constabulary was formed, but provincial growth placed too many demands upon it, leading to provincial councils forming their own police forces in 1853. This fragmented law enforcement system changed in 1867 when the national Armed Constabulary force was formed. In 1877, this Armed Constabulary amalgamated with the provincial police forces to become the New Zealand Constabulary force. At this time, there were approximately 580 men in the Armed Constabulary and 330 in various armed police forces. The new force was divided into two sections, a Police branch and a Field branch. The Police branch was expected to act as a support to the Field force in emergencies; their training was therefore on military lines, and until 1896, only men who had served in the permanent defense force could be recruited. The rules and regulations of 1852 laid down the requirements to join Governor Grey's Armed Constabulary Force: a man had to be of good character, sober, and able to read and write. His training was mainly drilling, with arms practice. The emphasis on foot and mounted drill was continued in the provincial Armed Police Forces and in the Armed Constabulary Force of 1867.

In 1886, Parliament passed the Police Force Act giving New Zealand its first national civil police force. This force was separate from the military and was to be unarmed except in grave emergencies and was to be based on the principles of policing devised by Rowan and Mayne, the first commissioners of the London Metropolitan Police.

The interview took place in the Commissioner's Office, Police National Headquarters, Wellington, New Zealand in January and February of 2012.

Career

GDH: What were the highlights of your career?

PM: I was fortunate enough to be posted overseas on three separate occasions. The first was to Australia as a Police Liaison Officer for a period of four and a half years, based in Canberra. During that time, I was working from the Australian Federal Police Headquarters building and had responsibility for extraditions, deportations, sharing of intelligence, and similar aspects of police work. In 2002, I was posted to Washington, DC to open up the Liaison Officer's position at the New Zealand Embassy, following the 9/11 events in New York. I was there for a two year period, interacting with State and Federal Law Enforcement Agencies throughout the United States, Canada, and South America. In January 2007, I was seconded to the Royal Solomon Islands Police Force (RSIPF) in Honiara, initially as Deputy Commissioner (Operations) and subsequently as the Commissioner of the RSIPF, following the sudden resignation of the Commissioner. I held this position until my return to New Zealand in February 2011 to become the Commissioner of the New Zealand Police. An obvious highlight was being appointed Commissioner of the New Zealand Police.

Of particular note, from my perspective, was that I was appointed Police Operation Commander for the Asia-Pacific Economic Cooperation (APEC) series of meetings convened in New Zealand in 1999. Auckland hosted the principal meeting, attended by 21 world leaders, including the then President of the United States of America, Bill Clinton. Foreign Ministers, Trade Ministers, and relevant spouses were also present, which brought the number of Internationally Protected Persons (IPPs) to 84. Bilateral meetings subsequently occurred in various parts of New Zealand, including Queenstown, Wellington, and Christchurch and involved the leaders from the Peoples' Republic of China and the United States of America and the Republic of South Korea. The APEC commitment and security provision was one of the largest Police operations of its kind at the time and involved the deployment of more than 2,500 Police Officers.

Following the APEC Police obligation, I was appointed the Police Operation Commander for the first America's Cup Regatta that was convened in Auckland Harbor during the latter part of 1999. This commitment was for a period of six months and also included overseeing millennium celebrations in central Auckland. The millennium celebrations were held against the backdrop of the proposed possible turn of the century computer date problem (known as the Year 2000 Problem or Y2 K). The possible computer problem was especially important because if the world's computers were going to stop working at 12 a.m. on January 1, 2000, New Zealand, being the first country to enter the twenty-first century, would be the first country to experience the problem.

GDH: What motivated you to enter police work?

PM: As a 19 year old, there appeared to be no other profession that offered the variety, interest, and overall excitement in terms of a career. That has proved to be the situation and I must have experienced at least 20 different aspects of work within the New Zealand Police since 1972.

GDH: What surprised you in how your career developed?

PM: No particular surprises, suffice to say that I never had any aspirations or intention to be the Commissioner of the New Zealand Police and in that context, my appointment to my current role has been somewhat of a surprise.

GDH: Did your work prove as interesting or rewarding as you thought it would?

PM: Unquestionably—particularly given the rare mix of national and international exposure that I have been fortunate to experience. I would certainly never have guessed that policing would evolve to the extent that it has compared to when I joined in 1972.

Changes Experienced

GDH: What do you see as the most important changes which have happened in policing over the course of your career?

PM: Whilst the basic nature of policing has not changed, there have been huge advances in terms of technology and associated developments. It is to be remembered that I joined the Police before the advent of computers and cellphones in the context of our work. The New Zealand Police was comparatively isolated in the 1970s and 1980s. However, in today's world, the New Zealand Police are inextricably connected to other law enforcement agencies globally. By way of example, we have New Zealand Police Officers in London, Washington, DC, Beijing, Bangkok, Jakarta, Bougainville, Timor Leste, Solomon Islands, Australia (Sydney and Canberra), South Pacific (Apia, Samoa), and Afghanistan.

New Zealand Police also accommodate the Secretariat for the Pacific Islands Chiefs of Police at our National Headquarters in Wellington. We also second three full time positions; the Executive Director (at the level of Superintendent), a Secretariat Officer (at the level of Inspector), and an administration officer.

Policing models have evolved and matured over New Zealand's history. In the period up to the 1950s, the model of policing in New Zealand was largely one of decentralized local policing (the *Police Act* 1958 removed the word "force" and replaced it with the word "service"). The Police have, since 1958, been known as The New Zealand Police Service, which better reflects Police operating practices and philosophies—policing by consent.

In the 1960s, centralized rapid response policing emerged. Then, in the 1970s and 1980s, technological developments allowed the New Zealand Police to refine its centralized command and control. This allowed for dedicated team policing units or task forces to be established to respond to particular demands. The expression "Team Police Units" in New Zealand refers to civil disorder units, which became a necessity in the 1970s and 1980s to deal large crowds of intoxicated and disorderly youths. At the same time, there grew an understanding that the policing "service" needed to focus on connecting Police closer to communities. From this understanding grew a formal commitment to community-oriented policing and was formalized with the implementation of Operation Blueprint in the 1980s. Operation Blueprint comprised of establishing a number of Community Policing Centers (CPCs) or small police stations. The organization and staffing of the CPCs was replicated across the country.

Later, in the 1990s, problem-solving policing and intelligence-led policing emerged, accompanied by a form of managerialism (including New Public Management and Management by Objectives), saw community-oriented and problem-oriented policing approaches being linked with targeted operational strategies aimed at specific organizational outputs and goals.

The nature of policing in New Zealand relative to other jurisdictions too, significantly reflects reassurance policing models that are aimed at early intervention. This early intervention has seen New Zealand Police shift to a style of policing where we are highly visible, known to the public, and target "signal crimes," exercising informal "social control" in local communities.

This form of policing is by nature citizen focused and depends on public confidence in the Police, as Police seek to motivate the community to work with us, engaging with them to help identify potential opportunities to prevent crime before it takes place.

GDH: What changes in external conditions have had significant impact on policing?

PM: First, the ongoing constrained fiscal environment and upward cost pressures. New Zealand Police is anticipating significant longer term pressures on publicly funded services in New Zealand. Leading into the 2020s, the main driver of the demand for public services, and especially policing services, is expected to be the ageing population. On the supply side, the primary source of cost pressures for delivering these services will be personnel related.

Second, demographic changes in relation to migration, and the population's age profile and ethnic mix. People are moving about, to, from, and through New Zealand more than ever. And like most other developed countries, the replacement rate of New Zealand's population is declining. As a result of these trends, the country's population is changing structurally, which will affect future demands for service and the makeup of the workforce of New Zealand Police.

Then there are rapid advances in technology, which are redefining privacy, authorship, participation, and personalization. Advances in existing technologies and the emergence of new technologies are changing people's lives faster than anything else. More than ever, individuals are shaping their worlds directly from the goods and services they consume to the governance of nations. These technologies are allowing businesses to interact intimately with customers on a massive scale, challenging traditional notions of privacy, and enabling the emergence of new types of crime.

We are also faced with changing demand for police services and changing expectations about the nature and quality of public services. The demands for police services are changing as populations become more diverse and the operating environment more complex. Expectations about the nature and quality of these services are changing too, and demands on New Zealand Police are no longer defined by this country's borders. We have to meet the challenges of countering globalized, technology-enabled crime. In committing their offending, organized criminal syndicates and terrorist groups continue to find new ways to exploit the movement of people and advances in technology. Combating these people and their crimes requires overcoming challenges of interoperability, coordination, and governance between enforcement agencies and internationally.

Finally, the changes that the New Zealand Police faced, from a management perspective, as a result of the 1984 series of New Zealand economic and labor market reforms designed to eliminate government debt and to create an internationally competitive economic environment. The government reforms were the most thorough in New Zealand's history, and the changes ranked amongst the most radical and comprehensive undertaken anywhere in the world. The scope and the scale of these changes were significant and placed an emphasis on the Police to do more with less. As a result, New Zealand Police have developed and implemented a number of extensive change programs to maintain service delivery levels.

GDH: Overall, has the quality of policing improved or declined?
PM: The answer is unquestionably they have improved. Accounting processes and measurements are an integral part of our day to day work. In past decades, police were highly reactive, and the "revolving door" in terms of the justice system was just part and parcel of the environment we worked in. Today, the New Zealand Police is highly focused on its Prevention First policy, that is, ensuring that as far as possible the New Zealand Police influence the environment that it operates in and takes steps to pre-empt criminal activity. The whole thrust of our organization is aimed at proactive and preventative approaches, with an absolute belief that we can influence the criminal environment within which we work.

I initiated the Prevention First strategy shortly after I was appointed Commissioner of Police in April 2011. The program was designed to be the operating strategy for the New Zealand Police and to place prevention at the forefront of the organization and people at the center. The strategy was implemented to operationalize policing actions and to enable the Police to deploy resources to "beat" demand, understand and respond to the drivers of crime, and to foster a change in mind-set that puts prevention and the needs of victims at the forefront of policing and ensuring that prevention was the responsibility of every Police employee. Prevention First was premised on ensuring that all Police employees understood their role, and to establish a link between operational information and an intelligence-driven resource management and deployment model, and the five drivers of crime (alcohol, families, organized crime and drugs, road policing, and youth). We believe that these five drivers of crime do not act in isolation, but that they intersect, overlap, and impact upon one another.

The final aspect influencing the improvement in the quality of policing is the establishment of relationships and working groups/committees. The New Zealand Police have extensive relationships at all levels within the community and have been instrumental in establishing a number of specific groups and task forces. An important group to assist with the investigation of serious crime is the Combined Law Enforcement Group (CLAG). The CLAG consists of Police, the intelligence agencies, Customs, and a number of other border enforcement agencies, and is further strengthened by the international co-operation through the embedding of Liaison Officers within Police. This structure means Police now work in a far more collaborative environment to achieve optimum success.

GDH: In general, is it more or less difficult to be a Police Officer now than in the past?

PM: I believe the answer is undoubtedly, more difficult. Today represents a very complex environment for Police, especially in the context of extensive legislation, accountability, and inter-government agency collaboration. The public and government scrutiny that I mentioned earlier has also added to the complexity of current policing in New Zealand. I believe the New Zealand public is well served by our organization and is better served by the New Zealand Police in 2014 than it was in 1972.

Personal Policing Philosophy

GDH: What do you think should be the role of the Police in society?

PM: Absolute adherence to the upholding of New Zealand's law in an objective, professional, and non-partisan manner. As I have said on many occasions, Governor-Generals, Prime Ministers, Ministers, and Members of Parliament come and go. The New Zealand Police is a constant, having been in formal existence since 1886 with its own proud history. We are a constant organization that provides structure to the democratic process in New Zealand. In 2011, Transparency International voted New Zealand the least corrupt country in the world. It is my submission that the New Zealand Police is central to the success of that positioning.

GDH: What should be their job, functions, and roles? What should be left to other people or organizations?

PM: Today's policing role is far more comprehensive and inclusive than it was in past years. Essentially, the role comes down to prevention of breaches of the peace, and the protection of life and property. That of course is quite an undertaking and it is up to the Police to work together with a number of other government agencies, NGOs, and the public in terms of those aspirations.

GDH: What organizational arrangements/structures do you think work and which do not?

PM: Clear lines of organizational structure and clear lines of organizational accountability. To ensure this within the New Zealand Police, I have extensively changed our senior management structure in the past 12 months. For instance, the Police Executive was previously 29 in number and has now been reduced to 15. Although not militaristic in nature, I believe a Police organization needs a clear hierarchal structure given the operational nature of much of our work.

GDH: What policies on relations with the community, with political groups, with other criminal justice organizations work well? What hampers co-operation with other agencies and groups?

PM: In the 1970s, there was a policy of centralization within New Zealand Police. Essentially, suburban Police Stations were either closed or had minimal staff aligned to them. Staff were focused in larger complexes which had the effect of reducing administrative overheads and creating certain efficiencies in terms of having staff under one roof. However, this approach had the disadvantage of withdrawing local Police from local communities. Police vehicles were seen leaving a central hub, attending events or incidents, and then returning to the one principal building. The Police were subsequently seen as being less connected to the individual communities, there was no ownership in terms of crime patterns or trends and it was very much a "fire brigade" type of approach to law enforcement. The disconnection had many disadvantages, the main one being the lack of cohesion between suburban areas and mainstream policing. In recent decades, however, there has been a move by the New Zealand Police to reverse the 1970s trend, with local "community policing" principles re-established and reaffirmed.

It is essential that the New Zealand Police remains apolitical and that there be absolute adherence to the principle of the separation of powers. The Police must be very even-handed, and it is fair to say that the New Zealand Police has been very conscious of this. Decisions have been made based on the law, and as a consequence, despite adverse commentary from time to time by political groups, the even-handed approach has prevailed. It has also been incumbent upon the New Zealand Police to treat each political group fairly, regardless of whether any particular party has formed the Government of the day.

As I mentioned earlier, last year New Zealand was voted the least corrupt country in the world by Transparency International, and it is my submission that the New Zealand Police, with an apolitical stance, has contributed significantly to that impressive result.

As a Police Commissioner, I am part of what is known as the Justice Sector Group, which involves Chief Executives Officers (CEOs) from the Department of Justice, Department of Corrections, the Serious Fraud Office, and the Crown Law Office. We work collaboratively in terms of finding efficiencies, whether in terms of a collaborative financial approach or in terms of shared resources. For instance, Corrections had underspent their annual budget with which Police was able to secure extra funding. Various organizations within the Justice Sector Group are embarking upon shared intelligence, procurement approaches, and administrative efficiencies for the benefit of all the Group members. No longer is the New Zealand Police a separate organization in terms of administrative matters. The absolute independence of the Police in terms of operational matters remains sacrosanct. Cooperation in this regard with other agencies would be hampered if there were particular personalities within the Chief Executive Officer group who were not committed to working in a collegial role. It would also not be as efficient if there wasn't Ministerial oversight of the joint approach to greater efficiencies. The personalities and attitude of the Chief Officers is fundamental to success in this regard.

GDH: How should policing be performed? What should be the preferred priorities and strategies?

PM: In early 2008, there was a change in the New Zealand Government, and the newly elected Government, in response to the 2007 international fiscal crisis, imposed a review of the New Zealand Police with the view of reducing organizational costs. To diminish costs, the Police commenced the development of the Policing Excellence Programme, which was a major change program comprising nine work-streams or initiatives, owned and driven by individual District Commanders. The work-streams were designed to enable Police to "become more effective and more focused on prevention" and to be better placed to deal with changing demands. The program was intended to increase service delivery effectiveness, free resources, and increase the use of technology to enable Police to spend more time on serving their communities. The aim of the program is to facilitate the transfer of officer time from administration and compliance paperwork to working more with the public and victims, and in preventing problems escalating. It was also intended that the implementation of the work-streams would have benefits across a number of other justice sector agencies.

New Zealand Police has also recently embarked on a Prevention First Policy, which has a number of tranches aligned to it. Prevention First puts prevention at the forefront of everything we do, ultimately to reduce crime and crashes, gain greater control of the criminal environment, and make New Zealand a safer place to live, visit, and to do business. It is a balanced approach which uses intelligence, enforcement, and alternative ways of resolving cases enabling us to better understand and respond to the drivers of crime. Prevention First will mean a raft of changes to the way we work with victims so they receive a better service and are less likely to become victims again. It will involve changes to the way we deploy staff so our workforce is more flexible and better placed to respond to what is happening in our communities before it is too late. Prevention First Policing is based on three principles. First, deploying to beat demand. Deployment is a crucial component and is about being prepared and flexible so that we can mobilize resources pre-emptively and quickly to stay on top of demand. The second principle is understanding and responding to the drivers of crime. Police will work with other agencies, service providers, and the community to address the underlying causes of offending and victimization. There will be an emphasis upon families, youth, alcohol, road policing, and organized crime/drugs. The final principle of Prevention First is changing the mindset of our people. It will foster a change in the mindset of our people which puts prevention and the needs of victims at the forefront of policing. This will require absolute leadership and a victim focus.

Problems and Successes Experienced

GDH: In your experience, what policies or programs have worked well and which have not?

PM: A community policing model which sees Police inculcated into far-reaching aspects of society in a proactive manner works very well in the New Zealand and the wider South Pacific context. What has not worked well has been the policy of centralization that the New Zealand Police experienced in the 1970s. Police Officers became isolated from their communities; they were not intimately part of those communities and were seen as being involved in a "fire brigade" style of policing, responding to tasks and then retreating back to large Police Stations.

GDH: What would you consider to be the greatest problem facing the Police at this time?

PM: The biggest problem facing policing at this time is managing to provide an efficient Police service to the population in the context of a new fiscal environment. This problem can be particularly challenging, especially when improving standards of service in a realistic manner at the same time.

GDH: What problems in policing do you find are the most difficult to deal with? What would be easy to change?

PM: There are a number of issues and one is to ensure that subordinates and rank and file members share the vision of the Police Executive and embrace those philosophies. In the context of New Zealand Police, the Prevention First approach has to be inculcated throughout the 12 districts, involving nearly 12,000 personnel. Whilst not every member of the organization will be on the "journey," the challenge is to ensure there is a philosophical and practical meeting of minds. Having been with New Zealand Police for nearly 40 years, it is quite apparent that the new generation of younger Police Officers does not necessarily have the same ideals and vision—that is the challenge. It is also a challenge to ensure that female Police officers are brought up through the ranks to take on Executive responsibilities. Whilst the New Zealand Police has approximately a 17% female component, the number of Commissioned Officers is very low. There are a variety of reasons for this occurring, and it is a challenge in today's environment to promulgate change in this regard.

GDH: Is anything about policing easy?

PM: Policing becomes comparatively easy when there is a mandate from the community to act in the manner which is adopted. The more "buy-in" from society and support for the actions of Police, the less problematical law enforcement is. Generally speaking, in the New Zealand environment, policing does have the support of the communities. Last year, the New Zealand Public had 82% trust and confidence in the Police.

Transnational Relations

GDH: Have you been affected by, and how, in the work of your organization by developments outside the country?

PM: As previously mentioned, the New Zealand Police is no longer an isolated organization in a country far removed from the rest of the world. On the contrary, we have been inextricably drawn into a raft of international obligations, whether in the context of mutual assistance treaties, international obligations, or various working groups.

GDH: Have those interactions been beneficial or harmful? What kind of external international influences are beneficial and which ones less so?

PM: Generally speaking, the interactions have been very beneficial in terms of the international sharing of intelligence and in terms of the practical application in relation to criminal investigations. For instance, our Beijing-based Liaison Officer has been able to successfully conclude a number of serious criminal investigations as a result of his personal interactions with Chinese authorities. New Zealand is involved with the Interpol network, Asian Police Network (ASEANAPOL) and other working arrangements throughout the world. The New Zealand Police Commissioner is part of the Australasian Commissioners' body involving the State and Federal Law Enforcement agencies within that country. As one example, when the Christchurch earthquake occurred on February 22, 2011 with the loss of 180 plus lives, the New Zealand Police Commissioner was able to call upon immediate assistance from his Australian counterparts and approximately 250 Australian Police Officers arrived in Christchurch within 48 hours. There is very close association with South Pacific Nations which has proved to be extremely beneficial in terms of intelligence and criminal investigations in this particular region of the world.

GDH: How have developments post September 11 affected your work?

PM: We immediately set up Liaison Office positions in London, Washington, DC, and Jakarta. We are well and truly embedded in those environments with greater understanding and mutual assistance.

Democratic Policing

GDH: What does democratic policing entail and how has this been implemented?

PM: We are faced with increasing expectations of transparency in relation to public institutions' decision making. There is a major shift towards the transparency of public institutions' and governments' data and decision making processes, with citizens and other commentators increasingly expecting to be informed as a matter of course. This shift is significant for New Zealand Police. New Zealand Police has an interest in New Zealand being corruption free, but, in performing its functions and meeting its obligations, some secrecy is necessary.

Whilst the operational independence of the Police has remained sacrosanct, there is far more accountability to central government. In times gone by, Police had their annual budget and spent it "as they saw fit." Today there is absolute scrutiny in terms of government, not only directing the priorities but in holding Police administrators highly accountable in terms of productivity and results. The financial management of the New Zealand Police is business orientated, with outputs and clear expectations from government. There is also far more connectivity with other government agencies. For instance, the Justice Sector (Police, Justice, Corrections, Crown Law Office, Serious Fraud Office) is working collectively in terms of shared services in ways to improve efficiencies. This is a comparatively new development, and in the past, each government agency has been somewhat independent in terms of working in their own silos.

There is also a greater accountability to oversight bodies in terms of policing activities. For instance, the New Zealand Police is now the subject of annual reviews by the Office of Auditor-General, State Services Commissioner, and the Independent Police Conduct Authority. All aspects of Police work is rigorously scrutinized against the Strategic Plan and business processes. *Official Information Act* requests from political, media, and public arenas are very much to the fore. The question of public accountability, primarily through media outlets, has changed markedly since the 1970s. The New Zealand Police prides itself on its interaction with minority communities and the democratic changes in this country have been significant over recent decades. For instance, Auckland City (population 1.5 m) has 20% of its population who identify with Asian backgrounds.

Looking Ahead

GDH: What are the most likely developments you see happening and which would you like to see happening? What is most needed now to improve policing?

PM: In today's world, we have complex problems requiring multi-player solutions. A simpler time of public institutions unilaterally solving problems has passed, and sophisticated mechanisms of cooperation and accountability, plus means of testing solutions as problems emerge, are now necessary. By its nature, New Zealand Police work is influenced by the actions of others and at times is accomplished through others. This networked nature of policing must address intractable, complex public problems by providing solutions that are enduring and fair, while avoiding the burdens of excessive administration and bureaucracy.

Not only is the nature of policing changing but the environment in which the New Zealand Police operates is changing in some significant ways. The Police Environmental Scan, "What's on the Horizon? The Next Five Years and Beyond: An Environmental Scan" (February 2011), describes major drivers likely to shape New Zealand over the next five years and beyond. In particular, three "mega" forces are likely to override or drive all others across the globe in the first half of this century. First, an historic shifting of power and wealth. Second, the multi-faceted imperative to get "more from less"; and finally, the technology revolution. The level of turbulence caused by these mega-trends is redefining what is meant by a "stable" operating environment. They are also framing the public policy challenges for New Zealand over the coming decades.

There are very few areas of the world where policing is respected as an honorable profession within communities. Throughout vast tracks of the African Continent, South America, Eastern Europe, and Asia, policing is seen as corrupt, politically influenced, and highly inefficient. The challenge is for Police organizations to be non-partisan and absolute bastions of professionalism in terms of upholding the law. Sometimes the law in itself is questionable! In the New Zealand environment, I am confident about the integrity of New Zealand policing, however, there needs to be absolute and ongoing scrutiny to ensure high standards prevail. The principle of the separation of powers between government, the judiciary, and law enforcement is sacrosanct as problems in policing occur when there is a blurring of responsibilities in this regard.

Conclusion

The major themes of this interview with Commissioner Marshall are obvious. Peter Marshall is a dedicated police officer with foresight, and trust in and respect for the institution of the New Zealand Police. Furthermore, he has been instrumental in introducing two extensive change programs in the New Zealand Police that have radically transformed how they view themselves and deliver their services. The first change program introduced was Policing Excellence that was designed to enable the New Zealand Police to become more effective and more focused on prevention, and to be better place to deal with changing demand. The second program, Prevention First, was designed to be the operating strategy for the New Zealand Police to place prevention at the forefront of the organization and people at the center. The intention of the two programs is not only to reduce New Zealand Police operating costs but also to assist Police with achieving the Government's outcomes of reducing youth and violent crime, total crime, and the reoffending rate.

The implementation of both Policing Excellence and Prevention First will ensure that the New Zealand Police is strategically placed to be able to take advantage of the future environment and that the organization is able to develop and implement extensive change management programs that fundamentally affect how the organization delivers its services. His is a truly lasting achievement for a Commissioner who is seen as a leader and a statesman.

Jean-Michel Blais, Chief Constable, Halifax Regional Police, Canada

7

INTERVIEWED BY
STEPHEN B. PERROTT

Contents

Introduction

Although the city of Halifax has been policed since its founding in 1749, first by naval shore patrols and then by Day and Night Watches, it was not until 1864 that the Halifax Police Department was formed as an official entity in this bustling port city. Sister city Dartmouth formed its own police force in 1874, as did neighboring town, Bedford, more than 100 years later in 1982. In 1996, all of the villages and communities of the former Halifax County, then policed by the Royal Canadian Mounted Police (RCMP), were amalgamated with Halifax, Dartmouth, and Bedford to form Halifax Regional Municipality (HRM), all situated on the eastern coast of mainland Canada. The entire municipality of nearly 400,000 people is now policed by a joint force of about 500 Halifax Regional Police (HRP) officers and about 200 members of the RCMP, making it the only integrated police force in Canada. The commanding officer of the RCMP contingent is currently Chief Superintendent Lee Bergerman, whose office is directly adjacent to Chief Constable Jean-Michel Blais.

In practice, patrol functions in the urban core of Halifax, Dartmouth, and Bedford are handled by HRP with the outer suburbs and geographically dispersed rural communities of the former Halifax County patrolled by the RCMP. All specialized units are completely integrated: Public Safety, Special Investigations, Special Enforcement, and Court Liaison.

Chief Constable Blais was interviewed in December 2013 at police head-quarters in Halifax, Nova Scotia, Canada. He addressed all questions asked of him in a forthright and open manner.

Career

SP: Begin by telling me a little bit about your career, how you got started, and what sorts of twists and turns came along the way.
JMB: I've over 26 years of policing experience here in Canada and in the southern hemisphere of the Americas. I started out with the RCMP. I took a look at it being a job slightly out of the ordinary. I didn't want to have a 9–5 regular job; I wanted something that had a bit more excitement. I wanted to be able to contribute in a very visible manner to my community. And I didn't want to stay in Toronto or Montréal, two cities where I had grown up and attended school and university.

The Mounties "came a calling"—I had also applied to the Ontario Provincial Police—and the Mounties came first. I went off to Regina for training and then to my first posting which was south of Québec City where I was for about six and a half years in various types of work, mainly drugs, immigration, and customs. I went to Haiti for the first time in 1995 for six months— my first experience in international policing which I found very rewarding. When I came back from Haiti, I completed my law degree at Laval University and then was promoted to the rank of Sergeant in the Montreal Drug Section. I stayed there for a few years and then, in 2000, I was commissioned to the rank of Inspector. That was out in Winnipeg and I ended up in municipal policing in Portage la Prairie, Manitoba, and doing major crime investigations for the entire province of Manitoba outside of Winnipeg. And then, by virtue of my legal training, I was sent to the RCMP Adjudication Directorate, and became an adjudicator for the internal disciplinary tribunal and ended up becoming its Director.

In 2008, I sought and received a transfer to Haiti as the Deputy Police Commissioner in charge of 1,700 United Nations police officers down there. I came back from Haiti and became the Chief Prosecutor in the RCMP's internal disciplinary tribunal referenced earlier in charge of a group of 10 lawyers from across the country. Then, in 2010, by my request, I was transferred to

Halifax where I was in charge of labor relations within the Atlantic region for the RCMP. I was promoted in 2011 to Chief Superintendent in charge of the Halifax district of the RCMP, an integrated policing model along with HRP. When the Chief of HRP retired, after a 42 year career, I chose to put my name in to become Chief. I was accepted, and in October 2012, I became Chief—and here I am today.

SP: Would you say that you had a pretty eclectic background getting here? Any major areas in policing that you've missed?

JMB: Yes, strangely enough, it's basic patrol, front-line patrol. I've been very limited. I've always had to force myself to get out there as a supervisor of these individuals. If you take a look at the areas I've been in, obviously, international policing has been important. I've had three tours of duty in Haiti, worked in training people in Cuba and Columbia, and undertaken training international police officers in Canada. I have spent a significant amount of time in provincial policing, but at the investigative level as opposed to patrol. It has been fascinating getting to watch over Code of Conduct aspects; and labor relations has been a strong suit. And then, the last two and a half years have been in municipal policing, but as a police executive.

SP: So, you were moving around so many jobs so quickly that you didn't get much time to spend in patrol itself?

JMB: That's correct.

Changes Experienced

SP: What of the changes you've seen now in 26 years in policing?

JMB: At the beginning, it was the application of the Canadian Charter of Rights and Freedoms. I came in 1987 and the Charter was just starting to ramp up, especially the development of the case law from the Supreme Court of Canada. With each new decision would come a new responsibility on policing: probably the biggest was the Stinchcombe decision on disclosure that the Crown (State) must disclose to the defense all potentially relevant evidence, regardless of whether or not there is any intention to call it.* Added to that was the judicial scrutiny that came about from the Charter as well as from various inquests and inquiries, specifically those related to wrongful convictions, particularly the Sophonow, Marshall, and Guy-Paul Morin Inquiries, and in the changes in the execution of

---

* R. v. Stinchcombe, [1991] 3 SCR 326A.

how we do things.* And, then you have the continual evolution and the more recent issues such as the McNeil decision stipulating that the police reveal to the Crown any history of misconduct on the part of an arresting or investigating police officer potentially relevant to the case of an accused.† And, so, from a legal point of view, we've seen a lot of changes and, added to that, has been the attention to the whole issue of scrutiny and accountability.

I very often lecture and I show a graph of a declining line from left to right representing crime going down and an inclining line from left to right that shows the costs of policing and of public safety going up. Obviously, we can say that one of the big drivers of that is going to be the cost of police officers and their benefits, but the other issue is that it is taking a lot more time for us to do investigations today. The reason for that is because of accountability. There's a desire in our society for police as agents of the state, representatives of the government, whether it be municipal, provincial, or federal government, to be more accountable. And, so those are some of the major things that I've seen. A very good example, very recently, is what happened to the 18-year-old man shot in the street car in Toronto. And going back to the Dziekanski case at Vancouver airport 2007, where the immigrant from Poland, unable to speak English, led to a failure for him to clear Customs Hall for many hours and his growing agitation, until eventually four RCMP officers arrived, "tasered" him four times as they tried to arrest him, causing his death. These really highlight the importance of accountability and we see that today in Nova Scotia with the Serious Incident Response Team, in Ontario with the SIU, and other models in other provinces.

Obviously, there is the demographic change: we've had four generations working at the same time in policing. You have the Boomers, Generation Xers, Gen Ys, and the Millennials. As the Boomers slowly go out, in the next 5 to 10 years, that will change markedly how we do things.

Policing at its most elementary level is risky business—it's problem solving—and solving those problems that people themselves, would not, could not, and, in some cases, should not solve, and we're called in to solve all of those problems. A good portion of that is the whole issue of mental health. Individuals who are walking our streets and who in the past would have had society's supports—they don't have that anymore and we have to go in and be the first responders and, in many cases, policing is really not adaptive. We are

---

* The Sophonow, Marshall, and Guy-Paul Morin inquiries all involved wrongful murder convictions overturned only after each of these three men had been incarcerated for years and, in Marshall's case, raised questions of racism in the criminal justice system. These inquiries challenged much conventional wisdom, and provided important recommendations for change regarding how police investigations are conducted in Canada.
† R. v. McNeil, [2009] SCC 3.

there to deal with criminal problems and the underlying causes of criminality. Mental health issues lead to many other problems in society, including acts of crime.

SP: How do you see the greater need for the police to be involved in mental health and a greater need for multidisciplinary connections? How do you see that playing out when there are cutbacks for important services for people at the fringes?

JMB: Yes, it's a challenge to do more with less. For example, taking a look at my budget which this year is at 73 million Canadian dollars—93% of that is for wages and benefits for our people. Only 7% is for vehicles, guns, office space, and what have you, and that's a fairly small margin with which I can maneuver.

The challenge within our society is what the expectations are. One thing that I didn't mention that clearly fell under the preceding question is the change in our society as it relates to the information exchange, and this is where social media comes in. And the one thing that I have learned from case law, and this is perhaps where my legal side comes out, and from the various inquiries that I mentioned earlier on, is the notion of the rule of law and that the police have to be not uninterested, but we have to be professionally disinterested. We bring the case to the courts and the courts then will deal with holding the individuals to account if they are indeed found guilty. Whether or not they are found guilty, well, we have to abide by that. We can't go out and exact justice by our own hand. In recent years, what we're seeing is the beginning of a series of hydraulic pressure points that are going to occur as society mobilizes, and can easily mobilize itself through social media, by saying "we want to see certain things happen." Take a look at a 1932 study by a Yale professor that examined wrongful convictions in the United States and the UK (Borchard, 1932). He found that in 13 of the 65 cases of wrongful convictions a crime had not even been committed and yet people had been convicted and jailed and, in some cases, executed. If you take a look at the high profile cases: the Baby Lindbergh case, for example, and the Fugitive case with Sam Sheppard. These are cases where you had that hydraulic pressure from the media and from the public. Well now we are going to see that hydraulic pressure even more so come to bear as you have people able to flick a switch and send off a diatribe that has no basis in reality, but has a basis in their own reality. That's one of the biggest challenges we're going to be facing in the years to come.

SP: So, would you say that the problem grows exponentially or has something changed qualitatively?

JMB: I think it's both. By virtue of the type of pressure that comes down. What we've seen is a gradual deterioration of the public trust in policing, in spite of the fact that we have more accountability today than we've ever had. People are more vociferous and vocal in voicing their displeasure, and it's a lot easier to just say "the police screwed up." On what basis? "Well, the police aren't able to tell us anything about the case." That's another issue that comes from our privacy legislation that we have to deal with. It's coming from all parts. It is quantitative. It is qualitative. It is something that the velocity of which is very difficult to comprehend and follow. A term that I coined recently is *nebulosity*: the speed at which something is opaque. The author Nicholas Nassim Taleb talks about Black Swans and outlying events (Taleb, 2007). Well, those things are happening more and more frequently. And we as police officers—as police executives—think that technology is going to solve our problems. No, the reality is that technology is going to create more problems than it is going to be able to solve for us. It's the ingenuity gap that we're missing. As the challenges and problems become more and more sophisticated, our ability, our sophistication, in finding resolutions and solutions to these problems doesn't quite keep up to that. That's an ingenuity gap.

SP: What about the nature of any changes you've seen with various communities, across various constituencies, special interests, ethnic and women's groups?

JMB: One of the good things about living in a democratic society, particularly a parliamentary democracy, is that we are very good at managing conflict between groups through discussion. We don't have the same litigious society that they do in the United States, but we do follow a bit. What we are seeing is that the various communities out there, and we're not just talking about ethnically diverse communities, we're also talking about women, sexual orientation, sexual identification, gender identification, youth versus non-youth, etc. It's the individual identification that people have to a specific group. We're seeing that those groups are being more and more vocal about what their expectations are. And, it goes beyond expectations to demands. How do they want to be represented? How do they want to contribute to the dialogue? And when it comes down to policing they want to have their say. So, these are all challenges. And I think that society as a whole has recognized these challenges. Here in Nova Scotia, it's a relatively homogenous society, but we are aware of the challenges that we have in properly integrating and accepting differences and that other groups, not just visible minorities but also invisible minorities, have a legitimate role and place in our society.

SP: So, you are saying that the police have become better at learning to work with and appreciate diversity but at the same time these group distinctions are becoming more magnified?

JMB: Yes, the cleavages between the groups are getting bigger, and between the police and the groups, the gaps are also being magnified. Perhaps it's not that the gaps are becoming larger but that the texture of those gaps is becoming scrutinized more. Obviously, if we were living in an ideal situation, 50% of all my police officers would be women and of the total about 20% would be from cultural communities. But the reality is that's not the case. The cultural communities aren't large enough, especially here in Nova Scotia, to provide us enough candidates. Additionally, a lot of individuals from those communities choose not to be police officers. We do have a police officer of middle-eastern background, but we have no Muslim police officers. We have no Jewish police officers. Aboriginals are few and far between. And there are many reasons for that. Women, for example: people want to push to have 50%, even 52%, of police officers being women. The reality is that we do not have that number of eligible women who want to be police officers.

SP: There have been some papers published recently that suggest the likely settling point for women in policing is about 20%, and that it's not going to move much beyond that. What do you think?

JMB: It seems there is a ceiling. It's certainly not an official ceiling but a demographic one. Women will continue to want to have children and policing is not the best profession to reconcile those needs. Just as there are some men who wish to have large families, or to be very involved in their family, and when you have the type of job we do, it's not conducive to allowing that.

That being said we are seeing individuals who look upon policing as not necessarily a lifelong career but something to do in the medium term. The challenge is that individuals have to put so much effort into becoming a police officer by virtue of the training that is required, that by the time they are through that process they end up saying. "Hmmm, maybe I don't want to leave."

From my experience in two separate police services, the retention rate is very high, upwards of 97%–98%. We're not getting that in other areas. My son-in-law is looking at another job in the same area with a third different company in four years. That's his way to be able to seek promotion, whereas in the police service you stick it out, you acquire tenure, and you apply for promotion.

Personal Policing Philosophy

SP: Can you tell me about your personal policing philosophy? And, has it
        changed over the years?
JMB: There's something called the "in-group bias." One of the biggest changes
        I went through was breaking down that barrier. When I was tak-
        ing a course with the RCMP in Ottawa many years ago, I talked to
        a senior constable who really impressed me. He said "there should
        only be one police service across Canada and that should be the
        RCMP. That way we wouldn't have any jurisdictional battles, infor-
        mation would flow clearly." It sounds in theory like that would work
        out, but the thing that is missing I learned over the years is that when
        you have one group, one service, you miss out on innovation. There
        is no intellectual competition going on. And I saw that by work-
        ing with different police services, with Québec City, the Sûreté du
        Québec, Montréal City, in the UN, and with many others. I got to
        see that these people were doing really good things a lot better than
        we were doing them in the RCMP. And we were doing some good
        things, and they were seeing that as well. So I realized that by having
        different groups, and by having them interact, and to certain degree
        participate in intellectual competition, we could make things bet-
        ter. Another valuable lesson was about "Group-think" and avoiding
        that. So, those are two major things that have evolved with me.

Another thing that has modified and changed over the years with me has
been the absolute critical importance of leadership development: for myself,
for my peers, for my subordinates. I saw that through being around bad leaders; individuals who really had no business being where they were at the
local level and I saw it again in Haiti. But I got to see other leaders who were
highly competent and yet were missing out on specific leadership qualities.
Or had no leadership qualities at all, for example, former Commissioners
of the RCMP: Zaccardelli and Elliot.* Two very different individuals, one of
whom was a highly charismatic individual who, by virtue of his charisma,
essentially wiped out the leadership aspirations of an entire generation, so

---

* Giuliano Zaccardelli was RCMP Commissioner from 2000 to 2006, a particularly difficult era for the force encompassing several significant scandals and controversies.
Zaccradelli ultimately resigned after the credibility of his testimony before a parliamentary committee, struck to investigate the Mahar Arar affair in a matter of so-called
extraordinary rendition, was called into question. William Elliot, a lawyer and career
civil servant, followed Zaccardelli as Commissioner from 2007 to 2011, the first civilian
to ever be appointed to that post. The appointment was intended to provide the force
with a fresh start with a leader not already immersed in RCMP culture, but concerns
about his civilian status and leadership style underscored another unsettled period for
the Commissioner's Office.

that when he left abruptly, the government was forced to go get an individual who was a functionary and not a charismatic leader. The pendulum swung in totally the opposite way. You had an individual who was not competent socially, who was missing social intelligence, and hence couldn't be trusted and couldn't trust others. So I got to see those dynamics and those individuals working and I had to scratch my head and say that I do not want to repeat those errors.

SP: How did Zaccardelli's charisma wipe out leadership aspirations?

JMB: He made a fundamental error, I think, by telling people that he wanted to be the longest running Commissioner in the history of the RCMP. The longest running, sometime between the 1920s and the 1940s, was about 26 years. What does that do to the cohort of leaders to follow? "Hey, I'm not going to have a chance to become the Commissioner." One of the first things I acknowledged when I became Chief of HRP was to realize that I was an outsider coming in. I was very public in saying that the next Chief of Police was going to be from within and if it's not the case then I will have failed in my development of the leadership cadre. Unfortunately, leadership development is one of those things we haven't done a good job at in our society generally, and in policing in particular.

What is leadership at its most basic level? When I lecture at Dalhousie University or in front of the Salvation Army leadership cadre, I ask the same question, "In one word, what is leadership?" People say, "well, direction … advancement … strength." They come up with all of these qualifications without really touching the center of what leadership is. Leadership at its most basic, elementary level, is influence—how do you take a group of people, how do you take one person, how do you take yourself, from Point A to Point B in order to achieve a common goal? I think this is one of the challenges we face by racing after all of these other golden idols. Those golden idols would be community policing, problem-oriented policing, now it's intelligence-led policing, and forgetting about the importance of leadership development. I include in that, of course, the basic values of integrity, honesty, and courage and being able to have those qualities, those skills, and those values that will allow us to leave a positive wake everywhere we go.

SP: It seems that you are saying that there has been too much pursuit of notions that are abstract and not enough pursuit of the development of the person. Does that capture it?

JMB: You look at policing as a science, as an art, and as a business without realizing that policing is all three of these things packed into one. But it starts with the individual police officer. Communities are driven by three things: number one, to obtain an environment that is devoid of crime; number two, to bond with this police service, to understand what policing does; number three, to be able to contribute to their society in general. People do this in many ways.

We as police officers have to be attuned to that and fulfill these needs. The question is, how well do we do this? When I first started this job people were really concerned that I would get rid of community police officers. The reality is that I said we're not going to throw all of our eggs into the community-policing basket and we're not going to throw all of our eggs into the intelligence-led policing basket either. It's a matter of getting a good cross-section of community-policing where it's needed and wanted, and intelligence-led policing where it's required and needed.

SP: So, you see these as separate but not contradictory components?

JMB: No, that's interesting, because I know people who view them as contradictory, but I see them as complementary. The question, though, is they may not be intersectional, which is what people like to see: nice and clean and neat. I remember working in Portage la Prairie where the community really wasn't that interested in community policing at the time. Community policing is, at a basic level, when you go out and ask the community, one, "tell us what your problems are," and two, "help us to deal with those problems." Community policing is not cooking breakfast for kids in a high school—that's community–police relationship building, which is far from what community policing is.

Something that we have coming up now is the whole issue of performance management where they say "what can't be measured can't be improved upon." How do you measure perceptions in policing? You give somebody a paper to read that talks about a shooting, a pedestrian collision, a home invasion, and then you ask them, "do you feel safe in your community?" And they say, "well, no." Well, of course. That is another cognitive bias, the negativity bias, because people will gravitate to the negative. Why? We're hard-wired for survival. Our worries are about the threats out there, not about the opportunities.

Problems and Successes Experienced

SP: I wonder if you could identify one or two of your greatest successes and then the failures.

JMB: I'll start off with the positives. Having gone to RCMP disciplinary adjudications, I was proud that I was able to make the transition from police officer to a judge. At one point, I had a case where there were 27 straight days of hearings. I had eight lawyers at the outset appear before me and it was, for all intents and purposes, the same thing as a criminal trial and I was able to deal with the apparent conflict. It ended that I recommended that the individual, a commissioned officer, an Inspector, who had essentially been found guilty of a sexual impropriety, be dismissed. After five years, the decision was upheld by the Commissioner of the RCMP. So I had great pride knowing that I left that unit a lot better than I had found it.

From a tactical point of view, my greatest achievement was when I went to Haiti following the earthquake that devastated that country on January 12, 2010. I was sent down there with the Canadian Armed Forces to find, recover, and repatriate the bodies of RCMP officers Doug Coates and Mark Gallagher. Mark Gallagher I didn't know, but Doug Coates had been a friend of mine. In fact, he sent me down to Haiti as the Deputy Police Commissioner and then he replaced me in the same capacity. I spent 40 hours searching for his body in what was left of my old headquarters, along with dedicated Brazilian and Chinese search and rescue technicians. And then bringing him back … having to deal with the mental fallout, the stress that I went through there, I view that as a very strong personal success.

In terms of greatest failures, these were when I was starting out and dealing with old school mentalities and being shy of conflict and confrontation. It was not going into bars for a patrol or busting down the door of a drug dealer who wanted to fight us. It was dealing with the cops in the office. I see it today in my own organization—you have individuals who are afraid of conflict with one another. They are afraid of being labeled racist or having a harassment or human rights complaint leveled against them. They are afraid of calling a spade a spade. I guess it's because we don't expect conflict to occur in our own home, so to speak. I learned to embrace conflict. I became a Hockey Canada referee—I was put on the ice where you have to deal with conflict on a minute-by-minute basis.

SP: You have learned to embrace conflict?

JMB: Absolutely. It came to me from Sun Tzu's *the Art of War*. Probably, the best lesson you can learn from that is to embrace conflict—not being afraid to say, "hang on, this is the issue. This needs to be recognized." That's where you get the whole issue of moral courage. If you don't have that moral courage then you really have no business being here. You really are the Thin Blue Line separating anarchy and chaos from order.

SP: It's no secret that Halifax has received a lot of bad press over the last decade for being, on a per capita basis, one of the most dangerous cities in Canada. I know this has been a challenge not only to you but to the previous Chief as well. Any projections as to where you see yourself going with this?

JMB: We're trending down, significantly. Two years ago with 19 homicides, we were number two behind Winnipeg. When the statistics are published for last year, we'll be far from the top. This year, with two weeks to go, we are presently down 33% from last year's totals. That being said let me tell you about the town of Gary, Indiana, with a population of 87,000 people. Gary, so far this year, has had 51 homicides. We are four and a half times the size of Gary. Can you imagine if we had 200 homicides to correspond to Gary's rate?

SP: Another lesson in not chasing the negative?

JMB: Of the eight homicides we've had this year, two have been vehicular homicides, individuals who were drunk or were driving dangerously and got in an accident resulting in the death of a person. We had one where a 74-year-old dementia patient pushed a 94-year-old dementia patient, who fell, bumped her head, and died. One of the remaining five classified as a homicide was a drunken stupor fight between roommates. Two were, unfortunately, linked to domestic violence and two were connected to the drug culture. So, things have improved remarkably.

That being said, we still have attempted murders at the same level as last year. We still have a huge number of firearms out in the community; we have seized a considerable number of firearms, just below last year which was a record. And we still have issues with regards to people leaving their doors unlocked, resulting in numerous thefts from their cars, their houses, and their sheds.

SP: To what do you attribute the decline in the homicide rate?

JMB: I'd say we have effected some change. One of the premises of intelligence-led policing is targeting prolific offenders. Well, that was done by my predecessors. They did a good job developing a Guns and Gangs Unit, a proper patrol response, bringing in Compstat and other intelligence products. I'm just carrying that out and bringing it to its next iteration, just as those people who follow me will do the same thing.

Theory and Practice

SP: I'm interested in the new breed of police officer. You have two degrees yourself. What sort of importance do you attach to the blending of research with evidence-based police practice?

JMB: This gets to the issue that I view as anecdotal bias-free policing, so we just don't fall into the trap that we do in our personal lives of "where did you hear about such and such and what happened" and instantly draw an inference. That being said, intuition is a really important part of policing. That is, taking all of your experience and being able to apply all the facts to it and being able to draw patterns. What we're trying to do in HRP right now is to develop that empirical skepticism in our management, our decision making, and in our investigations that allows us to say "well, why not? what exactly happened here?," rather than saying "well, it had to have been this or it had to have been that." As Sherlock Holmes said, "It is a capital mistake to theorize before one has data. One begins to twist facts to suit theories instead of theories to suit facts." The whole idea is to be able to get us to a point where we can look at the data and say, what do we see from it? Sometimes, you don't see anything, but most times, you're able to say, ah, there are patterns there. That's the future of predictive policing, but it's not the only future that's out there. We still are dealing with human beings, with all of their strengths and weaknesses, and we have to be able to foresee what can be done, with all of those strengths and weaknesses, dealing with people from the outside and especially dealing with police officers on the inside.

SP: Do you see the potential for useful input coming from academia?

JMB: Oh, absolutely. It's key. I've heard people say before, "it's very rare to see a police chief with a university degree." When I went through Regina in my basic training in 1987, 27 of our group graduated. We had 21 undergraduate degrees, two masters, and one individual who had interrupted his doctoral studies. That was almost 30 years ago. So, things have changed considerably now. Within HRP organization, out of the 500 police officers, we have about 300 who have university training of all types. In senior management, I have an individual with two degrees and I have one manager with an MBA and another two working towards their masters.

The question is, how do we use and leverage that academia presents to us as part of the data-driven package? Not deal with academia?: we fail to do so at our own risk and peril.

Transnational Relations

SP: Can you comment on the future of policing the global village?

JMB: The issue of international cooperation is key. However, we will continue to experience difficulties as legal systems are different and the role of police is also different in each country. In the world today, we have three major legal systems: common law, continental or civil law, and socialist law. Each one has subtle and not-so-subtle differences when it comes to dealing with crime.

Beyond these distinctions in systems is the important role of cultural differences. Consider going down to Haiti, which doesn't have a history of trust in government agents and representatives. So, when we as Canadians went down there and said that we were going to teach the Haitians community policing, well, that was a total error, because we didn't take a look at the terrain and see that these people weren't ready for it—they could not even recognize it. So, in the 1990s we were saying "Oh, yeah, community policing. The end all, be all." Well, we were wrong.

Democratic Policing

SP: In this age of terrorism, of cutbacks, and of young people discontent that they are finding it increasingly difficult to obtain meaningful employment, how do you think democratic policing is going to be able to handle the challenges of this new era?

JMB: I spoke earlier on about the negativity bias, where people are hard-wired to look to threats rather than opportunities. Take a look at when I graduated from university. I worked cleaning theaters. There were no jobs in Montreal where I was studying in the 1980s. So with my Political Science/Economics degree I went to Toronto to drive taxicabs. At the time, I was disaffected. I didn't know where I was going and what was going to be done, but at least I had some faith, not much, but some faith in my ability to eke out a life. And what were the biggest worries in the 1980s? The biggest worries were nuclear war, the spread of communism, and there was something called AIDS. Now fast-forward 30 years, we've got all these other worries replaced with terrorism. Terrorism, when it comes down to it, is not about weapons of mass destruction, but rather weapons of mass disruption.

People don't like change. I think that's what we are going through today. We have a tendency to view things as being static, instead of realizing that things will change. "Plus ça change, plus c'est la même chose" as we say in French. Yes, we are going to see some incredible changes over the next little while, but the intensity of those changes, and our reactions to them, are going to be the same as it was 30 years ago. We get on. We adjust.

SP: Without losing the essentials of what we are as a society and what society wants policing to be?

JMB: Well, that's the thing. We're going to have more and more expectations put on us as individual police officers, and as individual police executives, managers, and leaders. You have to justify things more and, so, we will justify them. But we should not fall into "analysis-paralysis" where we are really worried about doing something because of fear of accountability or being chastised by the media.

And, yes, we are in a time of fiscal austerity. But 20 years ago when the federal government went through two program reviews, all policing across the country went through the same thing. What I'm saying is that some of these problems are really rehashed problems that we've had in the past.

Ultimately, democratic policing relies on trust. Trust is garnered through proper communication with your community and its constituents to let them know what you do, and to have them understand what you do. And, if we don't do that, that's when we risk losing the support that is there.

Looking Ahead

SP: Chief, before we wrap up, is there anything else you'd like to say about the future?

JMB: Policing is complex. It's a risky business. And it's not going to get any simpler. We can train people as much as possible with this expectation that they should know how to deal with specific operations, they should know how to deal with tactical considerations. But at a very basic level, we're only human beings and if we're going to be constant problem solvers, we cannot do it alone. And this is where we are going to need help from the community itself. We're going to need help from stakeholders and partners. And we have to be able to look at things with a more complete, integrated approach. Sometimes as police officers we are going to have to just step back and let other community actors deal with some of the challenges that we have been expected to deal with these past few decades.

We also have a tendency to believe that technology will solve all our problems or at the very least, mitigate many of them. I am of the opinion that as much as technology will assist us in dealing with our challenges, it will create even more. We will simply have more information available to us which, in the end, will consume more resources.

Add to that the latest trends when it comes to policing, such as community policing and intelligence-led policing. We are constantly looking for the silver bullet that will eradicate social deviance. The reality is that we cannot eliminate it totally. We are dealing with human beings and all their traits and, in any society, there are bound to be social deviants, asocial attitudes and behaviors, and individuals who are advancing their own individual agendas leading to some form of criminality. Perhaps the goal of policing should be to better manage expectations and perceptions of various publics, while working on social deviance from a systems approach that deals with the root causes of the deviance, rather than simply reacting to crime.

Conclusion

I found Chief Blais to be both enthusiastic and open during our time together. Going into the interview, I found myself quite taken with the Chief's educational credentials, especially thinking back to the levels of schooling police officers had when I served in the 1970s and 1980s. That he did not find his scholarly achievements especially remarkable compared to his peers left me struck by how rapidly the educational profile of the typical police officer has changed in such a short time. I was further struck by how genuinely optimistic Chief Blais was in contemplating how the policing profession will adapt to our increasingly uncertain and changing times.

References

Borchard, E. M. 1932. *Convicting the Innocent: Sixty-Five Actual Errors of Criminal Justice*. New Haven, CT: Yale University Press.
Taleb, N. N. 2007. *The Black Swan: The Impact of the Highly Improbable*. New York, NY: Random House.

Ellison Greenslade, Commissioner Royal Bahamas Police

8

INTERVIEWED BY
PERRY STANISLAS

Contents

Introduction

The Bahamas is an archipelago consisting of flat islands and islets (or cays) numbering 700 in total, extending 100,000 square miles off the Atlantic Ocean from the Florida coast past Cuba, and covering an area which is the size of California. The overwhelming majority of the population is of African descent, reflecting the slave origins of the former British colony and a significant white population by Caribbean standards. The population of the Commonwealth of Bahamas is approximately 319,000, of which 85% are of African origin, and 13% whites, with Asians and Hispanics making up the remainder. The diversity of the Bahamian population can be seen by its "out islands" which differ from each other with some islands such as Long Island consisting predominantly of long-established middle and upper class white residents. Other islands have historically been the home of poorer whites, while Cat and Andros Islands consist largely of black residents. The capital of the country and its center of government and commerce is Nassau on the island of Grand Providence.

The Bahamas, like many of its Caribbean counterparts, has a relatively limited economy with sea sponges at one time being a major international export, along with agricultural products. Tourism is now the mainstay of the economy. Approximately 80% of the tourists to the Bahamas are from the United States. The Bahamas is one of the leading merchant shipping registration ports in the world. During the 1970s, the banking sector emerged as a major source of foreign investment which led to its prime minister espousing the aspiration of the country becoming the "Switzerland of the Caribbean region."

The interview with Commissioner Ellison Greenslade of the Royal Bahamas Police (RBP) took place in November 2012 in London. It explores his career and route to becoming the leader of his country's police force, and organizational developments which it has undergone. An important aspect of this process is how the RBP transformed itself from a former colonial police organization to a more modern policing organization responsive to citizens' needs. Also explored are the challenges facing police leaders in the Bahamas and regionally.

Career

Ellison Greenslade joined the RBP in 1979, carrying out basic policing duties at Central Division, where he worked at Government House among other places of importance. Shortly after a near fatal incident in which he was stabbed while on duty, he was posted to the Special Branch. In the early 1980s, he was transferred to the Research and Planning Department as a sergeant, later on to become a systems manager and head of Information Technology. He was made Acting Superintendent and Divisional Commander of Central Division in 1991, and returned to headquarters for a short spell, before he was made Acting Assistant Commissioner responsible for Northern Bahamas, where he served for 7 years. In 2008, he was appointed as the Acting Deputy Commissioner and 2 years later he was made the sixth police commissioner of the RBP. He undertook postgraduate police studies at the University of Leicester, England, and earned an MBA from the University of Miami, where he is currently a PhD student researching organizational management. In 2010, Ellison Greenslade was elected as the President of the Association of Caribbean Commissioners of Police.

One set of questions put to the Commissioner was about his career experiences. The path from police constable to Commissioner follows the pattern of other Caribbean chief officers and that found elsewhere in Western policing, highlighting a generalist approach to career development where police officers start their working lives as constables carrying out basic duties, leading to a number of other roles which enables them to develop a sound overall working knowledge of the police organization and its core functions. The actual motivation for the young Ellison Greenslade initially wanting to join the police is explained:

EG: I joined for a very simple reason. I grew up in a very poor household, and never liked to see people taken advantage of. The police service for me represented this impressive symbol of authority, but the word I hold dearly to and that comes to my mind first is respect and the second word credibility. As a teenager, the people who in my mind's eye were very credible and commanded a tremendous amount of respect from the population at large were the police.

An important characteristic of policing is that it has provided a means of social mobility for individuals from lower social classes. In the case of the future Commissioner he faced more than the usual hurdles in joining the police:

EG: I didn't have very much going for me entering basic training, compared to others coming from very humble beginnings. I was told initially I could not join as I was too young. They looked at my physical profile and said I was much too small. I weighed around 130 pounds and they told me I didn't look much like a copper.

An important set of characteristics of the young constable, not from the type of background with well-established connections which is important in Caribbean societies organized on the colonial legacy of color, caste, and class, was the importance of self-belief and a commitment to hard work. This earned the young Greenslade recognition in graduating as the best recruit from his cohort:

EG: To step out as the youngest in my squad to receive the highest award for my achievement as a new recruit was something my family was quite proud of and I must say I was very pleased. It showed that if you worked hard enough sometimes good things can happen.

During the careers of many individuals who are fortunate to reach the rank of police Commissioner, there are critical incidents or opportunities that have an important bearing for their future progress. In a particular instance constable Greenslade demonstrated his willingness to go against traditional expectations of the police occupational culture at some risk to himself. He explains:

EG: An officer had broken the law and it was in my presence. I was asked to give an account and could have looked the other way. I was called in by a senior officer to explain what I witnessed, and I said that while I had every sympathy for my fellow officer and could understand what he did, I nevertheless had a duty to say exactly what

I saw. That attracted a great deal of positive attention and I was transferred to the Traffic Department, which was a good transfer if you like.

Changes Experienced

One of the most important and defining factors that helped transform crucial aspects of the RBP was the Royal Commission of Inquiry into Corruption launched in 1983. The inquiry was an outcome of international controversies about the impact of the growing criminal drug trade on the RBP, the Bahamian government and its banking system which led to conflict with the US administration of President Ronald Regan.

One of the recommendations coming from the Inquiry was the need to employ foreign consultants to assist in introducing organizational change. A specific area identified for change to increase efficiency and reduce forms of corruption was automating RBP manual administrative processes and the introduction of information technology. The then Inspector Greenslade was to play a leadership role in this process:

EG: I was fortunate to be given the job as systems manager—in essence the head of IT for the whole department. At that time I was an acting Inspector and that was a major undertaking because I was not a technocrat, I was just simply a police officer. But my superiors took the view that I had the right attitude to take it forward. I took ownership of the task and drove the program forward and today we can brag about our technology, and an IT platform that can act as a model for many countries our size and larger.

The issue of technological change has been cited as one of the defining features of postmodern society, along with a number of other important developments, such as the ability to travel and new forms of crime. Another important feature of contemporary society is greater ease in the sharing and dissemination of ideas, whether human rights or extremist views that can contribute to conflict, such as increasing racism, anti-western sentiments, or homophobia. The significance of technological change for the RBP is explained by the Commissioner:

EG: We have undergone a phenomenal amount of changes as a result of technological advances. I would venture to say a police officer who retired five years ago would have a difficult time if they re-entered our force today. Within the last five years we have seen the introduction of the I-Pad, Smartphones and any one of these applications that work on these devices. I mean the world is very connected now.

A distinguishing feature of contemporary societies with considerable implications for policing is the speed at which information can travel. The Commissioner illustrates this point:

EG: We had an incident involving a youngster called the "barefoot bandit" by the American media, and we were amazed at the speed with which information travelled and brought the international media to the Bahamas. I mean, it was amazing the speed at which the media mobilized and wanted interviews. This teenager stole an aircraft and a boat and came to the Bahamas. He had never been to flight training school, had very little education, but was smart enough to teach himself how to fly and was confident enough to do it and the story caught fire.

How the nature of police work has changed and its impact on the way tasks are carried out are matters with which police leaders around the world have had to grapple. This can take many forms, for example, moving from a colonial policing model primarily concerned with order maintenance, to more democratic and citizen focused forms of policing. Even when the important changes have taken place, many traditional aspects of policing remain the same, such as attitudes towards the use of force. Differences in the way police work is carried out in the Bahamas today compared to earlier periods are elucidated by Commissioner Greenslade:

EG: I think it is just easier now to get things done. 50 years ago we had a small number of police officers going point to point on bicycles, if they were lucky. Today, we have access to the best weapons available, best uniforms and protective clothing, and equipment. So the tools to carry out police work have come on in leaps and bounds. Look at the police cruisers we use today, which are more like a mobile police station than simply something to carry and move people about.

While the technical resources available to relatively affluent Caribbean police organizations such as the RBP have contributed to improved efficiency and effectiveness in crime-fighting and other instances; normative changes in society have made particular aspects of police work more unpredictable and hazardous:

EG: The types of things police are expected to respond to now have changed. I remember a time, and we are not talking about that long ago, when a person who pulled out a sword in most Caribbean societies would be seen by society, never mind the police, as a very bad man and subject to the most extreme social stigma. Now we have youngsters with automatic weapons prepared to shoot and kill people or confront police officers, with very little notion of shame.

Personal Policing Philosophy

A number of questions during the interview with Commissioner Greenslade explored matters concerning the RBP's leadership and management philosophy. The first concerned the RBP's guiding philosophy:

EG: Our guiding philosophy is to fulfil our mandate to the people of the Commonwealth of Bahamas in partnership with stakeholders, citizens and visitors, and by serving them with care and respect.

The Commissioner's statement highlights the shifting values of the RBP to now include viewing policing as a collaborative enterprise involving other criminal justice, and community stakeholders, and a service orientation sensitive to the needs of citizens and users. The importance of police organizations being sensitive to the needs of those who require their services is illustrated by the Commissioner through his personal experiences:

EG: People can immediately sense when words and deeds do not match up, or where people are not being authentic and just going through the motions. If you are just going through the motions with me, I, as a normal rational human being, will just go through the motions with you. Let me give you a common experience that I have had in foreign countries, where someone passing by says to me, "how are you doing?" I respond "not good" and they reply "fine" and carry on walking by. They aren't actually listening or interested, but it is clearly part of their daily ritual of greeting people in that manner.

The role of police leaders in bringing about the desired transformation in organizational culture is elucidated by the Commissioner:

EG: I believe if people do not feel good about themselves, they cannot do good. So if I, and the other leaders of the organization, can engender a culture of treating each other with respect on a daily basis and demonstrate that we care how people feel, that must impact on the public.

Making the RBP more responsive to the needs of its citizens and members of the public is in line with the service orientation of advanced policing jurisdictions and highlighted in a range of strategies and practices such as problem-orientated policing, community policing or in efforts to improve the quality of policing received by the public and hard to reach groups. Essential elements in the Commissioner's philosophy are improving the transparency of the working environment of police managers, and eliminating practices that diverted attention from day-to-day policing priorities:

EG: When I was made Commissioner, one of the first things I did that same week was to change all the doors of senior managers at headquarters from wood to glass doors; because it meant that leaders could not hide themselves away and were clearly visible to all who visited headquarters. Now, to be honest, not all senior officers were happy with this change.

Similar changes were made in regards to police vehicles:

EG: Prior to my appointment, the Commissioner had his own parking spot and vehicle. I bought all senior officers the same vehicles as my own, and made similar changes in terms of parking spaces. These things seem very small, however in the culture of the police service these forms of distinction are seen as important and speak to status and those issues which in my view are irrelevant to what we should be about.

Problems and Successes Experienced

One characteristic of contemporary policing leadership strategies is the introduction of new management arrangements and performance standards in achieving organizational objectives. Probably the most important requirement of the *Police Force Act* concerns the Commissioner's annual report and its impact on his management of the organization. Describing how the Act has contributed to present reporting arrangements, the Commissioner explains:

EG: It has required putting into place processes where I can know what is happening to keep my commanders accountable on a daily, weekly, and monthly basis, so I can fulfil the requirements for policing. This enables us to identify early in the year our key strategic priorities, and how we must work to accomplish them.

The Commissioner provides an illustration of the management process utilized for one specific aspect of the Commissioner's Policing Plan (Royal Bahamas Police Force, 2012).

EG: If we are talking about our priority of community partnerships as part of the broader strategy of increasing community safety; I say to my commanders, when writing their monthly productivity report, how many neighborhood watch groups have they formed or how many community meetings have they attended. They can't gloss it because I want to know specifically, what meeting was attended and specifically where and what time?

An important aspect of improving the quality of policing to meet the ever changing expectation of citizens is developing more focused and structured responses and forms of management accountability in achieving policing objectives.

A crucial factor for the Commissioner is the matter of the treatment and development of personnel which was informed to a significant degree by his predecessor. Speaking about his career development:

EG: I had the greatest amount of support from a very good Chief who firmly believed in giving young people a chance, and had no hesitation to give me, with only 20 years' service, an opportunity to be an Assistant Chief. He was certainly ahead of his time and was very much about building and developing the force for the future, and succession planning.

The influence and attitude to career development of Commissioner Greenslade's predecessor is apparent around the question of sexism and the representation of women, which is symptomatic of the limited opportunities available to women in the region:

EG: We have not in the past paid any attention in fast-tracking and developing women officers for leadership at the most senior levels and that is very clear. I can look at the career development of many male colleagues who have benefited from training and learning opportunities. There is a clear need for me as Commissioner to encourage and support our talented female officers with potential to take up opportunities that are available, and pass that message down to other leaders within the organization.

How these beliefs have contributed to changing practice is illustrated by the following remarks:

EG: We have made important progress in that regard. We have a number of female Superintendents and many others with a lot of potential to move to the next stage of their development.

Theory and Practice

One area where the link between theory and practice is particularly salient is in discussions around the selection, training, and development of police leaders. This is highlighted by Commissioner Greenslade's experience of higher education:

EG: I started a PhD on leadership, and am having just a wonderful time doing it. I have always enjoyed my work at the ground level, but once I started my PhD, that was a completely new ball game and forced me to think in different ways. I found it amazing. I find myself now being able to go back and draw from the literature depending on what I want to communicate or am thinking about.

A specific example of how the Commissioner's learning and exposure to advanced academic teaching is translated to everyday practice is illustrated in the following:

EG: I remember speaking to an officer who was very frustrated and I asked her to get hold of a copy of the *Gods of Management* by Charles Handy (Handy, 1985), because she was having some issues with her manager's approach. I asked her to read some of the chapters of the book and we would speak again. We discussed some of the things she was telling me, relating it to what she read and how to thrive under a leader who had a particular approach which she did not understand.

Transnational Relations

The improved ability to travel for business and leisure has created new challenges for Caribbean police organizations and the policing they provide. These challenges are particularly acute in countries where tourism constitutes so much of their earnings, and is highlighted in controversies around Bahamian homophobia, involving local religious interests in response to foreign travel operators catering to the Western gay and lesbian market. How these changes impact on local policing is explained by the Commissioner:

EG: On any day, you can have somebody from another country who has been exposed or conditioned in another country, with some of the most advanced policing processes and practices in the world. That is how much the world has changed, and that has implications for our institutions.

The RBP improved their responses in assisting visitors and holiday makers in any number of areas, from providing information, preventing harassment, and crime similar to other Caribbean countries, often creating a two-tier policing system in the process. The character of contemporary crime and its transnational nature have contributed to changes in the way local law enforcement responds. The emergence of international drugs trade and its association with firearms has driven the RBP's priorities. Drug activity witnessed the presence of well-known figures from Columbian organized crime world establishing themselves in the Bahamian "out islands," along with private security firms protecting their illicit activities.

Concerns about the impact of the drugs trade on Bahamian society spurred the government into action resulting in significant investment of resources into the RBP which contributed to its modernization. For example, in the doubling of police budgets, increasing police staff, the establishment of forensic facilities, and improving the basic hardware required to respond to the growing crime problem.

The present size of the RBP establishment is 4,500 people, of which 2,900 are sworn officers and over 1,000 auxiliaries, with civilian staff making up the remainder (Royal Bahamas Police Force, 2012). Reflecting on the significant changes that have taken place in the basic police establishment the Commissioner remarks:

EG: I can cast my mind back when the police force consisted of 16 officers for Nassau alone and we are not talking that long ago in historical terms.

Increasing the capacity of former colonial police organizations to respond to the contemporary crime has often accompanied other reforms in terms of policies, procedures, and structures. Police modernization in the developing world is often reliant on expertise drawn from advance policing jurisdiction which has generated discussions about the effectiveness of this approach to change. In the Bahamian instance, the appointment of a foreign advisor proved very successful in introducing a range of changes to the workings of the RBP. Summarizing some of the benefits of this approach the Commissioner recounts:

EG: One of the reasons I believe we have been successful in tackling matters around officer conduct is due to the fact that we have always been open to outside influence. We had a British police advisor who came to the Bahamas and spent 12 years with us. Some things worked, some things didn't, but he brought a lot of his policing experience and really contributed to our development in terms of policies and procedures. For example, establishing an Anti-Corruption branch and proper arrest and detention procedures.

The Bahamian experience suggests that policy transfer can be very effective in improving police organizations in developing countries under the appropriate conditions. While the Commissioner admitted efforts to introduce change in some areas did not work, he failed to elucidate what these were. The response of the RBP to the drugs trade has been robust and has been assisted by transnational partners in the Caribbean such as the US and by Britain with its training of the Bahamian coast guard. Reflecting on the effectiveness of some of the strategies used by the RBP to address these problems:

EG: We have done some good work in reducing the amount of guns in circulation. During the mid-1980s, 80% of drugs on their way to the US passed through our region. Now, it is down to about 2% and that's predominantly cocaine. The majority of this trade now goes through Central American countries and we can see this by the increase in violence and the crime rate in these places.

While improved policing and targeted raids, such as "Operation Rapid Strike" (Royal Bahamas Police Force, 2012) have been vital aspects of the response to drug and gun crime; actions taken by the police in other parts of the region have also been of particular importance to the effective policing of this problem. The Commissioner elaborates:

EG: We have spoken recently about the good work that is being done on the South Mexican border into the United States. The Mexican authorities have ratcheted up their responses to drug traffickers working in partnership with US agencies, and that is paying good dividends for us.

The Commissioner expressed concern about the drug trade and guns and the violence associated with them which have contributed to a culture of violence hitherto unknown in most of the Caribbean islands. A worrying development is how access to high powered weapons has emboldened those involved in criminal activity. The Commissioner elucidates:

EG: There was a time when it was unheard of for criminals to challenge legitimate police organizations. We saw news reports in other countries of police officers being targeted and murdered for doing their jobs, and interdicting in this drugs and guns trade. This is not something we have experience of in Bahamas, but we have seen it elsewhere in the region and have to be vigilant.

One area not explored during the interview was the pattern of alleged police brutality in poor areas where many police raids take place, which have led to tense community relations, and have similar hallmarks as the culture of policing in other Caribbean countries. The Bahamas has a very high homicide rate in common with other Caribbean countries, which has important implications for how the police operate (Amnesty International, 2013). New technology and transnational relations facilitate and inform the everyday work practices of the RBP in tackling gun crime. The Commissioner illustrates this point:

EG: Say we are talking about one of our strategic priorities of working closely with our international partners, and specifically, The Bureau of Alcohol Tobacco and Firearms and Explosives, in respect to illegal firearms trafficking and firearms offences. An officer in a city CID office can read or be informed of this priority in a very simple and practical way. They need only ask themselves when was the last time they used the ETrace system or other mechanisms we have to obtain pertinent firearms-related intelligence.

Technology and the capacity to operate across borders has created new forms of crime, such as Internet-based fraud, that are creating challenges for the RBP, as they are in other parts of the world. These contemporary policing problems are an important component in driving the modernization process. Reflecting on these changes the Commissioner comments:

EG: Many senior officers can tell you that only a few years ago we would never be called into matters regarding high-tech crime. But today we receive them on a daily basis, with people trying to access company computers and banking machines, accessing other people's personal mail and accounts, and now online fraud.

The technological challenges facing former colonial police organizations are not simply reduced to matters of white collar crime. The issue of terrorism and use of technology is a concern in advanced policing jurisdictions which has become an issue of discussion in regional police networks such as the Association of Caribbean Commissioners of Police. The Commissioner elaborates on some of the issues being discussed by Caribbean police leaders:

EG: They are even talking about cyber-attacks on critical infrastructure, such as the banking system, electricity, and other key infrastructure. So the issue of proactivity is crucial for many Caribbean police leaders in understanding these emerging threats; even if it is not an issue now or we don't have the capacity at this moment to respond to it.

Democratic Policing

An important area of questioning during the interview concerned the issues of accountability of the RBP and what form this took and whether it has changed. Historically, colonial police organizations were highly centralized systems that were primarily accountable to foreign powers whose principle concerns revolved around ensuring the smooth economic exploitation of local people and their social and political control. In the Bahamas, the legal system was dominated by white Bahamians. Since independence in 1973, making the institutions of the state accountable to citizens has been a priority and an ongoing project. The influence of previous generations of Bahamian leaders on the political culture of the country is expanded on by the Commissioner:

EG: We had a relatively peaceful transition from minority to majority rule. The power elite were white people with the money, so racism and race was a factor. We also had the influence of Dr. Martin Luther King and the civil rights movement in America and Sir Lynden Pindling, and others who became very important leaders. Many of these individuals knew each other in London, and came back as lawyers, and were crucial in leading a peaceful transformation from minority to majority rule. They knew the law and how to use it to change the country, which they did. Today, we have a country which is a thriving little democracy because of what they started.

A feature of the political history of the Bahamas is the relative lack of conflict compared to other Caribbean countries in the transition to independence or shortly thereafter. The absence of conflict has been important in shaping the political and administrative culture of the country:

EG: We don't have a history of police and public conflict in the way it is in other Caribbean countries. We are a democratic country, so we are prone to demonstrations and public articulation of grievances. But I can't really remember us having any major public order issues where the public have damaged or destroyed buildings, or any of our officers have been hurt.

Important aspects of Bahamian society that have contributed to its relatively peaceful and tolerant character are the absence of conflict on the basis of class or race and improving attitudes towards women and sexual difference:

EG: We don't have any tensions around race or the past in the Bahamas. We might feel there are people with mega bucks who use their influence to support the party that favors their interest with an association with the previous minority rule, but that is really not a point of major conflict.

The picture painted by the Commissioner is somewhat oversimplified. Class conflict in the Bahamas may not be as acute as other countries, but the type of communities which have become susceptible to drugs crime and victims of police violence, by and large, are the poorest sections of society. The small size of many Caribbean countries can facilitate heightened levels of fear and tension, for example, due to tit for tat violence. But it can also contribute to peace and stability, given the close nature of social affiliations in these societies. How the issues of small population and geographical size contribute to the lack of conflict in the majority of Bahamian society is explained by the Commissioner:

EG: I think a lot of that turns on the fact we are a small country with strong familial ties, and those types of links which I think help create stability or a sense of agreement on how people conduct themselves, because we can negotiate and come to a reasonable resolution.

How the aforementioned factors combine is important in shaping the relationship between the public, government, and the police. Describing the quality of these relationships, the Commissioner comments:

EG: I can say we have a very good relationship with the government. I can say without equivocation that I enjoy the full confidence of the Prime Minister, Minister of National Security, the Attorney General and, I would say, both sides of the House of Parliament and the Senate. I am very close with our politicians, because that is the way our political system works.

The Bahamian government and its key institutions have proven to be adept at learning from other countries in order to increase the accountability of the police. An important piece of legislation which seeks to further this aim is explained by the Commissioner:

EG: We recently made changes to our *Police Force Act* of 2009 based on the British model that brought in a whole host of accountability measures regarding the Commissioner of police and his force. The law requires me to produce a Commissioner's Report for the year, outlining policing priorities and how these have been met.

The *Police Force Act* of 2009 covers a range of matters pertinent to the professional and legal conduct of the police and the performance of the Commissioner. It also addresses the rights of the citizens and suspects around the use of police powers that demonstrates a clear effort by government to bring the RBP in line with international good practice. Perhaps one of the most important influences on police accountability has been the region's courts:

EG: Greater accountability is being demanded of police officers from magistrates, judges in High and Supreme Courts, and from the average man and woman on the streets who make up juries.

Significant cultural changes have taken place across the Caribbean, including the improving levels of education. The cultural influence of US television, and the Internet have made the public more aware and increased its sophistication around matters relating to police practice and the use of forensic sciences inter alia. Personal familiarization with North America and Britain through travel has had an important impact on attitudes regarding criminal justice administration, which has resulted in the Bahamian police being held to higher standards. The Commissioner elaborates:

EG: If you think you can just turn up to court and make a pretty speech and pass it off as evidence, that is not the case, because the average man and woman who comprises the jury, is not gullible and is going to challenge your case or the forensic or other evidence that you are relying on.

The popularization of human rights and role of the courts in promoting these values has had a major impact on the public and their expectations of the police and how they conduct their affairs. These sentiments are expressed by the Commissioner:

EG: The days of thinking you can ride roughshod over those accused is gone; it is not going to be accepted. This is an international issue, an ongoing debate, where governments around the world are being encouraged to ensure sufficient respect is given to the human rights of individuals. Judges are highly attuned to human rights issues and the proper application of the law, and will not permit democratic countries to violate these values.

The rise of human rights as a form of international standards has many sources which include local and international activists and journalists. However, none have been as influential as transnational organizations and agencies such as the United Nations. The RBP have recently been criticized by a human rights watchdog over allegations of police violence and deaths in custody (Amnesty International, 2013). Commenting on the UN's importance the Commissioner remarks:

EG: Organizations such as the UN highlight important weaknesses in police practice around the world, so is the observation that the challenge for governments and police leaders is much more than simply building capacity and making police organizations more efficient and effective in enabling them to catch, arrest, and process people and take them to court.

Looking Ahead

The developments which have taken place within the RBP and some other Caribbean police organizations and the steady consolidation of professional and regional policing networks is evidence of the increasing policing capacity in this part of the world. At bare minimum, it highlights that some police chief executives possess the requisite understanding and social capital to introduce important organizational reforms. The nature of the contemporary world and its interconnectedness is particularly important for relatively poor Caribbean countries. The Commissioner remarks:

EG: Previously, many of the much smaller or less developed Caribbean islands would not have as much contact and familiarity with some of the more advanced countries, or leaders of their various institutions. We are now at a point in our development where Caribbean countries are starting to look at other Caribbean countries as models of good practice and expertise, which has so many mutual benefits.

In this context, the RBP has a potentially significant role regionally and beyond as a model of an organization that has successfully introduced change in important areas. This demonstrates how former colonial police organizations that have benefited from the influences of advance policing jurisdictions can, under the correct conditions, become a source of expertise for others. These sentiments are expressed by the Commissioner:

EG: We have done some things in policing which others have not done and we have qualified people in all sorts of policing areas who are capable of speaking and sharing their knowledge to colleagues worldwide, and it's about giving them that opportunity and aspiration to do so. I also think that is a major benefit of belonging to associations such as the International Association of Police Chiefs and the IPES.

Conclusion

The examination of the RBP and its Commissioner throws light on how contemporary policing challenges and strategies have played an important role in successfully driving organizational change and modernization, in some areas of activity, in a relatively affluent Caribbean country. Independent evaluation of these changes would assist in understanding how successful the RBP has been. Initial signs are promising. The case study highlights the importance of a historically positive attitude to learning from advanced policing jurisdictions. This has benefited the RBP, its leadership's thinking and practice, which is epitomized in its progressive Commissioner, whose career has been intrinsically tied to organizational change. These developments to a significant degree reflect the attitude of the government to policing and its support and vision for the Bahamas and the unique history of the country. This underscores the observation that the effective transformation of former colonial police organizations reflects broader matters around governance and improving the quality of democracy.

References

Amnesty International. 2013. *Annual Report: The Bahamas*. http://www.amnesty-usa.org. Accessed November 15, 2013.

Bowling, B. 2010. *Policing the Caribbean*. Oxford: Oxford University Press.

Handy, C. 1985. *Gods of Management: The Changing Work of Organizations*. New York: Oxford University Press.

Royal Bahamas Police Force. 2012. *Commissioner's Policing Plan*. http://www.royalbahamaspolice.org/

Joe Arpaio, Sheriff, Maricopa County, Arizona, USA

9

INTERVIEWED BY DIANA
SCHARFF PETERSON

Contents

Introduction

In the United States, it is important to distinguish between the policing role of a sheriff and that of a police chief. According to Burch (2012), the historical framework for the sheriff can be traced back to tenth century England. At first, the "shire-reeve"—a political figure—served as the King's right hand to protect his interests by collecting taxes and taking suspects into custody. The foundation of the "shire-reeve" was adopted in the American colonies. The political dimensions of the sheriff originally included those sworn by the Crown (State), but changed within America in the seventeenth and eighteenth centuries evolving to an elected position, thus molding the sheriff to be accountable to the citizens. In most cases the sheriff's position is constitutional, which is stipulated in charter documents. Currently, in the United States, 98% of the 3,083 sheriffs are elected by the voting public within the county/parish. Therefore, the position cannot "be abolished, have its power and responsibilities reduced, or have its personnel decisions made by the county boards or commissioners" (Burch, 2012: 126).

In contrast, local police chiefs are administratively created and are a part of a department (division of the executive branch); they are not an office (independent entity), and not elected. The elected sheriff does not have to have minimal educational or experience requirements, which is usually in a direct contrast to a chief of police. In addition, the sheriff's responsibilities go beyond simply maintaining the peace. The local sheriff must also collaborate with and provide assistance to both courts and corrections. Furthermore, the sheriff has a larger jurisdiction (a county), which can include unincorporated areas, meaning different legal powers have to be utilized, as compared to municipal agencies. Functional dimensions of the sheriff provide a vast array of responsibilities such as criminal law enforcement, correctional services, court proceedings, security in the courtroom, additional services (transportation of mentally ill), seizure of property, collection of fees, and sale of licenses.

In the United States, the office of the sheriff is an independent agency and not connected to a county department. The sheriff is responsible to the citizens of that county and not a governing board or city council (as is the chief of police). The office of the sheriff cannot be dictated to by a small politically driven organization. This political disconnect allows the sheriff's office to be more accountable to the public at large and offer his/her services without concerns over being fired. LaFrance and Placide (2010) and LaFrance (2012) found that the local county sheriffs are more willing to work with all segments of society (local, state, and federal). Police chiefs are appointed and tend to be more concerned with managing their own department's needs. The direct electoral link to the voting public makes the sheriffs more attuned to the geographic areas in which they serve.

The interview took place on October 18, 2013, in Sheriff Arpaio's office, Phoenix, Arizona.

Career

DSP: Tell me about your career.
JA: I was born on June 14, 1932, in Springfield, Massachusetts. In 1950, after graduating from high school, I joined the US Army at the breakout of the Korean War. At age 21, and after three years in the US Army, I joined the Washington, D.C. Metropolitan Police Department. After moving to Las Vegas, Nevada, to work for the Las Vegas Police Department for a short time (six months), I became a federal narcotics agent in Chicago, Illinois. I spent 27 years with the Drug Enforcement Agency (DEA) in Mexico, the Middle East, Central and South America, as well as in the United States in Arizona and Texas. In 1978, I retired as head of the DEA Arizona. In 1982, I joined my wife in a private business for ten years. In 1992, at the age of 60, I ran for sheriff of Maricopa County, Arizona, which is

the third largest sheriff's office in the United States. I have been re-elected six times and plan on running for a seventh term, just for spite.

DSP: What motivated you to enter and stay in police work?

JA: My mother died in childbirth, but I grew up in Italian families here and there. From a young age, I was encouraged by my family to enter law enforcement. They always told me that I wanted to be an FBI agent or a cop, and that is just what I did. When I was discharged from the army, an opportunity was presented to me at the Washington, DC police force. I have stuck with law enforcement for over 50 years.

Changes Experienced

DSP: What were the most important changes which have occurred within law enforcement over the course of your career?

JA: The main thing that changed for me personally is the fact that I'm elected. It puts me in a different category. I've been a bureaucrat my whole life and, quite frankly, when I ran for sheriff in 1992, against the incumbent Republican, no one thought I could beat him and I thought that the sheriff should be appointed and not elected. That was the worst thing I ever said, because I learned quickly (right off the bat), if I was appointed, I would have been fired 20 years ago. Now, do you really think that if I were an appointed sheriff, I would be talking to you like I am? We always must have one law enforcement official elected by the people. A lot of local police chiefs don't like me because I will go right into Phoenix (Arizona) with my posse. Actually, when I finish this interview, I have a press conference, and then I am heading into Phoenix with my posse. I'm not criticizing police chiefs, but they can't really do anything; they have to worry about the city manager, about the mayor, and the city council. I think, as far as I'm concerned, the biggest change in my 50 years has been that I am an *elected constitutional* sheriff.

DSP: What about the organizational culture of law enforcement? Has that changed since you began your career?

JA: It has changed. I used to have a blackjack, a nightstick, and a '38 when I was a cop in Washington, DC and Las Vegas, Nevada. I worked probably the toughest beat in Washington, DC (14th street). I was a young and aggressive officer, and there was no gray area. Everything was black and white to me. I locked up everybody. There's an old saying that it takes about five years to become a police officer. I

think what they are talking about is maturity, not how many college degrees you have.

When I went to Vegas, I locked up Elvis (Presley), but that's a different story.
I spent six months there with my partner. We were kind of novices, stopping
a bus for speeding five miles an hour over the speed limit. Then I changed
my police philosophy to "give these guys a break." I believe that comes as you
get more mature. Don't forget, I was young (21 years old) and had spent three
years in the Army. By the time I became a federal agent, a narcotics agent
(back then we were called the Bureau of Narcotics), we only had 200 agents
worldwide, and I was probably only the second one overseas in Turkey, to the
Middle East. I was one guy stationed in Turkey. My job was to lock up all the
dope peddlers in a foreign country.

In 1969, President Johnson moved us from the Treasury and put us in
the Justice Department, which he called the US Bureau of Narcotics and
Dangerous Drugs. In 1973, (President) Nixon changed the name to the Drug
Enforcement Administration, DEA. In the politics of it, it looks like every
time a new President comes in, he changes the name and they merge and
make it look like something's happening. But going all the way back to the
federal agent in the old days, and the cop on the beat, we could do things a
little differently than you do now, when everyone is worrying about being
sued and everybody's got video cameras. You have tremendous public access
with the Internet and YouTube. With everything you do, you are going be on
YouTube. So, I think it's changed in that regard, when you are policing.

I think the culture has changed somewhat with our younger people that
we hire. Many, or some of them, look at the money. It's always the money and
overtime—the "I want to get paid" philosophy. When I grew up, I couldn't
have cared less and I worked 24 hours a day. My job was primary, and all I
did was work. As a result, I advanced in my career. I became a regional director and all that, so the work paid off for me. Instead of playing cards with
the boss, I was out there locking up dope peddlers. To answer your question,
things have changed. We have to be more cautious these days. Not that we did
anything wrong in the past. However, when I look back at my career, I had
18 assaults on me in my last year in DC. I was aggressive. As I said, there's no
gray area. I'm not that big of a guy who walked a high crime neighborhood
alone. Anyone that did anything (put the handcuffs on, take them across the
street, call the police wagon and keep going), got a lot of assaults. Now as I
look back, what would have happened if there were video cameras running?
Some people make comments and say, "wait a minute, who assaulted who?"
Do you get the point? I just didn't take any nonsense. I didn't do anything
illegal. Even today, if someone resists arrest or tries to punch me, I'm taking
them in (into custody). Today, you have to be careful because you've got this,
"everybody's suing you now" philosophy. I think that is the biggest change.

DSP: Have current economic conditions resulted in budget cuts and how has this impacted your organization?

JA: Once again, I'm elected. I do not report to anyone but the 4,000,000 people in this county. I am *part* of the county. I'm an elected official. I'm not an appointed official in the county. We have a board of supervisors, whose only job is to make sure that I get the money that is allocated to the county. They can't tell me how to use that money, and I feel very strongly about that. I make all of the decisions, and we have received money back every year since I became the Sheriff. No one gives money back, but I get criticized. You know, I get criticized for everything. That's another big problem. Our budgets are nearly $250,000,000. I used to have 4,000 employees, but that has gone down.

One significant thing that I have done as Sheriff is that I have built up my volunteer posse. I love the challenges! Right now I'm going into Phoenix with my "Crime Suppression Operation," which has caused federal judges and the Department of Justice to come after me. I just had a ruling against me by a federal judge about monitors (*Melendres et al. v. Arpaio et al.*, 2013); but, I know how to work around that. I'm telling you what I'm doing firsthand. You can just go to the Internet and 50% of what you read about me will be garbage, but that's all right—it's all lies.

DSP: Regarding external relationships, what changes have you observed?

JA: Do you have 10 days!? Well, it's interesting and sort of sad in a way because I was a regional director in Mexico City, in South America, and offices in Panama, and Argentina. I was a federal drug enforcer. Plus I was the head of the DEA in Texas and in Arizona. So I think I know where the US/Mexico border is, and yet, I never hear from President Barak Obama. Of course he's worried about my birth certificate investigation. I never hear the President call me, or all of these politicians who come into my office. They just want my endorsement. I think everyone running for the Republican Party came to see me here, or I met with them to discuss the border. It is a big problem.

I believe when I started enforcing immigration laws (in 2006), I was put into a different category. I took a lot of heat (criticism), and continue to take heat. I think that's the foundation and the bottom line on my recent reputation. Don't forget that I became sheriff in 1992 and took office January 1, 1993, and I built up a reputation with "Tent City" and pink underwear. I can go on and on. So, I had built up a lot of notoriety over that because I operate all the jails. I take a little heat sometimes, you know, accusations that "it gets 140° Fahrenheit" in the tents. I can go on and on, but that's where people came to know me—by how I run my jails. By the way, there are some sheriffs out there that all they do is just run the jails. I do everything. I'm the top law enforcement officer for this county, not the police chiefs, but the sheriff is. I can go anywhere. I enforce all of the laws—murders in unincorporated areas,* in contract cities,† and in Phoenix, which is the fifth largest city in the United States. I don't go out there and investigate murders, but as you can see, I do go into Phoenix (with my posse) to catch dope peddlers and all that.

I may have caused some problems with police chiefs and mayors in the past, but it is my immigration policy that has caused them to really go after me, from the White House down. There's one judge who just ruled on racial profiling—he said we "racially profile." He listened to the ACLU (American Civil Liberties Union of Arizona). They are going to put a monitor in here, but I am still going to do my job, because I'm elected. We will be appealing all of his (the Judge's) rulings, especially the one telling me how many detectives I should have. That is *not* a federal judge's jurisdiction. I have got a lot of good appeals coming, but that is going to take a long time. Right now, I am going to have to work around it, and try not to violate his decision. I'm comfortable. I can do that. I'm not worried about it, but it is harassment. Forget the immigration! I'm very concerned by a judge trying to tell me, an elected Sheriff, *how to do my job*—that's going to be a big appeal. I have two appeals coming: one part will be immigration, and the other part is about a judge telling me how to do my job.

I told you at the beginning of the mistake I made. I am going to protect the Office of the Sheriff, and that will always be my biggest fight. We have about 3,100 sheriffs in the US and, by the way, even sheriffs do not stand next to me. We've got 15 sheriffs right here and I am larger than all of them put together. There's an association in Washington, DC, the National Sheriff's Association, that I used to take part in and attend. I do not waste my time anymore. Not that I'm against sheriffs, but I don't find that it's really interesting. I don't see sheriffs standing next to me through everything that I'm going through on the immigration and everything else. *Where is everyone*? I'm the Lone Ranger riding alone, but yet everyone wants my endorsement. It's really funny, all the heat that I take and being investigated criminally by the Department of Justice. Of course, that all went nowhere; it all just disappeared.

There were headlines for three and a half years regarding the Department of Justice (DOJ) investigating me for alleged racial profiling. That has been going on and on, and nothing ever happens, because it is political. And, once again, the bottom line is that I am elected. I would never take a job as a chief

---

* Geographic regions of land that are not incorporated into the jurisdiction of a municipality.
† Cities that contract with other entities (public and private) for services that they do not offer themselves

of police. Not that I couldn't survive; I'm pretty good. I used to meet with Presidents (of the United States), but I would never take the job of police chief. I think when you talk about me and my 50 years in law enforcement, the relationships between appointed police chiefs and an elected sheriff is very important. Some people should write about that, and show in law enforcement that there is a distinction between an elected sheriff and a bureaucratic police chief, who is always very afraid to do things; sometimes afraid because we all work for lawyers today. We all seem these days to work for lawyers, which costs us millions. You are going to get sued if you are doing something, or not doing something. I believe that it is the liability that is causing law enforcement to *not* police like we used to.

DSP: And have things changed regarding police education?

JA: It's really ironic because when I grew up in law enforcement, everyone did not have all these degrees. Here you have a guy with a bachelor's degree, and I think, *he wants to be a cop*? *Why do you want be a cop with all of that education*? It's ironic that we all go for education these days. It's all about how many degrees you have. I've got my guys here and I promote them, such as my deputy chief. Most of them have a degree or a Master's degree, but I don't care. I've got some people who don't have degrees and are just better workers than those who have degrees. I'm not impressed. I am not against education, but I'm not impressed when my deputies say they have earned a Master's degree. You know what? I want to know how you do your job. And don't give me the attitude that this degree will make you better. I believe the more degrees we see today, the more problems that we see happen. I am not blaming the cops on the street, but they do not police like they used to. Maybe, it's the system that we have. To me, I don't have a degree. I was too busy working, and in court every day. I was locking up everybody from Washington to Turkey. My college was in Turkey, while I was in the *boondocks* (a rural area), shooting at dope peddlers all while working undercover. That was my education. I came up the hard way in my law enforcement career, without all of these degrees. I say the ironic part of education is that the more educated police are becoming does not make them better cops.

What makes good cops is the common sense, experience, hard work, and to not spend all of one's time learning how to get college degrees on the government's time. One may disagree with me; I'm just giving you my opinion. I think I did okay. How did I do? I became a regional director, the youngest one in the DEA. I did it all by working. I didn't get all these degrees. I just worked myself up there, *big time*. I have been married 57 years. I happen to have a wife who doesn't complain to this day, and my two kids, but all I ever did was work.

DSP: And what about changes in technology?

JA: The whole country has changed somewhat, and not just law enforcement. People sometimes do not work that much or they always just want the money, so we changed a little in our society. Let's talk about what's on television; kids can watch anything. All I have is a mobile phone, and I have my old Smith Corona typewriter. I don't have computers. I have none of this technology, and I don't have email. I can have someone in the next office, all they have to do is to hear the word, *email*—everything is about email! You see, I believe that you lose contact. You lose communication, and you lose everything. In police work, too, it is the same thing. We have all these computers in the car, and all this technological equipment. Come on! That's what I see, as the big change. It is the technology, the philosophy, and the social problems that we have now that we did not really have in the past.

Personal Policing Philosophy

DSP: What is your policing philosophy?

JA: The philosophy of how I run an organization in law enforcement is just like any other private business. I ran a business with my wife for 10 years, and I am pretty conservative. I like to save money, believe it or not. Being the sheriff, I operate a little differently. I am not as formalized as the police chiefs or some sheriffs. I talk to everyone, every deputy. When I have staff meetings it is not so formal. I run a very loose organization, in that regard. However, I think I know I am smart enough to get the right people into the right positions. Management is about getting things done through the people. I am only as good as the people who work for me. I set the policy. I go out knocking doors in, which I love to do, but people say, "Hey you have 4,000 people, why the hell are you knocking doors in?" I go undercover, which I love to do. I know the media will say that I want more publicity. I know all that, but I still like to get out on the streets. I have a uniform on today, which is very unusual, but I am going to have a press conference. We are going out there today, after the press conference, to lock people up. I am going out into Phoenix with 150 of the posse and my deputies. So, we are going out there to lock people up, right after the judge ruled that I can't even go to the toilet! I am not violating his ruling. I am not going after illegal aliens. I am going after dope peddlers.

I try to motivate people who work for me, but not through fear. They can't deceive me, because I know every trick in the book. I'm not some sheriff who was not a deputy at one time, where they bring him into the office. I have been there, so I know all the tricks. They can't con me, and they know it. So yes, we do okay. I have been able to survive 21 years. That should tell you something, and it is not because I am tall, dark, and handsome. It's because I know what I'm doing, through the media and in running this organization, which is the 3rd largest in the United States. I always get asked:"Hey Sheriff, how much money do you make?" I have 400 people that make more money than I do. Every sheriff here, and I didn't contest it, earns what I earn. A five-man department makes the same as a department with 4,000 men. That's not right, but do you know what? I didn't do it for the money. I make just under $100,000.00 each year for the 3rd largest county in the United States. Go anywhere in the country and see what sheriffs get paid. Moneywise, every police chief makes more than I do, even those in the small departments. I am not worried about it. I don't want a raise. I didn't take this job for money. You know I can use money; I have four adopted grandkids who are black and Mexican, but everybody calls me a racist! They (protesters) are out every day in front of my office for the past three and a half years holding the signs, calling me Nazi and Hitler. Why don't they defend me? They call me a Nazi and Hitler? It's okay to call me that; it doesn't bother me, because every time they demonstrate against me, my polls go up. You see, I'm a little different than anyone else. Anyone else would say, "Oh this is awful!" They blast me in the newspapers, but the more, the merrier. I have a different philosophy from everyone else. We might get 200 demonstrators today against me, but that's great! My polls will go up another 10%–15%.

DSP: What do you think should be the role and functions of the police?
JA: Here's another thing—all I hear is about "community policing"; that we have to have community policing. That is the big thing with all of the police chiefs. Let's not tie up a whole police department with community policing. I have a lot of great programs, and the jail especially and now there's the judge that says I have to have community policing. I have to go talk to a judge, but that's another issue. I believe that it is good to have community policing, as right now cops have to be very careful when they stop someone.

The role of the cops is really to protect the public. The number one rule is "to protect" and that is the rule of our country too. The safety of our country is the "number one rule," from the President on down to the guy on the beat. I am not against community policing, but let's not go overboard with it, and tie up all our officers with community policing. That's what we hear all the time.

I believe that it is kind of a cop-out, if we are not locking everybody up, then let's have community policing.

DSP: What facilitates or hinders good relations with the community?
JA: I treat people politely, but I believe that sometimes we tend to go overboard on community policing. I am going out today with my posse and I am doing *my community policing.* I'm going to lock everybody up that violates the law! That is my community policing. I'm *not* going into the community today to say, "let's all get together; here's my deputy, do you have any problems?" The Sheriff's Office is here to protect you, which is important. My idea of community policing is to put people in jail to protect the people and the victims from the criminals. I think that cops wear a gun and a badge because we are supposed to arrest people. Why would you have a gun and badge, if you're not going to arrest someone? This is not Citizens on Patrol, or city block watches. We are out there in the community to defend the people, and our lives are at risk, too, when we do that.

Of course there are obstacles. Now, there's one that I can blame myself for. It's the media, as I am very high profile. When I ran for sheriff, I made three, three, promises: I'm going to put tents up; build up my volunteer posse; and be an active sheriff, not one that plays golf or goes fishing. I don't have a hobby, none. The only hobby I have is sometimes I like to watch movies and television, which I cannot even do. I have security issues. I have and have had many, many threats against me.

With the media, I admit that I caused some of my own issues by being very open to the media about everything that I do. I like to think that I am pretty good at public relations. I think I have had about 4,000 interviews and profiles about me overseas. I'm talking about media in foreign countries. I talk to everyone, locally to internationally. I speak to the media. Many of them don't like me. I never get a headline, saying that, "we have a great sheriff." Are you kidding me!?

I think that the media drives everything. It drives the politicians from the President down. It drives elected officials. One has to know sometimes how to handle that. You will never see police chiefs talk like I do. No, because they are not elected officials. I'm elected and in a different category. I have a gun and badge, but I am also elected, so I guess I am a politician too. It puts a sheriff in a different category. The media are going to love this—going after me—because they are going to say a Federal judge just ruled against me. But, I know how to do it. The media triggers a lot of what goes on. But, I have been able to survive with all the negative publicity. I deal with the media. I never turn them down, even when they blast me. Really, it is a love hate/

relationship. But you know what? When you really look at it, why should one bite the hand that feeds him? I know they do their thing, and I do my thing. However, if I did not get any media attention it would be very difficult for the people to know what I am doing as Sheriff of Maricopa County. I don't have the money to let people know what I am doing. With 4,000,000 people in my County, what am I going to do? Everyday send something through the mail? I can't do that. So how do you get what I do to the people? I go to and through the media. That is really one of the big problems that I have had as the elected sheriff, which I did not have as a bureaucrat in all my different assignments over the years.

Problems and Successes Experienced

DSP: What do you consider to be the greatest problems facing the police at this time?

JA: Probably one thing could be the politics. My example would be immigration. This is a political situation, from the President down. It affects the cop on the beat because he can't do what he feels he should be doing, such as arresting illegals—that's just an example. You have rulings by judges that put the handcuffs on the police. You have the police now who are trying to act in good faith. Some of them are indicted for shooting someone that they are trying to arrest. I can go on and on.

DSP: What about the problem of corruption, how do you deal with corruption in your force?

JA: I went after some corrupt members of the Board of Supervisors, and, of course, I became the bad guy. Believe me. I worked corruption on and off in Chicago and in other places. So, when you say corruption, we have an internal affairs unit to handle that. There's a balance. I think with my department, we are the lowest paid, which is an insult. Yet, I do not lose that many people. I like to think that my deputies enjoy the freedoms that I give them to be a cop. I back them up when they are acting in good faith. We may have a big incident today, but do you think I'm going to throw one of my guys under the bus? No. Even though they screw up a little, I am still going to back them up. It gives them the freedom, *not to be afraid* to turn on a red light and a siren.

Today, if you hit somebody, here come the big lawsuits! And we have all of these policies; a book full of policies. It is a big balance to make sure that you abide by the laws, and yet, give your people the opportunity to do their job. It's a balance. I do not go around using my internal affairs to set people up. If I am going undercover, I am going after dope peddlers. I believe that if you get more satisfaction out of arresting or firing your own people, then *you* are the bad guys. Don't think that doesn't happen! The sheriff that I beat in the election got kicked out for getting rid of his deputies.

Theory and Practice

DSP: What part has theory played in your practice and that of your organization?

JA: None—I do not write to other sheriff's departments. I'm the lone ranger. I do my own thing. I don't waste my time with all the magazines or to get my name in the paper. I get my name in the papers around the world. I do not have to "get" into a professional journal. I'm beyond trying to get my picture in a journal article and writing research papers. I just advise everybody to put people in hot tents. I saved the government $80,000,000. Everyone in law enforcement and corrections should think of putting tents up! Don't even talk to me about overcrowding. I wrote a letter to the Governor of California last month when it was reported that he had to release 10,000 inmates. *Do you really think for a minute that I thought he would answer me*? He is not going to answer me. But I gave it to the media, just to put it right in there. I can do it because I laid the foundation. I have the experience. We had our 20th-year anniversary of Tent City last month. Is anybody going to say it is wrong? I have had four presidential candidates visit me in the tents, along with Amnesty International, the Department of Justice and all that.

External Relations

DSP: How have you and the work of your organization been affected by developments outside the county? Do you believe your practices could be utilized in other countries?

JA: First of all, there one reason that I go on all of these television programs overseas, and I'm not bragging, but I am probably on television in any country you go to. If you say you are from Arizona, you know about Sheriff Joe. Why do I take on interviews in other countries? They can't vote for me. I know that, but I like to spread the word. England? They call me and ask me for my advice about their prisons. Canada and France? They call and ask, "We know you do this, what do you think about that?" When people visit here with the state department officials from other countries, they come in here. I was a diplomatic officer overseas in Mexico, South America, Turkey, and so on. I do have a connection, a feeling for the people.

My mother and father came here from Italy. I like dealing with the Internationals, and I am not talking about just those from Mexico. We could have a big book written about Mexico. On the other hand, with Mexico, I've always advised them to build up their economy so they will not have the illegals coming in to the United States. It is an economic problem. I like to go and deal with consulate generals and ambassadors if they want me to, and give them my side of the story. As I always say, who else has the experience that I have? I like to lend that experience. They may not listen, but at least I can talk about what and how I used to do it over there. Maybe they could pick up a couple of ideas, but they are not going to talk to me. I'm talking about the Mexico part of it.

We are the greatest country in the world. On the law enforcement angle, there's a lot foreign police can learn and a lot of things that we can learn from them, if everyone is willing to communicate. I will always remember when we closed the border, they hated us in Mexico for those two weeks. Then by chance, I became the regional director. So here, I was in Mexico City. The President hated me, the Attorney General, everybody hated me! I had agents working undercover; we used to do it in those days. So what did I do? I had the Attorney General of Mexico over to my house. He liked blueberry pie. So, my wife started cooking blueberry pie. I got more done with whiskey and blueberry pie than with the big stick.

There is a lot of sense to talk about communication, especially with foreigners. Mutual respect and also a warm personality mean a lot. At times, one can get things done better that way than being the typical Secretary of State. And I did. I proved that I was actually going to be good. I got anything I wanted. I did not get my cases screwed up, that I knew of. I got along great with the Attorney General of Mexico actually, and my being a little more personal, like going out and having a pizza. That goes a long way. That's my philosophy. I put the word out that if the President of Mexico wants to meet with me, I would be glad to fly down there. I will tell him about my background, have a couple of martinis, and let's talk. Forget all this bureaucratic garbage that's playing into the television all the time.

Looking Ahead

DSP: What are the most likely developments that you see happening in law enforcement or that you would like to see happening?

JA: Maybe for it to go back to what it was, but we will never do that. You'll never go back on history on any subject, not this long. We are too far gone. I know that money isn't the answer to everything. The more money you get, the more you spend. I remember when I was the head of federal drug enforcement, and I was pretty conservative in a way, and tried to save money, like I do as sheriff. But they used to call and say, "Hey we've got to go before Congress, so make sure you spend your money." You know, instead of buying an ounce of coke (cocaine) undercover, buy a kilo. Because they don't want to go to Congress and say that I don't need any money. We got to play it. That's the trouble. You save money, and you're not rewarded for it! That's why we have the budget problems that we have. There's an old saying, you should run the government like you run a private business. There's a lot of ways, believe me, and these politicians, all they do is talk. This will be resolved. Fox News (a major US news broadcaster) took me off the air. They couldn't interview me because they were too busy talking about the budget. Come on! We knew it, guarantee you. I even predicted three weeks ago that it will go right down to the wire. Is that how you run a government? It's all got to do with politics and getting on that tube (TV). Getting on that tube. If they didn't have the TV we might get more things done.

We have a newspaper called the *Arizona Republic*. My son-in-law works there. He married my daughter and my daughter was a pretty good reporter. He's the head of the editorial board. I get blasted every day by the editorial board! Think of that, right? Hey, I'm 81. I'm going to be the poster boy. I'd run it again. You see, the day I got elected last year, they tried to recall me. It didn't work. I just got elected in November. Try to recall me? I had a bad beginning of the year. A guy sent me a bomb, a real bomb. The feds are trying to catch the guy. It'll take them 20 years. All this in four months, and all this is coming down on me. So, people say, "You're 81 years old, why don't you retire?" I'm not going to retire. You know what? The more they go after me, the longer I am sticking around. They know they can't get me. They're probably praying that I break my head next time. So, I'm running again, as I said the day I got elected last year. I've got my campaign for 2016. I've already raised $3,000,000 in eight months as the sheriff. I raised $8,500,000 for my last campaign. How many sheriffs can do that?

Evidently, somebody likes me. I'm going to protect those people out there, and I'm not going to surrender, and I'll be 84 years old in the next campaign. I have four more years! I'll decide what I'm going to do when I'm eighty-nine. I'll be all right. I'll get a wheelchair, like *Ironside* (a late 1960s/early 1970s television show). I'll put a machine gun on it, and I'll keep going. I'm a fighter. And you know what? All those people who don't like me, and there are quite a few, ganged up on me last election, they thought they had me, but they didn't get me. I still won by 7%, which is a little lower than normal, but boy, they zero in on me every day. I still survive. And so, they think I won't be around three years? I'll be around.

Conclusion

Sheriff Joe Arpaio has been in law enforcement for over half a century. Along with his many years of experience, he has developed his own individualistic style of management and leadership. It would appear that as much as his voting public approves of his style of leadership, there are many opponents to his approach. Irrespective of how different people hold him in regard, it is difficult to argue with his success in protecting the citizens of Maricopa County, Arizona. He is a firm believer in giving the taxpaying public the best return for the money, as he claims the use of "Tent City" has saved taxpayers considerable amount of money. The field of policing has changed over the years, but Sheriff Arpaio utilizes his own style when it comes to his environment, such as not using a computer (he has a typewriter). He considers college education unnecessary for effective policing and utilizes his own brand of community policing, which is to "lock up criminals" to protect the people of Maricopa County. His ongoing "battle" with the federal government is well publicized; it is something that he holds as a badge of honor. Sheriff Arpaio will continue enforcing the law to protect the people of Maricopa County, as his age does not seem to be a barrier, but more as a source of strength. Currently, he is exploring the possibility of running for the Governor of Arizona in the next election.

Glossary

Monitors: The U.S. District Judge G. Murray Snow ruled (October 2013) for an independent monitor (person or team of people) to be placed in the Office of the Sheriff (Maricopa County, AZ) to certify the department is not racial profiling. Judge Snow's ruling found:

> unless the officer has reasonable suspicion that a person is in the country unlawfully and probable cause to believe that the individual has committed or is committing a crime, the MCSO shall prohibit officers from (a) questioning any individual as to his/her alienage or immigration status; (b) investigating an individual's identity or searching the individual in order to develop evidence of unlawful status; or (c) detaining an individual while contacting ICE/CBP with an inquiry about immigration states or awaiting a response from ICE/CBP (*Melendres et al. v. Arpaio et al.*, 2013, p. 17).

Racial Profiling: Referred to as racially biased policing or biased policing, Ramirez et al. (2000), describe racial profiling as "any police-initiated action that relies on the race, ethnicity, or national origin rather than the behavior of an individual or information that leads the police to a particular individual who has been identified as being, or having been, engaged in criminal activity" (p. 3).

Tent City: Sheriff Joe created the "Tent City Jail" in 1993, as an extension of the Maricopa County, AZ jail. The capacity of Tent City Jail is 2,126 inmates.

Volunteer Posse: Posse members are volunteers over the age of 18, who are enlisted to assist, cooperate, and support the Sheriff's personnel in enforcing laws and promoting safety among community members. Thousands of posse members are currently active in different types of posse units—including but not limited to street crime prevention; divers; cold cases; medical rescues; school safety prevention; youth education; emergency support; cybercrime; rangers, and communications. Posse members must be U.S. citizens and should hold a valid Arizona driver's license.

References

Burch, A. 2012. *Sheriff's Offices, 2007 – Statistical Tables.* Bureau of Justice Statistics.

LaFrance, T. 2012. The county sheriff's leadership and management decisions in the local budget process revisited. *International Journal of Police Science & Management,* 14(2), 154–165.

LaFrance, T. and Placide, M. 2010. Sheriffs' and police chiefs' leadership and management decisions in the local law enforcement budgetary process: An exploration. *International Journal of Police Science & Management,* 12(2), 238–255.

Melendres et al. v. Arpaio et al., 2013. In the United States District Court for the District of Arizona. Case 2:07-cv-02513-GMS, Document 606. Filed 10/02/13.

Ramirez, D., McDevitt, J. and Farrell. 2000. *A Resource Guide on Racial Profiling Data Collection Systems: Promising Practices and Lessons Learned.* Washington, DC: U.S. Department of Justice. Retrieved January 23, 2014, https://www.ncjrs.gov/pdffiles1/bja/184768.pdf.

Per Svartz, Chief Constable, Blekinge, Sweden

10

INTERVIEWED BY DAVID BAKER

Contents

Introduction

Sweden comprises approximately 9.625 million people who are policed by 23,000 officers, of whom about one-third are women. In addition, there is also an auxiliary staff of approximately of 8,500 civilians. The Swedish Police Service, one of the country's largest organizations, is a national police system that is accountable to the Ministry of Justice. The Swedish National Police Board is the central administrative, coordinating, and supervisory authority of the police service, its resources, and employees. The government-appointed National Police Commissioner heads the Board and is responsible for operations.

In 1965, the police service adopted a national character and partial centralization to form a more uniform and effective police organization. The 1980s saw police reform that lessened control and increased local self-determination. In the 1990s, the number of police authorities was reduced from 117 to the current 21, in accord with the number of counties. Each county has a corresponding police authority which is headed by a County Police Commissioner, although there is currently considerable debate about reducing the number of police authorities. Each police authority, which has the autonomy to determine organizational structure, police districts, and police deployment across its geographical jurisdiction, is responsible for daily police operations. These police authorities conduct police work at the local level, including crime investigations, crime prevention, and responding to emergency calls as well as issuing passports and various permits and licenses. The Stockholm Police Authority is the largest with approximately 6,000 officers.

The Swedish Police mission statement advocates the reduction of crime, increased public safety, and crime prevention procedures. Operational crime prevention is based on police visibility, availability to the public, and efficient delivery conducted on a local basis. Community policing is a feature of Swedish Police, and during the 1990s, a Community Police Service was established to foster work in a specific geographic area. Problem-oriented policing strategies have concentrated on the causes of crime and public order disturbances.

A unique feature of the Swedish Police is the deployment of Dialogue Police, who create opportunities for negotiated arrangements with protesters, set parameters for crowd behavior, seek to avoid police–protester confrontation, and facilitate protest. The Swedish dialogue model was developed in response to the violent Gothenburg protests during the European Union Summit of June 2001 when police lost control of the streets. Such loss of authority threatened Swedish Police legitimacy and acted as a catalyst for public order reform. The final report of the investigative Gothenburg Committee highlighted the importance of dialogue (Baker, 2014: 98). The dialogue police are specially trained officers, who wear yellow vests amidst crowds but are linked and teamed with trained commanders, mobile units, plainclothes arrest officers, and transport units. Dialogue police, who initiate communication with protesters, use knowledge of protesters in order to reduce the risk of misunderstandings, avoid surprises, foster tolerance of minor disruptions, and avoid unnecessary provocation—a pivotal peacekeeping tactic. Besides involvement in pre-event discussions, these dialogue teams mingle "within" protest crowds whenever police anticipate that a demonstration might potentially turn aggressive, disruptive, and violent. The Swedish model places certain well-trained police amidst the demonstrating crowd, rather than at a distance anonymously locked and hidden inside vehicles or control rooms. Dialogue police have been an effective communications strategy at various public order policing events such as marches, festivals, local protests, group disturbances, political protests. and football conflict (Baker, 2014: 98–99).

The Swedish National Police Academy is responsible for the basic training of police officers and the national advanced training of both police officers and civilian staff. Police training currently takes place at three locations in Sweden: at the Swedish National Police Academy in Sörentorp and as vocational training at the universities of Umeå and Växjö. Police training is also available as a long-distance course. Police use of lethal force training instructs an officer aiming a gun to temporarily injure a person (this is different from many countries, such as Australia, where police aim for the greatest body mass if they use a firearm).

The Security Service's mandate is to prevent and detect offences against Swedish national security, fight terrorism, and protect the central Government. It encompasses counterespionage, counterterrorism, protection of the Swedish constitution, protective security, and dignitary protection. The National Security Service conducts police operations with regard to combatting terrorism.

International police cooperation has an increasing impact on Swedish police work. Swedish police cooperate in operational international policing together with foreign police organizations. This work takes place within the framework of criminal investigations, directly or through Europol, Schengen cooperation, Interpol, or the Nordic police cooperation. The police are also involved in international strategic police cooperation with various working groups and institutions primarily within the EU to jointly combat organized cross-border crime and drug trafficking. They participate in international development cooperation and support foreign police organizations in their efforts to become more democratic and effective. Swedish police officers participate in peace- and security-promoting operations as well as conflict-preventing activities.

Swartz has had a distinguished career as a police officer since joining the Swedish Police service in 1972 until his retirement in 2013. He entered the profession for the anticipated "excitement." His extensive education began with the Gymnasium Exam in 1966 and the completion of a Master of Laws from Lund University in 1972. As a serving police officer, he undertook Police Chiefs' Education (1973–75, 1978) and the Higher Management course (2004). During his lengthy career, Per studied various internal education courses, including international studies in management and leadership while in England and Germany.

With more than forty years of service in the Swedish Police, Per's service record covers both considerable operational and leadership experience. He worked in eight different police districts, most of them in the southern part of Sweden, before he was promoted to command level duties. From 1994 to 2004, Per was the Area Commander for Malmo, Sweden's third most populated city of over 500,000 people. He then became the Tactical Leader for the county of Skane from 2004 to 2008. His final appointment from 2008 to 2012 was as the Chief Constable of Blekinge.

Chief Constable Svartz is noted for the specialist use of citizen surveys in the management of police personnel and the public. His management philosophy has been to maintain a balance between the needs of government, the needs of the local public and the police staff and the economic imperatives. His objective has been that the police service needs to respond to the demands of a changing and developing society.

During his lengthy police service, Per has examined and reformed management issues within the police service at the local, regional, and national level. He describes his own management style as that of a listener and a delegator. In the past 15 years, he has been occupied not only with the reorganization of police areas but also with the introduction of new methods in the field of riot policing, community policing, and intelligence-led policing. In 2007, he was responsible as a coauthor for the introduction for the Swedish Police of the national book (digital) on intelligence-led policing. Also, he has been active in development projects in Montenegro, Croatia, Albania, and Slovenia.

Further community service includes working on the board of the Swedish Police Sports Organization, the last 4 years as the chairman of that organization, and during the past 2 years, he has been the chairman for the five Nordic countries.

Per is not only positive and enthusiastic about policing achievements but also realistic about some of the problems faced in his country. He is proud of the reforms that he has introduced, especially those during his 10 years as Area Commander at Malmo. Although he does not use the term, he has adopted a "holistic approach" to crime prevention: police, educators, social workers, politicians, and local officials, all have a part to play in making safer communities.

A preliminary interview was conducted with Chief Constable Svartz at the conclusion of the Stockholm Criminology Conference, June 12, 2012. A lengthy, recorded telephone interview was conducted on the February 20, 2013 with him in Malmo. This interview was conducted in English and it was digitally recorded and transcribed in full. The interviewer has attempted to keep the original flavor of the interview despite a few language difficulties. Parts in brackets are supplied by the interviewer for purposes of clarity. Much of the interview focuses on Per's diverse and lengthy career as a leader and manager in the Swedish Police.

Career

DB: Tell me about your time as the Area Commander of Malmo Police from 1994 to 2004. What were some of the major issues that you faced at that time?

PS: During that time, we started to have "biker" problems and at first I don't think we realized how deep that would become. They had been in Denmark for a long time and the Danish police had warned us, saying, "Watch out; this is going to cause some trouble." And it did!

Malmo is a town of immigration. The reason for that is it is in the southern part of Sweden, and people who come from the Balkans and from the southern part of Europe don't want to go any further north. They want to stay as long as they can in the south of Sweden. That meant that refugees fleeing the Balkan War arrived in Malmo—quite a lot of them. Many of them are not very well educated and so we have social problems.

Then there are public order problems such as narcotics. These have been brought into the Malmo area by car since the opening of the Oresund Bridge in 2000—a journey of twenty minutes from Copenhagen. We also face problems associated with young people drinking openly in the streets; violence at football matches and demonstrations. In other words, in Malmo, we have of course, the full range of criminal behaviors that afflicts a modern city.

DB: How did your career develop after Malmo?

PS: In 2004, I moved to Skane as a Tactical Leader. I was recruited to what was called a Tactical Leader position which is a kind of Deputy to the Commissioner and that means that you're responsible for development and checking up on what's really going on in that field. I also became the Chairman of the Operational Group. So that's what I did for four years. Finally, I finished my career as Chief Constable in Blekinge (2008–2012), which is a quite small county if you compare it to Skane. You could say I went back to basics again because of the way Blekinge is organized.

Changes Experienced

DB: What changes and developments have you seen over the years?

PS: When I started with the police in the seventies, we actually had bad relations with the social workers, because they didn't want to work with us at all. Not at all! At the time politics was very much more left wing—and I remember I met a lot of people at the university reading social sciences—and there was a lack of cooperation. In some parts of the country, some parts of the cities, that's still a problem. But on the other hand, you could say that the climate has changed dramatically.

As the Police Chief, I met the Headmaster of the school system and the Chief of the social welfare system. We met every third month and discussed different problems. About three years ago now, police started a new version of this program and it's very much more specific because it is about young people going into crime and how to deal with that immediately. And you should do that together with the school and the social workers by talking with them.

That, we couldn't do in any official way before. Police don't know what social workers know and the social workers don't know what the police know. And though the school and the teachers can see something is wrong, they don't know what to do. You should actually work all together and you should do it in a very specific way saying, "This guy, he has this and this problem—he has problems at home, problems on the street, he has problems in the school; so let's help them and let's have a program that we can all be together in." Previously, we were very afraid of that kind of cooperation because it didn't look very nice if you involved the police with a fifteen year old. But this project is still working in small towns; it is making a tremendous difference. It's very good. In the big cities, they are overwhelmed with work, so I don't think it's working out that well. But in the small cities—and Karlskrona was one of them—you could see fantastic results. Fantastic results actually!

DB: Have the nature and functions of police work changed over the years?
PS: Some of the policing doesn't change and some of the things that change within the police are changing very slowly. But there are, of course, reasons for that because, to put it very, very simply, we do three things. We come when people call on us. We come with our patrol cars or however we come. Then we investigate crimes at the CID. Finally, we do problem orienting policing or something like that. If you keep it very simple, it's only these three parts. And you must have resources, but they are limited of course.

Politicians all the time are going to be upset if you don't do something about a new problem, for example, about the problem of pedophiles. Then you discover that pedophiles are all over the world and suddenly you have a hundred police officers who are sitting and looking at pedophile pictures. Then you discover you could occupy another hundred if you wanted. Yet, you still have to come when people call on you and you still have to investigate other crimes.

With the Internet also comes the problem of "threatening behavior." So we have another big political discussion now about that on the net and Facebook and everywhere. You could occupy a police force with this, hundreds of police, if you are going to do full investigations every time. You still have to come when people call on you and you still have to investigate other crimes.

I also talk about the intelligence-led policing of serial crimes, for instance, when it comes to elderly people who are being robbed or abused or something like that. We are better now at dealing with these problems than we were twenty years ago—I think so. And so it goes on and on and on. You always come back to these basic things that you must come when people call on you and you must investigate when somebody is hitting another person or robbing him or doing burglaries and so forth. Crime is not decreasing, so it's a dilemma, that is what police are for and improvement has occurred.

The main thing is that you must come when people call and you must investigate at least the most severe crimes where you have suspects. But if you don't do that, then you will lose the public's confidence. Also, you must take new challenges and put them into your system so that you can do something about them. That's the reason why I took the example of "threatening" on the Internet—it's an enormous business. Police can't do that—you can't just say that you should investigate every crime here because you can't do that. So it has to be a balance. That's my philosophy. It's always a balance.

DB: What is the situation with clearance rates in Sweden?

PS: Clearance rates are steady on a low level and that is a problem because it has become a political topic. The clearance rate is very difficult to discuss because, I think, if you doubled the police, it would not double the clearance rate anyway. Sometimes our politicians compare the clearance rate with other countries. You can't do that because we don't have the same system of estimating the clearance rate and we don't put in the same crimes and not at the same time. So you can't compare and therefore it is impossible to have a meaningful discussion. From the public's viewpoint, every crime should be investigated, but as a police officer, you know that isn't the case and never has been.

DB: What changes have you experienced regarding domestic violence?

PS: When it comes to domestic violence, we made great progress through the years from 1998 onwards. I think this is a part of the development that has occurred in all the Western world. In Malmo, we discovered that there were no shelters for beaten women. All that was available was voluntary, and the community didn't accept that. We lacked the shelters very much. I went to the community, telling them about the problems and, at the same time, there was a very big political interest over this subject. Together with some reformists and politicians in Malmo, we started a project of cooperation between the hospitals, the police, and the social workers. Reform about the shelters is still ongoing and it was actually a big change in policing direction and policies. Today, Malmo, at least from an organizational viewpoint, is one of the leaders in Sweden. I don't say everything is perfect because it's not, but we have a working plan together with the hospitals and we have social workers, we have shelters, and we have institutions for children who are beaten or abused. We also have institutions for men who beat their wives, and we have a common education and understanding of such subjects. Twenty years ago, when you came upon a domestic violence case, it ended with mediation. So a police officer sat down with the woman and sat down with the man, and it ended with mediation. Today, that same case could be an arrest and full investigation, and we have the support from the rest of the community to do that.

DB: Has policing become more difficult over the years?

PS: On the street, some of the differences today are that young people don't respect the police as much as they did say twenty or thirty years ago. They are raised to ask questions all the time and it's not for a police officer to tell them to do something if they don't want to do it. In general, there isn't that respect any more. Authorities are not that important any more.

On the other hand, police officers are more skilled when they start today. They have a longer education and they are better off in many ways. Yet, you have more traffic, you have more crime on the Internet, you have these Facebook problems. You have suspects today who initially deny committing a crime. If you have a suspect that you take into investigation, the first thing he will say is: "I didn't have anything to do with that." And then you have to prove and prove and prove that he did it. Twenty-five or thirty years ago he would say, "OK, I was there. I did this or I did that. And by the way, I did another thing as well." You don't have that any more. Investigation obviously is more difficult today because people deny everything—until charges are proved.

Personal Policing Philosophy

DB: How would you describe your personal leadership or management style?

PS: I've always been the listening type and that has helped me a lot in management. I'm not a big doer but I've learned to be a better one. So I have always gathered around me people who have plenty of drive and many police officers do. I want to think long before I decide and I want to be sure that you don't get into major conflicts every time you change things. When you change things, you always have a lack of energy in the organization, so you should deal with that. Many managers just do it and say, "From this date on we are going to do it this way, so we start now," and they create conflicts. I think I would do it a little bit in the opposite way. We talk about it for quite a long time and then we do it. And then we can go back and say, "We have discussed this now for half a year. The discussion is over, so let's do it." I think that I'm more that type.

DB: What is your view of the relationship between police and politics?

PS: We are a democratic police and that means you must listen very well to what people want from us. And you must have a dialogue on every level. At the moment (February 2013), there is a very tense but intensive dialogue between the National Commissioner and the Government and the Ministry of Justice and that goes all the way down to the local level.

My experience is that there are not enough politicians in this country who know the police questions very well. There are a few. Sweden's Minister for Justice, Beatrice Ask, does, because now she has been there for at least six years and she gets all the information. There are only a few, who know enough about policing. That's my opinion. And that means that you have a rather difficult discussion with politicians when it comes to what can we do and what we cannot do and what does it mean when you say: "you must be better on this and better on that because, what is 'good policing'?" How do you know what is good policing? And if you start to ask that question of politicians, I am very sure that they will not be able to answer—not in a proper way. And that's a pity, and that's a lack in the system. So Sweden could benefit from more interested and skilled politicians at the national level who understand policing. On the other hand, on the local level, I have had a lot of very good cooperation with politicians. But these days, the local police boards don't have a lot of power; so it's mainly sharing information and discussion.

Problems and Successes Experienced

DB: What would you perceive as the major achievements or highlights of your policing career?

PS: As others have said before you work all the time and you don't reflect so much and sometimes when you've had a good operation, you think this was very nice and then you go further the next day, so it goes on all the time. When it comes to some highlights that would be things that I have had a part in developing. For example, in 1994, when I started as the Area Commander of Malmo, we introduced community policing—we did it from the ground upwards. We studied how we should do this and whether we should re-organize community policing both geographically and in terms of attitudes. We did that by the book and it went very very well. The organization and everybody were quite happy. But I think it only lasted for two years because then we had severe financial cutbacks within the police and we didn't have it any more!

DB: So the community policing reforms were impeded by financial cutbacks?

PS: Yes, and I learned a lot of politics during that time. In every decision you make within an organization and with resources, there's politics. If we are having severe cutbacks here or in the next year or the year after, what would happen? You have that in your head all the time. So it was a good experience, but it wasn't fun. And, actually, that period of cutbacks lasted ten years—almost all these ten years, I think that I was Commander in Malmo. It started very well, but I became "the Chief that was cutting down all the time" (an ironic laugh). We worked a lot on reforms. You must do that even if you have cutbacks.

DB: What other major reforms were undertaken?

PS: One of the highlights during that Malmo period was that when we started reforming, we started with public order policing at demonstrations. I don't know if you remember that in 2001 we had severe demonstrations during a visit of President Bush in Gothenburg.* Yes, and it didn't go well because the Swedish Police were not prepared for such a big event. I think it was 35,000 demonstrators and we usually have a couple of thousand, and it really went very badly. I had a lot of officers from Malmo up there serving and I went there for the first day of the demonstration. You could see this wasn't all right and this wasn't very well organized. The truth is that we didn't have the competence. What happened was that because they "tore the town down" so to speak, there was a national investigation at the political level. Two years later, a book came out of that inquiry and a report. Based on that report, we started to reform, and I was a part of that reform team. We had to change the way we policed demonstrations in Malmo and in the south. I was also a part of the national team reforming public order policing. That was very exciting, but it was hard work. I think we managed very well. We went to Denmark, Holland, and England and looked at what they did there. I think today we are much, much better, but it took over ten years. The problem is that you don't have in any town—Stockholm, Gothenburg, and Malmo or in any town in Sweden—the resources to handle a big event, with a large number of demonstrators. So you have to have police from all over the country participating. It's not a problem to transport them there, but you have to have the same strategies; you have to work in the same way. Otherwise, you will not manage it. So that was the problem but, I think, we did it quite well.

Today we have departments of police officers who go to Stockholm or Gothenburg or any other part of the country and do service at these locations.

---

* During the antiglobalization protests in Gothenburg against the European Union Summit of June 2001, violent clashes between police and protesters occurred in the city's main street, and parts of the CBD were ransacked and stores looted. Police who shot three protesters in Gothenburg were under investigation but argued that the shootings took place amid life-threatening circumstances.

It works fairly well, I would say, fairly well. And we also use them at football matches when there are big ones. The dialogue police work fairly well.*

Another highlight that I was involved in was the intelligence-led policing model which comes from the county of Kent in England. I saw that your Commissioner (Mal Hyde, South Australia) had a lot of cooperation with Kent. I've been there several times as well and I think they are one of these constabularies in England that are very keen on cooperation with others and they are very forward thinking. So we went there to study their model and then we went home and made the Swedish version of it (2004–2005). And that was also on a national level and I was the project leader. We wrote a book, which is the national model for management operational policing. That was very interesting because we did that book as a project over a year. You have to use the specialists from all parts and put it all together.

DB: What is your view of the police union's role in Sweden?
PS: The police union in Sweden is a very strong one. When I started in the seventies and the eighties, they were very dominating in debate and strong when it came to negotiating about salaries and things like that. I don't think they are that strong today, but they still are a very important part of the Swedish police when it comes to development and actually when it comes to everything.

We have in every local police authority at every level different working groups. We negotiate about salaries and so forth. When it comes to salary, no one is ever satisfied, but when it comes to environmental things, I think it's worked quite well actually. As managers, we are listening and people get what they want if it's needed. We have good cars and I think at one time we had the best police cars in the world. But I don't think some police unionists are changing fast enough; they are quite conservative. When it comes to education, I don't think they agree that we need more academics within the

---

* The Swedish dialogue police model was developed in response to the violent 2001 Gothenburg protests when police lost control of the streets. Police officers in Sweden employ dialogue not only for preparatory negotiations but also deploy specific liaison teams, part of a broader public order unit, to enhance knowledge of protesters and their intentions. Dialogue police facilitate peaceful protest, identify potential risks to public order, and seek to avoid police–protester confrontation. The Swedish model places well-trained police wearing yellow vests amidst the demonstrating crowd. Malmo Police Dialogue officer, Gorgin Shoai (recorded interview, August 14, 2011), conducts "many" pre-event meetings with "the local fans" of soccer and ice hockey matches. He warns fans that unruly behavior means "they will not see the match" and their club will be fined. He gathers "a lot of information to pass on to his Chief" that assists in determining the number of police needed to control the upcoming event and in preparing strategy. Shoai mingles with the crowd: "I know the fans of the local soccer team. I talk to the fans." As he is recognisable to the fans, they are prepared to talk to him, "but they would not talk to other officers." When the team is playing away, he advises fans not to cause any trouble and ensures that they return to Malmo by bus. There is no official debriefing with fans after match, but, as the dialogue officer, he is prepared to explain police actions that occurred during the previous event.

police. They want all the career things, but they only really value the times when they went patrolling when they were twenty-two. So that's where you have a problem. That doesn't go for everyone who is in the union but as an official stance or opinion, I think they are too conservative.

Theory and Practice

DB: How important is the relationship between police management and academics in terms of reforms?

PS: During the last five or six years, we successfully employed academic people directly into the investigation on the local level to deal with everyday crime—could be thefts, could be assaults, could be anything. To do that you have to study law and you have to be good at writing and be good at talking to people, but you don't necessarily have to be 20 years out on the street—it's not necessary.

In Karlskrona, which is a place with a small population,* we had six or seven academics and they were very clever and they were working all the time from the morning until four or five in the afternoon. They were achieving very good results because a lot of investigations are not very complicated. You write down a story and you talk to people and you write down your story. If you need an arrest, then a police officer can do that. If you need some more thorough investigations, you can have help with that. But with most of the small thefts and when people hit each other over the head at a restaurant, you can deal with most of that without having been a police officer for twenty years. This is a tense issue with the union.

DB: You have been closely involved in citizen's surveys that were designed by academics. Can you tell us about this strategy?

PS: As a police manager for many years, I learned and cooperated with Senior Police Executive, Mr Kjell Elefalk, and we together explored the field of citizen's surveys.† We've had citizen's surveys since 1998.

---

* The capital of Blekinge is Karlskrona, population approximately 33,000. It is the smallest of the administrative counties of Sweden, covering only 0.7% of the total area.
† Police in Karlskrona have utilized "Citizen Satisfaction Surveys" as a guide to local policing and its problem-oriented police operations on the streets. These surveys, based on collective rather than individual responses, feature local concerns and the customers' perspective of police actions. The citizen surveys have formed the baseline for police action in curbing alcohol-fuelled violence. As a result of the customer surveys, police in Karlskrona have identified and monitored "hot spots"; established voluntary night patrols; assisted environmental improvements such as security walks; used powers in relation to alcoholism and drunkenness as crime prevention tools to detain drunken people for 8 hours; and collaborated with multiple stakeholders, including restaurateurs and doormen at hotels and clubs.

They are deeply involved with operational matters when it comes to policing. We made a balance score-card for police and the balance is between your goals—how they will be expected to be carried out from the Government or from your own working plans, and from the law, legislation. You also need the resources—that's the second part of it. Then what we talked about with the union is staff management and staff policies. The fourth and maybe most important sector is the citizens—service to the citizens. It's a balance between those four. If you put it very simply, and I talk as an experienced manager all the time to my own chiefs or managers, I talk about these four features—you can't only communicate with one of them or two of them. You have to balance the four of them, all the time, every day. And that's a challenge.

Since 1998, wherever I have been a police chief, I have used the citizen survey. It was designed by two professors (one at Cambridge, the other at Malmo). It has had international recognition because the questions explore what is central to policing and the relationship between police and the public. The citizen survey is a questionnaire that you put to people in a certain area or at least every question is about problems in their area—not problems in common or across this country but it is problems in their area. If you do that, you will get a very good picture of what are the local problems.

You can see the difference between areas and you can see the dark figures of crime that you don't have in your police statistics because there are a lot of crimes that are not reported. And then you can specify your police work against those problems that you can elicit from the questionnaires. We did it once a year and I think you could do it twice a year. At the same time, it will provide an evaluation as to whether your problem oriented police work really works. This has been very exciting, but there has been trouble with it because the national police didn't acknowledge its benefits. The surveys are being reinstated as they are spreading throughout important parts of the country. I am proud of being a part of the development of the citizen survey. I know that it works and that it works very well if you can engage your police officers to believe in it too.

DB: Has academic theory and research had much impact on policing and its management?

PS: There are exceptions, but in general, I don't think many managers have been interested in this kind of policy. We don't evaluate our own work very well and we don't do it in an academic way. Unfortunately, we don't implement policies after studying a thing very thoroughly, not on a regular basis. And that is a lack in Swedish policing. Some managers are interested and go to seminars like the Stockholm Criminology Conference but not a lot of police officers. As I wrote in my book on intelligence led policing, you must have knowledge if you want to manage. Without knowledge, you cannot do problem orienting policing in the right way. You must be familiar with all relevant discussion. And not a lot of officers are. And there is not enough of that at the Police Academy. Once you start on the job, you become more interested in how to drive a patrol car—and that's what everybody wants to do, go after villains and so forth—but they are not very interested in problem-oriented policing. Later on, they will be. This does not mean that we don't have learning. Of course, we do, but it's not enough. Every time that we discuss police education and what should we do at the academies, it doesn't work. Our Commissioner in Skane gave the Government a big report on police education four years ago and it hasn't happened yet. The Government has difficulties in discussing it.

Transnational Relations

DB: Has policing cooperation across borders increased in recent years?
PS: I would say yes. It's coming along quite slowly. And when it comes to the other Nordic countries—Denmark, Norway, and Finland—we have daily cooperation when it comes to severe crimes.

At Blekinge, for instance, the smaller crimes became quite serious. People were coming from Romania up to Sweden—robbing elderly people along the way. They do one crime in one town and then they go to the next and to the next and to the next. And every crime is not a very big one, so they are not much noticed actually. It's one crime amongst many others. We have investigated these things; in a week, they could be all over Sweden and they could be doing these sorts of crimes, getting them between five thousand and fifty thousand Kronors a day (US$760–7,600), which is a lot.

This is a very big problem and we don't have the organization for it. We have Europol, of course, but up to three or four years ago, they were not very interested in this type of crime. They are interested in the big crimes and the big villains who operate over the borders. So we started a project together with the Polish and the Lithuanians to have immediate contact over the sea because from Karlskrona, we have boats going to Poland and we have boats going to Lithuania. We started on a daily basis and that goes on now as well, so we go there and they come to us. They send their cooperation officers to us for a week and we send our investigators and so forth for a week. This program proceeds quite slowly and unobtrusively, but it goes on all the time. It's speeding up the information and that's what's important when people travel around committing crimes. Cooperation is on the local level now and over the borders as well.

Democratic Policing

DB: Would you describe the Swedish Police as democratic?

PS: The Swedish Police force look upon themselves as a democratic police in that they are there for the people. They are not there in the first place for the Government, although the system is such that the Government tells you what to do by creating new laws and creating the grounds for your existence and provides the resources. But the police force is for the people to make their life a better one. And I think that is reflected across most of the police work in Sweden.

If you look at the international comparisons when it comes to trusting the police, Sweden, Denmark, and Norway are always at the top. You can fairly say that we are a democratic police. In investigative reports and surveys as well, we have rather high figures for service and the way that we speak to people and our willingness to help. The disappointments are more about, "I didn't get any result from my report of theft or I was hit or I was raped." If you have very high expectations of a police service and you don't get what you expected, then you will be disappointed.

Looking Ahead

DB: What organizational changes do you see happening within the Swedish Police?

PS: In two years' time, we will go from 21 to one authority for the whole country. That will change both the chain of command and the world of the managers or the chief constables. I'm not sure that policing, everyday policing, will change that fast.

DB: And what do you see as the future of policing in Sweden?

PS: I think that the organization will be better. Computer systems will be better; yes, things are going to be better for that. We have to adopt more of a problem-orienting policing. We must have more task forces within the CID or the public order section or police as a whole so that we can deal with the problems that are coming. And look what is happening when it comes to the Internet. Just a month ago, we had a small riot among young people in Gothenburg because of what one girl said on Facebook. And that kind of problem will increase because things are going faster and faster and we are not really prepared for that.

Sweden is one of the most "Internetting" countries in the world. What happens when the rest of the world comes up to that level? Today, we have fraud letters from Africa—they send them all over the world. But imagine when a million of them are doing the same, or when China, does the same. What will happen then?

That will reflect on a small country like Sweden as well. To deal with that kind of trouble, you must have a more flexible organization, but still you must come when people call and still you must investigate when they are burgled and so forth. I expect that those aspects of policing will be better with problem-orienting policing, whether it is dealing with new types of crimes or things that happen in the streets.

Conclusion

Chief Constable Per Svartz's policing career has spanned four decades of both continuity and change in Sweden. His insights in this interview reveal a man proud of his achievements as one who has led and managed progressive strategies and who is conscious of the challenging nature of modern day policing. He acknowledges not only the need for traditional, fundamental police services but also the need to adapt to rapidly changing circumstances and emerging forms of crime. His comments include a frank account of some limitations that have slowed police advances in Sweden.

References

Baker, D. 2014. Police and Protester Dialog: Safeguarding the peace or ritualistic sham? *International Journal of Comparative and Applied Criminal Justice*, 38(1), 83–104.

The Swedish Police Service's official website: https://polisen.se/en/Languages/The-Swedish-Police/.

Fábio Manhães Xavier, Colonel of the Military Police de Minas Gerais, Brazil

11

INTERVIEWED BY
LUDMILA MENDONÇA LOPES RIBEIRO
ROSÂNIA RODRIGUES DE SOUSA
ALEXANDRE MAGNO ALVES DINIZ

Contents

The Brazilian Police Forces

In Brazil, the institutional arrangement for Public Security is described in Art. 144 of the Federal Constitution of 1988, which defines the competence of Police Forces in maintaining public order and the safety of persons and assets. There are distinct assignments, according to the level of the institution (federal, state, or municipal), and to the nature of the issue to be managed, with some of them having a restricted competence—given the fact that, in Brazil, a complete cycle is an exception rather than the rule. Each agency accounts for a part of the crime prevention and repression work. The Federal Police is institutionalized at federal level. Its aim is to investigate criminal offenses against the political and social order or damages to assets, services, and/or interests of the Union or its autonomous agencies and public companies, as well as other violations having interstate or international repercussions and requiring uniform repression, as provided under the Law. Its functions further include prevention and repression of illicit trafficking of narcotics and similar drugs, smuggling, and embezzlement, without prejudice to related actions by the Treasury and other authorities in their respective areas of competence; performance of maritime, airport, and border police functions; and, further, to perform, exclusively, duties as the Union's judiciary police. The Federal Highway Police is also institutionalized at federal level. It is dedicated to the ostensive patrolling of highways. Similarly, the Federal Railway Police is institutionalized at federal level. It is dedicated to the ostensive patrolling of railways. The Civil Police is institutionalized at state level. It performs judiciary police duties and investigate criminal offenses, except for federal crimes and those committed by military police officers. The Military Police is an auxiliary force to the Army. It is institutionalized in all federative states, having competences for ostensive policing and maintaining public order. Finally, there are the Municipal Guards. Municipalities are free to decide whether to have them or not, as they are not compulsory institutions. Their main role is to protect locally existing assets, services, and facilities.

In addition to the agencies described in the constitution, since 2004 there is also the National Force, an institution created without constitutional support under the Ministry of Justice's National Secretariat of Public Security (SENASP) with the aim to

> [...] meet emergency needs of the states with regard to issues requiring a wider interference of the public authority, or when an urgent need for reinforcement in security is detected. The National Force is formed by the best police officers and firefighters of elite groups from the federative states, who undergo a rigorous training at the National Police Academy (of the Federal Police) in Brasilia, which includes a range of topics from crisis management to human rights. Modeled after the UN Peace Corps, the Force is coordinated by the National Secretariat of Public Security (Senasp), of the Ministry of Justice. After the training or engagement in action, National Force police officers are reintegrated back to their respective functions in their original states, where they further pass on the newly-acquired knowledge to the other members of their corporations.

To realize how complex the arrangement of police institutions in Brazil actually is, it suffices to look at related figures: 1 National Force, 3 Federal Police organizations, 27 Military Police organizations, 27 Civil Police organizations and 993 Municipal Guard units, all having complementary or competing competences. Given the fact that Brazil is a federation of states, there is no hierarchy between these distinct institutions, with the engagement in action by each one being determined by the nature of the Public Security issue in question.

So as to reduce the problems arising from the complex coordination of these distinct police organizations, each federate unit relies on its own

Secretariat for coordinating actions to be carried out by them, even as they report directly to the head of the Executive Power in their respective level (federal, state, or municipal), the idea being that arrangements of such nature will enable the development of integrated actions—to be initiated by one institution and completed by another. At federal level, the SENASP coordinates the national policy for Public Security, while further managing the national fund for Public Security and the National System of Information on Public Security, Drugs, and Prisons (SINESP). In the states, the State Secretariats of Social Defense (SEDS) formulate the macropolicies for the area, to be implemented by Military and Civil Police forces, within the limits of their constitutional assignments. As the Municipal Guards multiply all over the national territory, city administrations have set up Municipal Secretariats of Urban and Asset Security (SMSEG), with the same purpose.

With a view to guiding police actions from a national perspective, the Federal Government, through the SENASP of the Ministry of Justice, has in recent years been conditioning the transfer of funds to states and municipalities to the implementation of certain projects—community police formation programs, in particular. This alignment of federate entities along Public Security policy lines was initiated with the first National Plan for Public Security (2000–2002), given continuity by the second National Plan of Public Security (2003–2006), and consolidated by the National Security and Citizenship Program—PRONASCI (2007–2010), which stressed "prevention and treatment of causes that explain the growth of violence in this society, while not disregarding the enforcement of law and order." (Adorno, 2008, p.16).

Our interviewee in this chapter is a newly retired officer of the Military Police of the State of Minas Gerais (PMMG), one of the most respected police organizations of the entire Brazilian federation (Ribeiro and Oliveira, 2014). During the military regime (1964–1986), by force of Decree Law 317, of March 13, 1967, the Military Police institutions were transformed into auxiliary forces of the Army, taking on a hierarchical and organizational structure similar to that of the Army itself. This situation was not changed as the country returned to democracy, but, rather, it was ratified by the Federal Constitution of 1988, which provides, in its Art. 144 § 6, that the Military Police and Firefighters constitute auxiliary and reserve forces of the Army.

From a practical viewpoint, the fact that the Military Police replicate the organizational and intellectual structure of the Armed Forces gives rise to a series of problems in terms of the provision of policing services under a democratic order. First, there is the problem of double entrance path—one way for the common soldiers, with less demanding requirements as to schooling, and another way for admittance of officers, with more stringent requirements. This means that a soldier will never take a commanding position in the corporation, unless he or she successfully undergoes another selection process. The formation of these police officers is marked by the Army's national defense ideology, which, insofar as it emphasizes the logic of war against crime, has caused the Brazilian Military Police to be ranked among the world's most lethal (Bueno, 2014). Finally, as a result of privileges deriving from the military profession—such as the existence of a specific Penal Code, and of a separate body for investigation and judgment of their crimes—violations committed by military police officers are almost never properly prosecuted and punished, as demonstrated by the few existing studies on the matter (Brinks, 2012).

Cel. Fábio Xavier was interviewed at his own home. As he had retired from the corporation a good deal of time before, the interviewee was rather at ease not only to revisit his own career but also to criticize the limits and possibilities of police reform in Brazil.

Career

LR, RS, AD: What were the main features of your career?
FX: I joined the Military Police of the State of Minas Gerais in 1982, the year that marked the return of democratic elections for state governors in Brazil—which had never happened following the 1964 Military Coup. I entered the force as an officer. My choice of a military career arose from my discontentment with the continuous strikes of Professors at the School of Electrical Engineer of the Federal University of Minas Gerais, the institution I was studying at during that period. In view of the disruption they caused, I looked for an institution with maximum discipline. I found this in the Military Police, which reproduces the hierarchy, discipline, and ranking system of the Army.

In 1986 I took on my first post as a Lieutenant charged with the command of the Special Operations squad, in the former Shock Battalion (riot control battalion). I remained with that unit for four years. As a Captain, I was transferred to the Police Academy in 1990, to perform the functions of course leader and coordinator of judicial activities. Following that, I was allocated to the highest body of the PMMG, where I worked in the Operational Planning and Deployment Section of Brazilian Military Police forces and the Logistics Section of Brazilian Military Police forces. After being promoted to the rank of Major, I returned to the Police Academy, where I took the command of the Corps of Cadets.

In the early 2000s, already as Lieutenant Colonel, I accepted an invitation to join a mission of the International Committee of the Red Cross dedicated to disseminating human rights among police forces in Latin America and the Caribbean. Upon my return to Brazil in 2009, I became a member of the Minas Gerais governor's military cabinet; commanded the 13th Battalion and the 22nd Battalion; and after my promotion to Colonel, I became Director of Education for the entire PMMG.

Then in 2012, I took on the General Coordination of Analysis and Staff Development (CGADP) of the Department of Public Security Research, Information Analysis and Staff Development (DEPAID), a body under Brazil's Ministry of Justice (MJ). After a year in this function, I returned to Minas Gerais to retire from the military police career. I could have stayed on as a member of PMMG until 2016, but decided instead to bring my retirement forward by two years in view of changes in the prevailing political and institutional environment, which pointed to a limited penetration of Human Rights ideas into police practice.

LR, RS, AD: What were the most remarkable events you experienced during your career?

FX: One of them was the episode of the kidnapping of some colleagues— who were Lieutenants like myself at the time (early 1980s)—by a group of prison inmates who escaped the penitentiary taking the hostages with them in an armored car and drove for two days until they were stopped and arrested at (the southeastern Minas Gerais city of) Juiz de Fora. In fact I had been assigned to be part of that group, but couldn't join them in the visit to the penitentiary that day and was replaced by a colleague. Yet, I was in command of the special operations squad deployed to stop and recapture the escapees. It was a very intense situation and in the event one of my colleagues died but the escapees were recaptured.

Another remarkable event was the police strike of 1997 for better wages and less oppressive treatment. I was in charge of coordinating operations of the Loyalist Force (FORLEG). This situation had great impact on me, as I found myself in constant anxiety and facing internal conflict over how to restore legality when legitimacy was rather compromised. I went through a very serious inner conflict, as I sought to perform my activities while, at the same time, believing that the motives for the revolt were legitimate from some points of view. Another outstanding experience was my involvement with the international dissemination of human rights. In Colombia, I was for 35 days in contact with the local guerrillas, which allowed me to rethink some of the concepts and values until then followed by the PM (Military Police); and to change my stance in order to face up to the effect of inadequate police respect for human beings and human rights, and the influence of that on the guerrillas.

LR, RS, AD: How did your experience as a military police officer influence the other dimensions of your life, such as your views on Human Rights?

FX: Of course, when I started my participation in the dissemination of Human Rights, I had this strong sense of isolation. I was rather alone and meeting with no responsiveness from others; what I said had no resonance. But little by little things were gaining consistency. External factors converged in my favor, turning Human Rights into an icon, a banner to be carried forward.

I got involved in this theme area during my graduate studies in human rights and citizenship at the Dom Helder Câmara School of Higher Education. I had around 40 classmates, of whom only two were police officers and all the others were human rights activists, with a rather antagonistic view of the police. I had to think very differently from what I did in the Military Police, and this brought about a great development in my ability to articulate arguments and ideas so as to find a common ground. As the program reached its completion, I was still a rather young fellow with a high rank (Major), and the older Commanders, Colonels, and Chiefs saw my presence as both something new that had arrived but that at times was not desirable. The lectures I started to give on Human Rights with police officers as the target-audience came to be seen as a symbol of modernity. Every new commander that took up a unit in the Battalion would show how up-to-date he was by inviting me to deliver a lecture on Human Rights to his troops. At times, some 200, 300, 400 would assemble at the strangest times of day to "to hear about human rights." On one occasion right before a lecture a commander told me: "don't you spoil my troops with this Human Rights business." I replied that I wouldn't spoil his troops, I would just make some comments on modernity in our profession. But this episode reflects rather well the resistance against the theme.

Changes Experienced

LR, RS, AD: What were the most important changes experienced by the Military Police of Minas Gerais during your career?

FX: One of the most important changes that the Brazilian Military Police forces went through was a change in police philosophy. This followed naturally from developments regarding human rights. There was a recognition of the need to shift the focus towards a higher regard for the human being, and to improve both the relationship between the police and society itself and, above all, to improve police legitimacy.

My generation studied, learned, and experienced a State police. Everything I learned, everything I studied, everything I practiced in the first ten years of my career, had as its focus the defense of the State, the protection of an already-defined *status quo*. Any reference to society, incredible as this may sound, was relegated to the background. If the interests of society coincided with those of the State, then we were ok, otherwise the interests of the State would prevail.

The shift in perspective happened within a wider political context, national or even global of other lines of thought than the prevailing one. In Brazil, the process leading to the new constitution in the 1980s, led to very intensive modifications in the philosophy guiding police practice. However, from a practical point of view, re-democratization contributed to the rise of two kinds of policing to coexist—defense of the state and concern for society. When the 1988 Federal Constitution (or "Citizen Constitution") was promulgated, intermediate level officers like myself saw below us officers calling for changes in favor of a closer interaction with society; yet we looked up, to the older, more senior officers, and saw a desperate attempt to keep the *status quo*, as they asked themselves "Now that it's my turn to be a commander, why change everything?" I heard this from several colleagues. So, the change in philosophy was a continuous process, imperceptible to many, but with some well-defined milestones. Priorities were altered, but big contradictions lingered on because the institution is heavy and naturally inert.

The gender issue was also pulled along with this whole process. The presence of the first class of female officers coincided with my own class. We lived side by side with these women during our course, as colleagues and not as subordinates or superiors. We valued and praised the presence of women, while repudiating any unfair treatment and unbalanced benefits towards one or another side. Issues relative to social and sexual-orientation diversity were also rather complex. Among the 700 or so cadets, there were clashes centered around the Military Penal Code, which listed pederasty as a crime, for there were self-declared homosexual cadets, both male and female, in the class. It was rather confusing at the time for alongside attempts at repression and categorical exclusion, intended to send a strong message that this was not the way to go; there was also respect and consideration for diversity, particularly with regard to each one's sexual orientation. This situation still hasn't yet been fully resolved and causes a good deal of difficulty. I remember a dialog I had, as a Major, with the commander of a Corps of Cadets—he was at the time the Educational Director and Commander of the Academy. I was telling him how, in my travels abroad, I had noted that some police forces recruited men and women with a homosexual orientation to join the ranks so as precisely to achieve a closer identity with that section of society. The answer I got from the commander was this: "Fábio, you're too 'fancy modern' for the way things are here. If the guy is a fag or a queer, he must be expelled from the police; there's no place for this here." And, as it turned out he prevailed and the young man was expelled. However, he was back three years later by force of an injunction, and today he's already a Captain. But, anyway, what was "fancy modern" at the time is already a reality today.

Another turning point was the arrival of the philosophy of community police. Somehow this new concept was imposed on our practice as middle-rank officers. This caused a distortion at all levels, even from the strategic viewpoint. For instance, I had thought that a good commander was one who had a good enough relationship with the community that he could get his vehicles repaired and get extra fuel quotas to conduct patrols, without having to rely on public funding. When that didn't happen, only 15 of our cars could run, out of a total of 70. That commander was best qualified who could put cars on the streets at no cost to the state. This practice completely changed as I, already a commander, took up the 13th Battalion. That was a time of more consistent investment by the state, as we had already outsourced the fleet, and I experienced different relations. I had new cars staying idle for shortage of drivers. In order to solve the problem, I had to double the shift of available drivers, for all the cars were in a very good operating condition, given their maintenance by the outsourced system. So, these were two moments in which the economic situations and, somehow, the wider context of the state had a strong influence in our relations with society. Thus, there was a shift in direction with this new view of community police, from the previous view which had looked at the community almost as if it were sponsoring the police, to a vision of the community as a participant of police activity.

Another important change has been the relations between the various police institutions—such as the Civil Police, the Federal Police and related bodies in general—for maximizing the potential of a complete police cycle. In Minas Gerais, the years 2003 to 2010 saw the inauguration of an entire framework for integrating police work. This was essential for the survival of the Public Security system, but which had been rejected for reasons of *esprit de corps* disputes. Today we are already in the 3rd generation of integration policies and they are beginning to consolidate. But our institutional discourse is different from the experienced operational reality. And here, again, we see how important it is to have new mentalities awakened rather than imposed. When institutionally imposed, integration ends up with forced attitudes, becoming simply the fulfillment of government targets. But now this change is irreversible.

With regard to *favela* dwellers, to the socially neglected population, the homeless, I believe that there has also been a marked shift of reference in the police. When we say there's been a change in the institution, it's complex, for at times a change in a group of people does not represent a substantial alteration in the institution as a whole. Anyway, one notices that there is now a different approach to this kind of social situation. It is no longer totally antagonistic as it used to be, when people would look at people who find themselves in a vulnerable position as potential offenders or as persons who should be arrested and removed away from the streets by police. I remember, during my time as a Lieutenant and later as a Captain, we had the famous *"arrastão"* (dragnet) operation, which is no more than deploying 10, 15, 20 police officers on a street to gather minors and beggars and put them on a minibus. A problem once irrupted when the minibus got overcrowded and I had nowhere to take those people to. I ended up riding about the city, round and round, with this overcrowded bus! After a while I ordered them all to step out and just released them back on the street; and this hit the newspaper headlines. But, at the end of the day, this was a failure of society. What were the police supposed to do in this sort of situation, and to what extent could the problem be solved by just taking people off the streets? As a result of this episode, the police's Chiefs of Staff instructed that this type of operation should no longer be carried out, thereby triggering a process that remains unresolved to this day, but which, anyway, proved to be a rather consistent change.

Therefore, from the point of view of police philosophy, I think the key issue is this transformation from a State-oriented police to a society-oriented police. This proved to be fundamental, as all issues pertaining to human rights would follow along, including respect and, above all, protection of people in fragile, vulnerable social situations. Gender differences also came along with this change. And with the focus on society came legitimacy of police action.

LR, RS, AD: What changes have there been in PMMG's relationship with human rights groups?

FX: In the beginning, those groups had a certain lack of knowledge about what the police do, while, on the part of the police, they had no relationship with or understanding of those groups. This situation has not yet been fully resolved; it's an evolving situation. It is a global problem since extreme action keeps happening on both sides—activists and police alike.

Recently we've had the episodes involving the *blackblocks*. Some police officers (or a good deal of them) still see the use of force and violence as the solution for these social issues. The backdrop to this situation is a lack of political definition and also a certain social hypocrisy, in the sense that society does not want nor praise violence, but, at the same time, in a subliminal manner, it approves of some police officers who act by doing a kind of "cleaning up" in society. I experienced this when commanding some units that worked in commercial areas. The traders would "enlist" some more violent police officers to clean up the streets because this was good for their business. And we, at command, had difficulty showing that this was not the way to go.

I think we need to analyze the implementation of human rights as a dynamic activity, not yet completed; and to define some stages, especially in terms of an approach based on institutional dynamics, with advances and setbacks. One has to analyze this issue by considering that there are moments of progress, and there are also moments of regress. Progress must be measured as the balance from advancements and setbacks, step by step.

In the case of the Military Police of Minas Gerais, the area least affected by such shifts towards a society-centric focus was the academic area, at school benches. For some reason, this area was not given proper attention—with disastrous consequences. Including the topic of human rights by simply rewriting manuals and books won't work. Just leaving it up to the schools, with their generations of new police officers—be it ordinary soldiers or officers—experiencing antagonistic positions towards their own teachers, this won't work either. It's crucial to prepare a consistent faculty. In other words, it's no use having one human rights professor saying one thing, and professors of other disciplines saying quite the opposite. An integration is necessary so that the topic of human rights can penetrate the other disciplines, especially those that involve the use of force and firearms. This is a basic strategy; but, still, lots of time and funds are spent in human rights seminars and lectures without attention being paid to the need for theme coherence and interconnection with the other disciplines. So, I think that, in the academic area, human rights still lack a full solution.

Of course, just to introduce the matter was hard enough, due to lack of knowledge among the people involved. This could be corrected, though, little by little. In addition, there was the problem that people wouldn't believe that positive effects could come from work and actions based on human rights parameters. Then we had resistance posed by the institutional culture, which also had to be overcome. To disregard the institutional culture is to neglect a crucial item. Nonetheless, one cannot disregard the institutional subculture, either; that which is not taught at schools, but which pervades operational environments. That which is not said, nor spoken, nor taught, but which prevails as the truth, and thus shapes that subculture. I believe that police forces in general have a very strong subculture, and we must pay close attention to its influence. It is vital to set standards of behavior, both ethical and professional, that can stand up to and override this police subculture that praises violence, disrespect for human rights, and often includes police corruption. Violence goes side by side with that, as the corrupt police officer needs the violent police officer: the violent police officer imposes fear, and thus the corruption is facilitated, as favors of other nature end up arising from fear spread among the population. Thus, there is the police officer who is violent by nature, but who believes he's doing the right thing, and there is the violent police officer who is violent because he's corrupt, because he needs violence in order to impose corruption. These are two different hues, two different aspects, and also two different approaches. In view of which, any change aimed at institutionalizing the human rights paradigm must also take into consideration both the police culture *and* subculture.

Another aspect making it difficult to disseminate human rights in the police is what we call social hypocrisy. The police officer finds him/herself routinely faced with a series of violent options, which are pointed at as a solution for problems of a social character, and we expect him/her to take a distinct position from these various courses of action. Today, you turn on the TV at 5 p.m. and watch a crime report show such as *"Balanço Geral"* and *"Cidade Alerta,"* which are pure violence and convey this subliminal message: the police must beat them up, must act, must shoot, must do this and that. This ends up having an influence on police work, giving a violent connotation to the police officer. I recall an incident at the 22nd Battalion, when I got a phone call from an elderly lady, who complained about police action. Incredible as this may sound, she was saying that she had watched from her third floor window, the arrest of two minors who were caught stealing a vehicle. She remarked that the police officers did not beat the kids up and teach them a lesson, so, they were bound to steal again! She expected the police to give the kids a beating openly on a public road, in the hope they would learn a lesson and never again commit an offense. This hypocrisy sets in on many police officers, who feed on this social demand for violence, causing extralegal actions to prevail.

The last point, which is also rather complex when considering the interface between human rights culture and police activity, is the issue of impunity. The violent police officer that goes unpunished is an extremely powerful diffusion of the message: what's wrong ends up being right in the police institution. In an antagonistic, paradoxical way, the exercise of broad defense in favor of the police officer himself, materialized through the exercise of his own human rights, leads to the prevalence of an incredibly high level of impunity. I once had, in the position of commander, more than 40 or 50 police officers who were supposed to be punished for violent acts, but whose punishment had been with-held due to the ineptitude of the system, precisely intended to protect the human rights of the police officers themselves. That is, the corporation plays with the human rights matter to its own benefit, to the detriment of a swift internal justice and administrative procedure, so as to secure the right of an ample defense and adversary proceedings. This way, we end up having full impunity, with the with-holding of penalties, which should instead be applied exemplarily so as to prevent perpetuation of this kind of problem.

Problems and Successes Experienced

LR, RS, AD: What did you personally find challenging about implementing change in the Military Police following the restoration of democracy?

FX: It concerned training and capacity-building. The first step was to convince the commanders at that time to believe that lack of knowledge, training, and specialization caused people to make mistakes. The entire Human Rights process on which we worked sought to open people's eyes to something that ran parallel to our activity, scarcely considered, but which is a part of the evidence of police legitimacy. This somehow changed the organizational culture. We were not imposing a new doctrine, but trying to awaken something new. The word "awakening" is important because I bring with me something experienced in this sense. I prefer to teach classes on human rights to older rather than younger police officers; it involves a different approach. Among older police officers, there would be a certain resistance. Some would say "these people...it's no use to touch that, because they are hardheaded." But I had the exactly opposite experience. Seasoned professionals in their 25 to 30-year long careers have realized that it's not with lots of bullets in the magazine and knives between the teeth that the Public Security problem is solved. Thus, I managed to open up a window and awaken them to a different way of looking at the issue. I recall the words of an old-school 1st Sergeant, who said to me: "Why didn't they tell us that before? Why they didn't explain it to us before? Why only now this is said? I always believed this would be possible, but it seemed that people didn't want it to be this way." It shows that older police officers are also susceptible to change, provided there is an awakening, and not the imposition of an antagonistic doctrine.

However when I was in command of the Corps of Cadets, which numbers some 800 youth aged 18 to 22, I took a very different approach. The young cadet already comes with an "acculturated" violence in him or her. He or she comes from an environment where violence is already established. It was hard for such an individual, at the moment he/she took on the authority conferred by the uniform, by the gear, by the institution, to properly handle the violence. So we followed a different course. For example, there was a games room for cadets for their relaxation. We had to forbid and recall all videogame machines that featured violent games, such as *Mortal Kombat* and the like. Just imagine a group of cadets aspiring to a career in the police and having fun killing people on videogames. Incredible as it seems, the resistance seemed much stronger among them than among older police officers. It's as if they had the aspiration to—together with the uniform and gear received, and with the authority vested on them—exercise some innate violence learnt in society in reference to the treatment of other human beings.

Personal Philosophy

LR, RS, AD: What has been your personal philosophy throughout your years in the PMMG?

FX: I have striven to mark my career by a coherence between what is said and what is done. I think this is the main line I sought to develop, not giving up my values, but always exercising, in attitudes and modes, the means to implement ideas. Doing something involves believing in what one is doing and leading a group of people (officers and soldiers) to believe in those values. Values are the most important dimension because they are perennial, but they need to be exercised in order to adapt to realities. So, I think my most important legacy was believing in the coherence between what one says and what one does.

This also happens with regards to the human rights issues, a title that came to be incorporated to my career as I went from Captain to Major. It was a coincidence. The police was going through a transitional period, we had gone through the 1988 constitution rewriting process, and things started to unveil differently, between police procedures and society's demands, the latter more up-to-date and the former somewhat lagging behind. I was given a position in top management, where I could incorporate values until then neglected from a police viewpoint. The topic "human rights" had moments of utter contradiction with police activity, and what I have tried to develop was to bring light to the matter; realizing that this antagonism is false, and that, in reality, the human rights activity is the mainstay and source of legitimacy for police activity. That is, without the orientation and support of human rights, any development of the police activity becomes impracticable.

Theory and Practice

LR, RS, AD: As regards theory and practice, what's the role of universities in transforming police practices?

FX: I truly believe in the development of police practice as conducted by an academic line of research. I do believe that the experiences described by academicians are applicable. The police need to do a kind of social reduction so as to adapt things, but such adaptation cannot lead to the impairment of some of the values proposed. The risk run when interpreting international experiences by reference to national experiences is that the interpreter naturally ends up by showing some bias, translating only what suits his own convictions about each reality as a whole.

I had to face this kind of situation during my three years in various Latin American countries. They numbered a total of 18 countries, always involving the same related issues: international standards of human rights and their application to police activities. The standards were the same and the police activities were quite similar in the different countries. The matter was how to interpret and experience them. As these were countries with different languages, our first difficulty was with translation, for there are, say, adjectives used in certain places, and depending on where they are placed in the sentence, their meaning may change and even diverge from the mindset of the legislator. Once this first barrier had been overcome, it was possible to see how the same rule may lead to disparate views from place to place, from site to site. Somehow, there is a resistance against international experiences being directly allocated to local experiences. I noted that particularly in countries of Latin origin, where there is a certain parochialism, something like "don't let the Yankees come here to tell us what to do." Dealing with these matters, bringing the philosophy without imposing it, but with due professionalism, this is a major challenge of a project intended to live on. This is not simple, it's a process that involves ups and downs, but as each progress is made steadily step-by-step, the situation ends up consolidating in a more positive way. To that effect, it's necessary to have a convergence of factors of both an institutional and a governmental policy character. When such orientation is not there, then it becomes hard to sustain those modifications.

I believe, therefore, that the issue of proximity between the academic world and the police involves two distinct but converging challenges. First, the international standards and philosophies require a translation that is in tune with the legislator's mindset, rather than affected by the translator's own perceptions—this is crucial. Second, imported standards and philosophies must be aligned to certain governmental policies, to give a sense of coherence between what's being done in terms of police change and renewal, on the one hand, and what's happening in broader governmental terms, on the other.

Transnational Relations

LR, RS, AD: What is your vision about Transnational Policing?

FX: One of the areas that I regard as very important in transnational policing is the application of the International Policing Standards. I have had the privilege, in particular, to be involved in international compliance with the Basic Principles on Use of Force and Firearms (BPUFF) and the Code of conduct for law enforcement officials. The BPUFF are "guidelines" and not a Police "procedure manual," hence work has to be done in individual countries to apply it in the local context. I have worked as an ICRC specialist delegate in eight

Latin American countries, providing technical assistance to their projects of integrating the BPUFF and other international norms to their police procedure manuals. I was, for instance, engaged in the working group charged with writing the Brazilian national regulation on the use of force and had the responsibility for guiding the training of 780,000 Brazilian police officers in the progressive use of force.

From my experience I have found that one of the challenges of international standards can be their imprecision with wording. In the case of BPUFF, confusion has arisen over the meaning of "use of force," since at times it is used incorrectly as if synonymous with "use of firearms." Similarly, there is confusion as to what exactly the BPUFF means by "use" of a firearm; whether it is only firing the weapon or whether having, holding, and pointing a weapon are also "use." These things have had to be clarified when I have sought to transpose these norms to internal legislation or to police procedure manuals.

Another issue has been the relative lack of attention in the BPUFF regarding the use of force when dealing with crowds. Most of the BPUFF principles are designed primarily for one-to-one situations; when the police officer is facing a single individual, or small groups. I believe the provisions for dealing with crowds should be widened and deepened. And there needs to be clarification regarding the use of "lethal" force. The 9th principle says "…in any event, intentional lethal use of firearms may only be made when strictly unavoidable in order to protect life." Please note that the adjective "lethal" deployed here is qualifying the noun "use," alongside with the adjective "intentional." "Intentional lethal use," therefore, can only be understood as "the use with the intention to kill." Yet, it is technically incorrect and morally inadmissible that a Law enforcement official assumes, under any circumstances, the deliberate intention to kill anyone. Even when the conditions justify the firing of the gun in the direction of an aggressor, the intention of the official can only be to stop the aggression—and not to take away the aggressor's life. If the aggression is neutralized by the first shot and the aggressor remains wounded after this, the duty of the law enforcement official is to provide him medical assistance in order to save his life. Where is the "intentional lethal use" of the firearms in these situations? Nobody would suppose officials are allowed to continue shooting the aggressor to death. The misemployment of the term "lethal," therefore, brings a dangerous loophole to the 9th principle of the BPUFF.

What I am trying to highlight is that, based on my years of field experience, international guidelines such as the BPUFF need improvement in order to be correctly applied. In addition, there is the challenge is to transfer the basic principles to the procedure manuals without jeopardizing the protective character of the norms. Nevertheless, I can assert that transnational policing can be an effective tool for all the problems with the interpretation of the meaning of each international principle.

Democratic Policing

LR, RS, AD: In your view, what are the main characteristics of a democratic police?

FX: The trend towards the constitution of a democratic police in contemporary Brazilian society is something real. If we want to search for the essence of police activity, we'll find out that it has this society-centric orientation, given that it's intended to serve society as a whole. Of course, the best way to promote a society-orientation and public service standards is through democracy. No doubt, this would be the most appropriate, both from an internal point of view and in regard to the other institutions.

As a military institution, PMMG has some characteristics that are extremely positive from the point of view of a democratic living experience, and others that may seem antagonistic. The latter is what often comes to the fore. There is a stigma brought about by the use of the word "military," in the sense of an assumption of being anti-democratic. Of course, military philosophy is, in essence, military. By the way, it's rather interesting that "military" can be used as an adjective in the sense of orderly, responsible, polite, hard working. These are indeed very suitable meanings for "military." But when "military" is used in the sense of rude, violent, authoritarian, forceful, these are not so desirable adjectives attached to the military.

What happens is that the military orientation of police forces went through a stage during which the negative aspects of this adjective were strongly emphasized, reinforcing their ties to the Armed Forces, and highlighting a certain legacy. Incredible as it may seem, the Armed Forces themselves have different standards of militarism. For instance, the Air Force have different parameters of hierarchy and internal developments from those of the Army or Navy. This is natural. For example, in the Air Force, if a Sergeant is a flight controller and a pilot is a Lieutenant Colonel, this means that the Lieutenant Colonel will take orders from the Sergeant, as the flight controller enjoys a technical prevalence that supersedes the military hierarchy. At the Air Force, this technical *versus* hierarchy opposition is very well worked out. Fact is, the Military Police ended up seeking inspiration, among the Armed Forces, from the Army itself, causing relations between individuals to be a little less technical and more forceful, by rank: the Lieutenant speaks, the Sergeant complies! This type of situation is antagonistic to police activity. It's necessary that the Lieutenant speaks and that the Sergeant complies, yes, but according to parameters of legality and legitimacy. In a way, as we sought inspiration for the Military Police in the Army, we found a broad foundation to sustain our corporation precisely in the Infantry, which is, incredibly, the rudest, the most elementary of all armed forces, perhaps of the most rigid treatment.

Therefore, the issue of militarism brings forth the need to determine what kind of adjectival connotation is being referred to in the use of "military." I recall, when I took up the command of the Corps of Cadets, we had to go on a trip for studies and development, and the Police Command wanted to send me to Agulhas Negras (Brazil's top military academy). I told them I didn't want to go to Agulhas Negras as the commander of the Corps of Cadets; I'd rather visit the Air Force academy, instead, because I thought that the police activity is more turned to the prevalence of technique, without prejudice to the hierarchy, but that the technical should prevail over full hierarchy.

To me, the opposition between democratic policing and militarism is going to adjust itself as time passes, as we shall manage to shed the undesirable negative connotations associated to the adjective "military," and keep the positive ones. I believe we can work on a military activity with its aesthetics, its concepts, with its positive adjectives evoking responsibility, hard work, diligence, dedication, while at the same time discarding the negative connotation of "military" insofar as it is associated to rudeness, violence, authoritarianism, and forcefulness.

LR, RS, AD: So you think that a Military Police fit into a democratic regime?
FX: I see the demilitarization of the Military Police forces as a present concern. There's been a certain trend in that direction for some time already. For instance, for some years now we've had a well-defined orientation of the federal government, a leftist orientation. The military issue raises a sort of "allergy" among these public agents (now in power), regardless of qualifications or quality of the services provided by the Military Police. The fact that they're military leads to a disregard for the activity in various environments, in various instances of activities and initiatives of a legislative nature. It is common to see initiatives that discredit, disregard, and depreciate the military profession. I think this is inevitable. There will be a change in name, a change in façade, and in fact nothing will be altered in the internal parameters, if this is not cared for in a better-defined, deeper way.

Looking Ahead

LR, RS, AD: What are the challenges ahead facing the PMMG?
FX: In terms of current challenges, the context of social movements has changed. It's necessary that our leaders perceive these changes.

If we keep on doing what we always have, we're not going to survive; we need an updated, modern, and prospective view on what police work means. I think that the survival of institutions depend on the prospective capacity of their leaders, in the sense of repeating what has been done while rearranging old rules, adapting them to new situations. But there's a limit to it, and we're close to reaching this limit. If we keep on doing what we always have, we'll keep on reaping the same results. The problem is, these results have not been proving very favorable. The main challenge is to be able to keep up with those social changes through the prospective vision of our leaders.

Conclusion

This interview with Cel. Fábio Manhães Xavier purported to unveil the key elements in the transformation process undergone by the Brazilian Military Police in general and by the Military Police of Minas Gerais in particular. The interviewee was chosen due to his trajectory as Commander of the Police Academy for several years, when he strove to institutionalize the theory of human rights as the basis for all police practices. Moreover, as a function of his mission with the Red Cross, the limits and possibilities of this transformation—from Military Police (*stricto sensu*) to democratic police—could become even more evident.

Starting from the principle according to which the police in democratic societies is the organization that, on the one side, secures the safety of all citizens without discrimination, and, on the other, operationalizes the legitimate and proportional use of violence and disciplinary power, this reconstitution of Cel. Fábio Manhães Xavier's trajectory was extremely revealing. After all, the responses reported here point at the difficulty of accepting human rights as something that will guide Military Police action regarding the limits posed to the use of force. Further, they point at how society does not seem to be prepared for this change in paradigm, given its continuous demand for more violence, including that practised by police officers illegitimately.

Within this context, Cel. Fábio Manhães Xavier argues that demilitarization by itself will not solve the problems of lethality and corruption that ravage Brazilian police forces. To that effect, it is necessary to rethink existing training procedures (always relegated to the background in operational planning) as well as the justice and disciplinary procedures that cover up police deviations, causing them to be perceived as legitimate by all troops.

Thus, adopting a sociocentric matrix, as suggested by Cel. Xavier, means rethinking the function of police in Brazilian society. Far from an organization that normalizes deviant behaviors by means of corporal punishment, or that takes away undesirable individuals who roam the city's streets, the function of the Military Police must turn to policing in favor of the community. The dissemination of training in human rights, in his view, would contribute to the rise of a modern police in Brazil, as this would transform the logic of police operation. From this new perspective, the police would start to look at itself as a service provider, with its actions guided by the principles of a public bureaucracy, instead of representing an armed organization seeking to defend their own interests.

References

Adorno, S. 2008. Políticas públicas de segurança e justiça penal. *Cadernos Adenauer,* 9(04). Rio de Janeiro: Fundação Konrad Adenauer.

Brinks, D. M. 2012. *The Judicial Response to Police Killings in Latin America.* Cambridge University Press.

Bueno, S. 2014. Letalidade Policial. In: Lima, R. S., Ratton, J. L., Azevedo, R. G. (eds.). *Crime, Segurança e Justiça no Brasil.* São Paulo: Contexto, 2014.

Ribeiro, L. M. L., Oliveira, V. C. 2014. Quando o Estado é o perpetrador da violência: Uma análise das vitimizações ocasionadas pela Polícia Militar. *Latitude,* 7(2).

J. Thomas Manger, Chief of the Montgomery County (Maryland) Police Department, USA

12

INTERVIEWED BY
MICHAEL M. BERLIN
MARCELLUS BOLES

Contents

Introduction

The Montgomery County Police Department employs approximately 1,200 sworn personnel (officers, first line supervisors, mid-level managers, and command staff) plus an additional 600 civilian personnel. The Department serves Montgomery County, Maryland, which has a population of 1,030,447 (U.S. Census, 2014). Montgomery County borders Washington, DC, the United States Capital, as well as several other Maryland and Virginia counties. The police department is organized into four bureaus, Patrol Services, Field Services, Investigative Services, and Management Services. Patrol Services is responsible for patrolling a land area of approximately 500 square miles, a mix of urban, suburban, and rural areas, including cities, towns, villages, and unincorporated communities. Patrol is divided into six geographical districts, Rockville, Bethesda, Silver Spring, Wheaton, Germantown, and Montgomery Village.

Montgomery County has a diverse population, including African-Americans (18.8%), Asians (15.2%), and Hispanics (18.7%). Montgomery County is a business, research, and biotech hub. It houses 18 federal agencies and installations and is the second wealthiest county in Maryland with median household income of $98,221, 6.7% of the population lives below the poverty level. The Montgomery County Police Department is large, sophisticated police agency, among the 50 largest cities and county police departments out of a total of approximately 12,000 local police departments in the United States.

Chief Manger was interviewed in his office on Monday, May 4, 2015 at the Montgomery County Police Department Headquarters Office in Gaithersburg, Maryland. He appeared comfortable and relaxed as he responded to the interviewers.

Career

MB & MB: Please tell us a little bit about your career, the organizations you worked for, key assignments and experiences, and what motivated you to go into police work.

JTM: I was born in Baltimore, and left for Montgomery County with my family at the age of 14. I remember being at college at University of Maryland and it was just after the Watergate scandal (when President Nixon's Committee for Re-Election of the President authorized burglary and surveillance of the campaign headquarters of the Democratic Party competitors in 1972. It resulted in the resignation of President Nixon). I had this notion that, like a lot of people, I wanted to save the world and bring justice to injustice. I had actually originally thought about being in journalism, becoming an investigative reporter and doing a lot of good things through journalism. I planned on majoring in journalism at the University of Maryland but very quickly became a bit disenchanted with some of my journalism classes and saw the way that journalists did their job. Then I thought, maybe I should be a social worker and save the world this way. So I started taking classes in sociology which led to some criminology classes and I really liked the criminal justice classes that I took. I think it took maybe a year or year and a half before I changed my major to Criminal Justice and really thought going into police work might be the career for me.

I graduated from college in 1976 at University of Maryland and back then, Ocean City, Maryland used to hire summer cops. Some of my friends had done that, and said, "Oh you should do it." I had just graduated from college and I had no immediate plan for the summer so I became a cop in Ocean City. Now, I will tell you that putting us out on the street with 2 weeks training, with a gun and a badge, I look back on it and am amazed they would do that. I had a blast and I'm not sure how much I learned about police work, but I sure learned that that was the right profession for me. I enjoyed it.

I applied to just about every police department in the District of Columbia (DC) area, as well as, the Baltimore area, where I was from originally, and was going through the processes, physical testing, psychological screening, and all the background checks. Fairfax County in Virginia just happened to be the first agency to offer me a job. I had never been to Fairfax before in my life except to take the test there, but I knew it was a good police department and I knew it was a big police department so I accepted their offer. It's funny, right after I accepted their offer, I got a call from Prince George's, from Howard, from Baltimore, all these agencies you know, that said, "we will hire you," and I told them all that I've already committed to Fairfax. Knowing that I hadn't started, I easily could have called them and said, "sorry," but that was just my personality, you make a commitment and you honor that commitment.

I spent the next 27 years with the Fairfax County Police Department, rose up through the ranks and actually became Chief of Police there when I was 44 years old. When I was appointed as Chief it was a young department, so it wasn't crazy that a 44 year old would become Chief. I was very fortunate and was a strong believer that if you work hard in an organization and dedicate yourself to the mission, you can become successful and that worked out well for me. As a Police Chief the job really changes you—you think you know what being a Chief means, but you don't. Not until you're in the job and understand the responsibility, the 24/7 pressure and responsibility for everything. I spent the next 6 years as the chief in Fairfax County. During that time we had the Sniper Case involving John Mohammed and Lee Malvo in 2002, and of course we got involved with that, the shooting at the Home Depot was ours, and the 9/11 (the Al Qaeda terrorist attacks on the World Trade Center, Pentagon, and downing of United Flight 93). Those were certainly huge moments for law enforcement. Being the Police Chief in a large jurisdiction really was exciting and intense, but again that same feeling I had in 1976 when I was a summer cop in Ocean City, the feeling that I'm doing what I need to be doing, I had that same feeling during the Sniper Case and during 9/11. I felt there was no place I would have rather been than working to try and help keep the community safe in whatever role I had as Police Chief in a large community.

In 2004, Chief Moose was the Police Chief in Montgomery County. I had previously lived in Baltimore, then moved to Silver

Spring when my dad got a job with the Federal Government. We moved to Silver Spring since he was working in DC and I'd lived in Montgomery for 10 years before I moved over to Northern Virginia, when I became a police officer in Fairfax. So I knew Montgomery County and my parents still lived in Montgomery County, my sister still lives here. So Montgomery County still very much felt like it was home and when Chief Moose retired to write his book about the Sniper Case, they were looking for a new Police Chief. I was eligible to retire in Fairfax but I thought this might be the next challenge for me. I could go back to Montgomery County and take on a new challenge. The challenges are very similar, the communities are very similar. The politics are a little more difficult here than they were in Fairfax, but it was a very natural transition. I won't say it was an easy transition, but it was a very natural transition for me to come over here and now I've been Police Chief over here for 11 years.

Changes Experienced

MB & MB: What do you see as the most important changes which have happened within your organizations over the course of your career?

JTM: Frankly, I think we are doing better in every category now. I think about when I began as a police officer in the late 70s and community policing was being talked about, but I don't think anybody knew exactly what it meant. In fact, the definition changed depending on whom you talked to. But one of the cornerstones of community policing was understanding that the police have a role in the community and it's an important, unique role. Nobody else in the community can do what the police do, and I think understanding the responsibility that you have as a police officer helps you and guides you in terms of how you do your job. There was a time when, in certain neighborhoods, you felt like it was "us against them." You went into that neighborhood thinking, "OK, we're going to have to fight our way out of this neighborhood." I don't think that we as police thought, "we're here to protect the residents of this neighborhood." It was almost like, "we're here to sweep up all the casualties of a particular neighborhood."

Understanding the relationship that you develop with the community really shapes how you are able to do your job. We were just learning that and understanding how to operationalize that in police work back when I started and when I was beginning to get promoted. I can recall vividly some of the hiring standards that we had. There used to be a height standard. My dad wanted to be a state trooper when he got out of the service in World War II, but he was 5′9″ tall and you needed to be 5′10″ to be a Maryland state trooper. We look back on that and think, "well what difference does it make what height you are on your ability to be a police officer?" You know, this notion that you've got to be big and bad, haven't we all learned that that's actually not the case? It's actually what you have between your ears that counts. If you know how to talk to people, have compassion and empathy and all those things you'll be a good police officer. Training is needed in teaching officers how to communicate with people. We can train you how to do the rest of the stuff. Let's hire the people that have the right traits, and height certainly isn't one of them. Or take sexual orientation. When I got hired, every single background investigation asked questions about sexual orientation, because if you were gay, they weren't going to hire you and made no bones about it. The notion back then was, "gee, if you're gay you can be blackmailed, and you can't have people in law enforcement that can be blackmailed." We just look back on all of these things and shake our heads and think, "it took us a while to understand what was really important."

I can recall when I started with Fairfax there were two black women out of 1,100 police officers at the time. They have many more now, but only two African-American women at the time. Now, how does that happen? I think I actually have a little bit of an understanding. You want to join an organization that you think you can thrive in, that you would feel a part of and, if there's nobody that looks like you in the organization, then you've got an obstacle to overcome in terms of trying to recruit people. I look at today and the hiring standards and the recruitment that we do and we really have an understanding that the police department should reflect the diversity of the community that we serve. I think we've really taken many steps in the right direction to ensure that we are hiring the right people and ensuring that the department has not only diversity, but the understanding of the diversity in the community. When you have a community that speaks 100 different languages, then you better have the ability to communicate in every one of those languages that the community speaks if you're going to give the right type of police service.

Yet for all these improvements, I will tell you that I don't know that we will ever come to a point where we say, "you know what, we're done, we've got everything done, we've got everything accomplished, we're doing just fine." There is always room for improvement, in terms of things like human rights and legal training, these are things that you can never stop training on and never stop talk-ing about. Even if you get this in the entrance level training acad-emy, every year in in-service training you need to remind people, "here's what you're allowed to do and here's how you're allowed to do it." Those are just some of the most important training issues that police have today: making sure that we're treating people with respect, treating people lawfully, consistently, fairly. We will always have work to do in that area, but we are doing much better than we used to. There has to be a continuous effort to train and develop personnel, to never stop training, in-service training and reinforc-ing the importance of treating the people fairly.

MB & MB: Have current economic conditions resulted in budget cuts? If so, how has this impacted the organization?

JTM: I don't know of any department that hasn't experienced budget cuts in the last 10 years. You really have to get to a point where we have to analyze what's important, prioritize our responsibilities, and say, "we've got to do the things that are important for us to do and make sure were doing them well." And sometimes there's other responsibilities where you have to say, "we just can't do it any lon-ger," or you have to find more economical ways of doing them. We have lost positions, some funding for some of the special initiatives that we would do, whether it was traffic enforcement or being able to identify a specific crime issue and attack it through overtime or some other strategy. Every police department that I know of has experienced some of those budget cuts. I don't like this saying "we've got to do more with less." Nobody's asking us to do more with less, they are just asking that we do our job with less, that we do the same with less. This is still difficult to do because you've got a lot of responsibilities and people are always calling the police ask-ing us to solve some of their problems. I think that one of the other things that police departments have done as a result of economic conditions, is we have to identify what is it that we were doing that wasn't really part of our job, issues that just fell to us because nobody else would do it. A good example of that is mental health issues. I mean, think about it, think about the times we responded to calls for service and you were dealing with someone who had mental health issues. And why was it the police? Because we're the last resort for some of these problems.

We've partnered with some of the mental health agencies in the county, and we've got a very nice relationship with our health and human services staff and with mental health providers. It's a more efficient way of dealing with some of those cases. Or take homelessness, it's not a crime to be homeless, but who deals with the problems created by the homeless? It's the police, it's the police more than anybody else, and our ability to work with some of the social service agencies and get a more effective response, has freed up some of the time of some of my officers, but it also got people the help they needed. Putting someone in jail because they're acting out, because they've got a mental issue or because they're homeless doesn't do anybody any good. It doesn't do the person any good and it doesn't do the community any good. You're just hiding the problem temporarily. One of the outcomes of the economic cuts has been to find more efficient ways of doing the job better.

MB & MB: As regards to external relationships, what changes have you observed in police relationships with public interagency cooperation, personnel within the criminal justice system, relations with minority communities, political influence, and human rights activists?

JTM: I know I answered a lot of that, but this goes back to community policing, one of the cornerstones of community policing is partnerships. It's developing relationships with folks that have an interest in public safety and human rights. I've got a great relationship with the Human Rights Commission in Montgomery County and after 11 years of working with them, I actually got inducted into the Human Rights Hall of Fame in Montgomery County. I'm very proud of that because a lot of police chiefs and police departments are not seen as a friend of human rights organizations and certainly most police chiefs understand there's a lot of commonalities to our mission with a lot of those organizations. Just developing those relationships and working on those relationships is tremendously important and that's all a part of community policing.

Regarding interagency cooperation, with maybe the exception of New York Police Department, there's no police department in this country that can do it all by themselves and never needs any help. Cooperation began with the protests in Washington, DC against the World Bank. Chuck Ramsey was Chief of the Metropolitan Police Department in Washington, DC and when tens of thousands of protestors showed up to protest the World Bank, he contacted me in Fairfax and contacted all of the other chiefs in the region asking for help. We were able to provide hundreds of officers. It started with the World Bank then it became inaugurations, all different kinds of events that happened in DC We created a model, and I give Ramsey credit that he was the one that started it, but we created a model that has proved to be useful over and over again when there's a big event and you need help. This works out great. The latest protest in Baltimore was a perfect example (civil disturbances, rioting, and looting which occurred in

Baltimore, April, 2015, following the in-custody death of Freddie Grey as a result of injuries sustained during his arrest and transport by the Baltimore Police Department). We sent officers up there and we had an executive of Baltimore Police Department assigned to our group and it worked out very well.

MB & MB: Can you say a little bit more about the model that you created?

JTM: The first thing you need to do, and this sometimes is the most difficult thing, is you need to get the attorneys involved to get a memorandum of agreement. Get a memorandum of understanding (MOU) signed so that you have the ability to work in another jurisdiction. For a long time, we'd have to go down to DC the morning of the event and I'd have hundreds of police officers from outside jurisdictions raise their right hand and be sworn in as US Marshalls temporarily. Now, we work through MOUs. We went into DC and Baltimore, and while we are on the front lines of trying to maintain safety and security, should there be reason to make arrests, it was Baltimore and DC officers that were making the arrests, so you didn't have officers from other jurisdictions making arrests and having to go to court. Someone from the home jurisdiction is assigned for communications. We got a lieutenant from the Baltimore Police Department. He would get word from the command center saying, "Move to this intersection and do this." The Baltimore executive would talk to the person who was in charge of my contingent and it just worked out very well. You keep everybody together. I know when we first got to Baltimore there was originally some desire, "hey can you send half of your platoon here and send the other half there?" We said, "no, keep us all together," because we train together, we want to stay together, our command structure is designed that way. So they were fortunate that they could send Prince George's County to some location, keep Montgomery County here, send Howard County somewhere, and send Anne Arundel somewhere. But keeping folks together, that was part of the original model that we had in DC and it's been very effective. For more on community policing, see Berlin (2012) and Oliver (2004).

Problems and Successes

MB & MB: During your time, how has progress been achieved and what obstacles have there been to progress? What policies or programs have worked well and which have not?

JTM: The most successful crime fighting initiatives involved the public and getting buy in ahead of time. Take Speed cameras—people love the speed cameras or hate the speed cameras. I tell you one of the things we did right here was we involved the community in the decision about where the speed cameras would go and all that sort of thing. We're not putting them in places just to make money, we're actually demonstrating the crash data and we have a community board that looks at the information and approves the location or doesn't. So, community involvement in decisions. I've said it over and over, people need to believe the criminal justice system is fair, that law enforcement is consistent and lawful, all those kinds of things. In a place like Montgomery County, I have large segments of the community that have great confidence in the police, but I will also take you to neighborhoods that have little trust in the police and don't get as much cooperation. Yet, we can't write off any neighborhood, not one street, not one neighborhood. We can't write them off and say, "forget those people because they don't care about us, they don't care about cooperating with us, so we'll just write them off." Can't do it! We understand that we need to make more of an investment in those neighborhoods and it benefits public safety everywhere. Today, we're hiring better people, people that are more suitable for this job. I mentioned this a little bit earlier, it used to be that when you hired a police officer what you had in mind was somebody that can handle themselves, when they walked in the room you probably said, "look at the size of this guy, lets sign him up, because we're the tough guys." I don't care. You get a bunch of tough guys, there's always tougher guys out in the street. You don't want a tough guy, you want somebody that's smart, has a spirit for public service, and has the right character traits to be a good police officer. We'll train you how to write a report, we'll train you about use of force, we'll train you how to do all that. Let's hire the person that has those right character traits. I think we're doing a better job of that today then we used to and I think that's taking us forward. I think people understand that you've got to sustain a level of integrity within a police department and if you don't, you're just going to lose the public trust and you're going to create a culture that's not good for any police department. So, addressing dishonesty within the police department has got to be something we care about and fight for. You get cops that do things that are dishonest and the easy thing to do is give them a little bit of discipline and move forward. No! If you got dishonest cops, you got to get rid of them, and that's not easy. It's not easy to fire a cop, it's a lot of trouble, it's a lot of work and it's a lot of aggravation, but you're either going to set the right tone for a culture in a department or you're not. I'll go back to when we started putting cameras on cops. On the one hand I get why some cops would resent the fact that they got to wear cameras because it sends a message we don't trust you. But think about the responsibility. Who else in our society, who else in our community can take so much freedom away besides a cop? That's an awesome responsibility to have. If people want to make sure cops are doing it right and held accountable when they're wrong, there's really no problem with that. I have every intention when we put cameras on, to wear one myself. That will probably be pretty dull footage—I'm not out locking people up every day. But I intend to wear one because I want to get a feel for what my cops are having to deal with. But I can tell you, if I'd worn a camera my whole career, there'd have been times where my mother could have looked at that video and said, "I'm not very proud of you, young man," for some of the things I said and that sort of thing. But you know, I never lied, cheated, or stole. Lie, cheat, and steal is not what you want your cops to do. I could have had a camera on and there could have been some very ugly moments in terms of me having to deal with some very ugly situations. 99% of the cops out here will do the right thing and that's what those cameras will prove. For those that don't, shame on them, we don't need them in our profession.

MB & MB: Is it fair to say that the way to address corruption and human rights abuses is through accountability?

JTM: Absolutely.

MB & MB: Can you say a little bit about the impact of technology? We've talked about speed cameras we've talked about body cameras, what is the impact of technology, both good and bad on policing?

JTM: Listen, it's mostly good. Think about DNA technology. Or think about license plate readers. It was unbelievable the usefulness of those technologies. On the other side, there's 'big brother'. The public is worried about how long we are keeping this data and what we are using it for. I wish I could explain and get people to believe that the only thing we care about are criminal investigations. Nobody cares about where you are or what you're doing. Unless you're committing a crime, you've got nothing to worry about with all this data. People walk through 100 cameras a day and they have no idea that they're doing it. The DNA technology and touch technology means that when somebody picks up a cup, you've got their DNA and we're solving crimes every day with those advances in technology. We're doing a lot better job of locking up bad guys with a lot less investigation because of this technology. This comes with a responsibility to use it properly and not misuse it. I think there's a bright line, that is you use it for criminal investigations, period. There's not one chief that I know that would not take that limitation and say, "that's fine with me." There's no other reason to use the data that we have the ability to collect now, other than criminal investigations, period.

MB & MB: I read that Montgomery County is getting 2 drones for the police and fire department, but that you're not going to use them until there is a policy in place on privacy?

JTM: Yes, people asked about drones and I said, "not interested," because my public, this community, is not ready for the police department to have a drone. It would be nothing but aggravation. I'd be spending all my time trying to explain to people that we're only using this to prevent crime. So I said no, my public is not ready for them. Do I think they have a use in policing? Absolutely. Here's the problem: the fire department wants them, and people say they want them because when they're fighting a fire they can put the drone up and have a camera on all sides of the building so they can direct their firefighting efforts. That all makes good sense to me. I can tell you that while I think that there is a use for drones in police work, my public is not ready for it and what I'd rather them do is pass a law and say, "here's what they're going to be used for," and then I'll say, "well I can live within those parameters." If I get a drone right now I'd be spending too much of my time trying to explain to the public what they're used for, people wouldn't trust us. I know my community is not ready for it.

Personal Policing Philosophy

MB & MB: What do you think should be the role and functions of the police?

JTM: To keep communities safe. It really comes down to keeping communities safe and whether you do that through preventive patrol, arresting bad guys, whether you do that simply through investigating crimes, those are all ways that you can keep communities safe. Locking up bad guys that are committing crime and being there to prevent crime keeps communities safe. Basically, there are a thousand different ways to do it, but it all comes down to responding to people that need help and being there in the community. I think we've all determined that preventive patrols is a bit of a shot in the dark; it's a bit of a crapshoot if you're going to be where you need to be, when you need to be there. It happens occasionally, but it's not a rock solid philosophy. However, I think it does have a role.

Then investigating crime, once a crime occurs. You have to have solid investigations that result in people being held accountable for the crimes that they commit. Then of course you have to have faith and confidence in the rest of the criminal justice system.

I just think that understanding the unique role that police play in a community and being able to fill that role is critical. It does require that the department be above reproach. You want to have a department that has a reputation for honesty and has a reputation for service. Those are all part of the culture of a police department. As a chief, I've got to instill that culture, maintain that culture, and ensure it. As a chief you can write policy and do a lot of things, but I learned long ago that it's the sergeants that are really the boots on the ground who are determining how the job is done. If they are making sure that the cops are doing the job the right way, then that's great. If they're not, then that's a problem.

MB & MB: What should be dropped or left to other public and non-state organizations, what should be done about unpoliced areas?

JTM: The Director of our Corrections and Rehabilitation Department, there's two jails in Montgomery County, he will tell you that he is the largest mental health provider in Montgomery County. I'm not sure that a jail should be the largest mental health provider in any jurisdiction. I think we need to do a better job at dealing with the folks that have mental health issues. Homeless people, the complaints I get about the people who are panhandling (begging) at intersections, I get a lot of complaints about that. Let's not criminalize all that and thus make the police the ones to solve this problem. I think there's other ways to solve some of these issues without criminalizing this behavior and saying, "oh we'll let the police deal with it."

MB & MB: What encourages and hinders good relations with the community, with government, other criminal justice organizations, non-state providers such as community groups, and commercial enterprises?

JTM: I think that the only way that you develop a good relationship with anybody is with good communication and trust. What hinders good relationships with anyone is if there is a lack of trust and a lack of good communication. You've got to earn trust and for police organizations, I can tell you, we've got to earn it every day. One police officer, one action, one individual event can just really harm that trust, I won't say completely destroy it, but it could. You could be starting from square one, you can have a great relationship with a community and something bad could happen and if the department doesn't react the way it should, you could be starting from scratch in terms of rebuilding that trust with the community. I preach to my cops all the time that each one of us has that responsibility. It can't just be the chief out there having a good relationship with the community, every one of my cops with every traffic stop they make, every person they stop and talk to, they are influencing how the community feels about the police department.

MB & MB: What should be the priorities of your police service?

JTM: The key is service. We've got to understand that we provide a unique service to the community, a service that no one else is authorized to do. We need to understand how reliant the community is on us to provide a police service and if that puts pressure on us to do it right, then so be it, that's the way it ought to be. Let's say somebody had had something stolen from their house, or had a traffic crash, or something like that, you have got to understand that this may be the first time they ever called the police. So, my handing of that call was going to influence their opinion of the police for the rest of their life. Every time one of my cops is dispatched to a call for service, I wish I could flash that message up on their computer screen, "remember, the way you handle this is going to influence their opinion for the rest of their life." It really does come down to treating people with respect and treating people like you're going to see them again. Too often we have interactions with people and treat it like we're never going to have to see this person again. If everybody kept in mind, "I might see this person tomorrow, I might see this person a week from now," maybe some of the interactions would be a little bit better.

Theory and Practice

MB & MB: Would you say that theory has played a part in your practice and that of your organization? We noticed you were on the IACP Research Committee.

JTM: I think that police departments have always done research. In the past, sometimes, it's been clumsy research, but it was some level of research nonetheless. I don't think we do as good a job as the academic community. I think we could learn a lot from them and some of the research that's done there. I think we're doing a little bit better at paying attention to some of that research. Too often, I think research in police departments is merely considering their own data and experience and that's all there is to it. I think that digging a little bit deeper sometimes can help make decisions and guide policy. I'll give you just a couple examples. One was police pursuits. It was always, if somebody ran, we chased them, whether it was just running a stop sign or a drunk driver. If someone had the audacity to run from us, we were going to chase them. Well fast forward, for me 38 years, and we're very judicious on whom we chase because we understand the dangers of these high speed pursuits. One of the things I've learned through research is that if a pursuit lasted more than 5 minutes, it was about 10 times more likely to end badly, to end in a crash, with somebody innocent getting hurt.

This conclusion was reached through research about all these pursuits and it influenced our policy. I did this many years ago back in Fairfax, that if a pursuit got to be 3 minutes long, a supervisor had to make an informed decision. The dispatcher would get on the air and ask the supervisor, not to the officer chasing—that's the last person that ought to be making the decision about whether the pursuit should continue. Ask the supervisor, "do you want this pursuit to continue or do you want to cut it off?" Often times the sergeant knew what the person was being chased for, they knew the area the pursuit was going on, and very often they would make the informed decision to have the officer cut it off. This is real policy and significant policy that was influenced because of the research being done. Research done on hate crimes, about the impact a hate crime has on a community, has also influenced police policy. Before I read the research that was done on hate crimes, somebody just spray painting some racial slur on a garage and you think, "OK, well its vandalism, a little bit of soap and water we can clean that up." For a police agency we never knew, until I read about the research, about the impact of hate crimes, how limited our response really was to those things. It's not just vandalism, it has an impact on everybody in that neighborhood. That has changed our response to things like hate crimes. Research is very important, we need to pay attention to that and it has had a positive influence on policy.

MB & MB: Do you want to say anything about police practitioner partnerships?

JTM: It's worthwhile to go back to community policing. One of the things that makes it successful is when the community gets to participate in the process. If the only people that care about crime and safety in the neighborhoods are the police, we're in trouble. Everybody's got to care about that. Quoting Sir Robert Peel, "the people are the police, the police are the people." Everybody's got to be a part of public safety and when you include different segments of the community, whether its academia, whether its advisory boards, when you have that input you get more buy in from the community and it makes for better police service.

Transnational Relations

MB & MB: How have you and the work of your organization been affected by developments outside the country—human rights demands, universal codes of ethics, practical interactions with police from other countries, travel outside the country, new crime threats, and the war on terror?

JTM: Before 9/11, if you asked most police chiefs what they were doing to combat terrorism they would have said, "well nothing, really, that's the FBI's job." Now everybody is paying attention to homeland security and to terror threats, not all of them are necessarily threats from outside the country. The biggest terror threat to the US is the lone wolf and every one of our communities can have a 'lone wolf' (individual terrorists not affiliated with any cell, organization or network). Think about the way the Internet can radicalize somebody. That can happen in any house in any neighborhood, anywhere. We've got to pay attention to what's going on in terms of domestic terrorism. Countering violent extremism is an important part of any police department. It's not just the job of the federal government, it's not just the FBI; all of us have a role to play. This is a development that's really just occurred for most of us since 9/11. In addition, we can learn a lot from places like Israel and other nations which have been fighting terrorism for a lot longer than we have. The relationship that we have with democratic countries around the world has also been very helpful and I know there's a lot of training going on across the globe which is influencing American policing.

MB & MB: In terms of the transferability of skills, I assume we can learn from others and we can help others, as well?

JTM: I think we have a tremendous amount to offer in terms of policing in a democratic society: treating people fairly, lawfully, and building trust with the community. I think American policing is way ahead of many other countries in that regard.

MB & MB: What is the role of local police in fighting transnational crime? For example, organized crime, drug dealing, and also with regard to the immigration issue?

JTM: I will tell you that local police have a difficult time with some of the transnational issues. We just don't have the resources to take investigations to other countries. We are really reliant on the FBI and other federal agencies to help us work these kinds of cases. We certainly have a responsibility to work with those federal agencies. When you investigate a crime only to find out that the person who is responsible for the crime is in some other country or continent, it's tough for most police departments. Again, maybe the New York City Police Department (NYPD) is the exception, but it's difficult for most police departments to battle that as effectively as we would like to. Because there's so much of this going on, so many fraud type cases, the FBI has to prioritize what they can do and what they can't do. So, there are victims of crime in your community that don't get the service you'd like to give them and that's frustrating.

MB & MB: I take it cyber-crime is also a large aspect of this?

JTM: Yes, absolutely.

MB & MB: Can you comment on the role of local police concerning immigration enforcement?

JTM: The immigration issue has been a thorny issue for local police for a long time. I remember in 1981 I got dispatched to a call for a woman who was the victim of an indecent exposure. She was walking to the bus stop early in the morning, before 7 a.m. and some guy exposes himself to her. She calls, gives me a description and I actually catch the guy. This is an individual who didn't speak English, and as it turns out, was undocumented, he was not in the United States legally. I charged him with indecent exposure. While the case was pending in court, I contacted immigration and said, "I've arrested this guy for indecent exposure, I think he's dangerous and here's the court date, so if you're interested in deporting the guy here he is." They asked, "Is this a misdemeanor or a felony?" and, upon learning it was a misdemeanor, said we're not interested and that was the end of the conversation. Now, this was 1981 and I sort of shrugged it off and said that's the way things are. Fast forward to today. There's so many folks, certainly in urban jurisdictions like mine, that are here in the US undocumented. If these folks live in fear of the police and they are victims of crime, but they never report the crimes because they are worried about the police, this makes a community less safe. Unreported crime makes a community less safe. Any victim of crime deserves police service. Any resident of your jurisdiction has a right to have good police service. Just because they're not a citizen or they're undocumented does not mean that they don't deserve police service; they do. And if you're going to provide that service, you're going to provide that service. You can't have any group of folks in your community to whom you say, "everybody else deserves a service but if we contact you we are working on getting you deported out of the country." That's not our job. Frankly, I've got enough to do without taking on immigration enforcement as well. This is right for my jurisdiction—it has the support of the community it has the support of elected officials and I think it's the right thing for my police department. Because of the number of undocumented residents we have in our community, we have to develop a relationship with them. This may not be right for every single community in the United States. I think that's why local communities need to make their own decisions. I don't' judge any community if they decide they want to be a part of the 287G program (287 g is the section of the U.S. Code which authorizes local police to enforce federal immigration law subject to certain certification and training requirements) and they want to make their officers do immigration investigations and that sort of thing. It may be right for their community. But if you police a community that has a lot of undocumented residents, you have got to be very judicious about your involvement in immigration enforcement.

MB & MB: In your role as the head of the Major Cities Chiefs, are there any particular issues that come to mind, any special issues, any advice for other police leaders?

JTM: The Major Cities Chiefs consists of the largest 68 police departments in the US, the largest police departments in Canada, and we've actually started adding a couple in the United Kingdom, as well. The value of Major Cities Chiefs organization is we're able to talk about problems that are shared by large police departments, we're able to learn from each other's experiences. One of the things we really focus on is legislative issues. And since Ferguson,* there's been a real blowback on police in a lot of ways, particularly the militarization issue and the seized asset issue. Many police departments are not involved in militarization. People are asking, "Why on earth do the police need armored vehicles and this and that?" There is a need for that and it's how you use them, making sure you use them appropriately. We are trying to make sure that Congress and their legislation doesn't react so harshly that it impairs us from doing our job. We try to play a role in terms of influencing public policy for the benefit of public safety. For most of it, it's just the shared experience. We have 3 conferences a year, we sit around a table, and somebody says, "you know the first transgender officer I had in the locker room, these were the issues we dealt with, here's what we did." So everybody learns from that experience; and there's always something. There's a lot of things post 9/11, post Rodney King,† post Ferguson that are really changing policing. We're all still learning lessons from Ferguson.

---

* Ferguson refers to the shooting of Michael Brown, an unarmed 16 year old African-American teenager by Ferguson Police Office Darren Wilson in Ferguson, Missouri, on August 9, 2014. Witness accounts of the shooting varied and weeks of protests ensued, resulting in a heightened local, county, and state police presence supplemented by the Missouri National Guard. Following the Grand Jury's decision not to indict Officer Wilson for Michael Brown's murder in late November, 2014, rioting, looting, and arson followed. A U.S. Department of Justice report issued in March, 2015 found extensive evidence of constitutional violations in Ferguson, Missouri, and mandated major changes in the criminal justice system. However, it found insufficient evidence to charge Officer Darren Wilson with civil rights violations.

† Rodney King was beaten by three Los Angeles Police Officers and a supervisor following a March, 1991 high speed chase. The incident was captured on video-tape and received international coverage. Extensive rioting and looting followed the officers and supervisor subsequent acquitted on state criminal charges in March, 1992, although two were later convicted of federal criminal civil rights violations arising out of the incident. Rodney King was also awarded 3.8 million dollars in compensatory damages from the City of Los Angeles as a result of his beating.

Democratic Policing

MB & MB: What do you see as the key elements of democratic policing and does maintaining law and order mean that policing is involved in maintaining the existing social order and power structures or can it allow serious protest against the government and laws and powerful elites?

JTM: I think it has to allow protest. It's in the Constitution that people can have the right to protest and free speech, and there have been enough decisions out of the Supreme Court that we know what that looks like. There are some limitations to those rights. We know what those limitations are. In fact, people do have the right to say what they want about the government and other folks. Last week in Baltimore (see previous discussion), our brief to our officers was that the protestors have the right to protest, it is their Constitutional right and you need to protect the Constitutional right of allowing people to engage in their free speech and engage in lawful protest. For us, we need to make sure our cops know when that crosses the line into criminal behavior, into unlawful activity. And you've got to have a strategy for dealing with that in a way that is fair, consistent, and lawful; you don't want to overact. One of the greatest things that we've done, and we've been doing it for a long time, but it wasn't done back in the 60s when some of the ugliest protests and police responses occurred, is we talk to the group who is planning the protest and ask, "what would you like to do, where do you want to go, do you want to be arrested?" We have all those conversations ahead of time and it certainly makes it go smoothly. But cops need to understand that this is a Constitutional right and training officers and making sure they know that it is their responsibility to protect that right, generally makes for a better event.

MB & MB: Can the police resist demands from the government to crack down on opposition and protest?

JTM: They have to. You have to have those conversations ahead of time with the elected officials, with your bosses, to make sure we're all on the same wavelength. I met with my executive just a few days ago, after the first 3 days that we were in Baltimore, to say, if this should ever happen here, let me tell you what we would do and how we would do it, to make sure he and I were on the same wavelength. You have got to be on the same wavelength; you do not want ever to have a mayor or an executive tell the chief, do this do that, if it's something that is not lawful and not appropriate in terms of a response to a protest. In this day and age, I don't know that too many mayors would risk their reputation by asking the police to do anything but handle these protests the right way.

MB & MB: Earlier you talked about politics and the police and civilian control of policing in the tradition of Sir Robert Peel. Your tenure as police chief is probably among the longest; what is the appropriate place for politics and elected officials as opposed to the independence of the police?

JTM: Elected officials are elected by the people and to some degree they may have sought election because they want to do things a certain way. I tell my colleagues, "as long as something is not illegal, immoral, or unethical, you got to do what your boss tells you to do." If a mayor gets elected and says, "I'm going to make a police oversight board," and the police chief says, "no, I don't think that's a good idea, you shouldn't do it," they can have that discussion privately between the two of them. Ultimately, if the mayor decides they're going to have a police oversight board, the Police Chief has to go on with it. You either quit or you go with it, because it's not immoral, it's not illegal, and it's not unethical. You have to abide by what your boss tells you to do. Politically, the boss of a police chief is the mayor, county executive, or the chief elected official. What's interesting are the sheriffs, especially the elected sheriffs. They are in a different position. They don't have to take orders from anyone, but they have to worry about getting re-elected by the public so they certainly do need to worry about what the public thinks of them.

You think about the case in New Jersey where the governor's office asked or created a traffic jam where people cross the bridge into New York (in 2013 the office of Governor Chris Christe of New Jersey allegedly created a traffic jam for vehicles entering New Jersey from New York via the George Washington Bridge in retaliation against a local elected official who did not support his successful bid for Governor). If they would have asked the state police or the state troopers and said, "Hey, we want you to do this," the head of state police would say, "absolutely not." But what would happen if the governor had said, "either do it or you're out of a job"? It's interesting. I was appointed by the previous county executive, 11 years ago. When the current county executive first ran for office, he visited me and we spent about an hour together before the election. He said, "If I'm elected, I'd like you to stay on as police chief," and I said, "Thank you, I'd like to stay on." He and I talked. We both needed to feel some level of comfort that we shared the philosophy of how police service ought to be delivered. I have worked for this man for 8 years now and not once has he ever told me how to do my job. We've talked about some very challenging issues, but we talk. I hear what his expectations are and it's my job to operationalize those expectations in terms of running the police department. Again, unless someone tells you to do something illegal, immoral, or unethical, then politics should have nothing to do with it; you do the right thing.

MB & MB: Thinking about the Zero Tolerance Policy in New York, what if your executive wants zero tolerance and you as police chief have got a community policing philosophy? How do you balance the two?

JTM: That's when you hope you have a good enough relationship to say, "zero tolerance is basically declaring war on a community. It is not going to give us the result we want. Here is a better way to accomplish that." If you look at what happened 5–10 years before a Zero Tolerance Policy is introduced and you find nobody was doing anything. It's as if we were just ignoring problems forever and now it's gotten so bad that we have to introduce zero tolerance. There's a middle ground here and the community needs to know what to expect from the police. You want people to believe that the police are treating people fairly, but if you go from ignoring problems to suddenly zero tolerance, the community is not going to think you're being fair and certainly not consistent. Having a discussion and explaining, "Here's a better way to get this done, mayor," is the direction you need to go. Here's the problem, you've got some police chiefs that are brand new, they don't have the experience and they say, "if the mayor is telling me to do this I guess I got to do this." I've got to tell you, after 17 years of being a police chief I can have that conversation with my executive and he's got enough trust and confidence in me to say, "I trust you, here's the result I want, I trust you, Chief, to get it." That's the best way to achieve the desired result. I'm always happy to listen what my boss wants and what my boss wants the result to be. Let me figure out the best way to get there. For more on zero tolerance, aggressive quality life enforcement, and Compstat related policing strategies, see Eterno and Silverman (2010) and McDonald (2001).

Looking Ahead

MB & MB: What do you see as the greatest problems facing the police at this time and what are the greatest opportunities?

JTM: Right now it's all about the impact of Ferguson, issues that have been around forever. Use of force, use of deadly force. The fact is that back when all of us went to the police academy, it was, "here, you can use deadly force if your life or the life of someone else is in danger; if you feel you're in danger for your life you can use it." But did they say, "Well let me explain to you how you might avoid getting into a situation where you would use deadly force"? It might be that when you get that call for a man with a knife to his throat in his apartment that you don't go rushing into the apartment and put yourself into a confrontation and say, "well I got in there, the guy came at me with a knife, so I just shot him." OK, well why did you rush in there to begin with? There's nobody else in the apartment? Why didn't you pull back, think about how else could we handle this? De-escalation of force is now as big a part of the training as anything else. Post Ferguson, the militarization—we need automatic weapons, we need armored vehicles. In Baltimore, we had our armored vehicle up there. You know when a protestor had a seizure right outside by the CVS drug store, we actually came back with the armored vehicle, went out in the middle of the protest, got the person who had the seizure, brought them into the vehicle, and brought them out so Fire and Rescue could get to them. Fire and Rescue would never have gone out into that protest, that person would have just laid there. But we went, rescued him, and brought him back. There's a reason to have these vehicles, but you have got to use them for the right reasons, not like Ferguson, oh my, the Ferguson police! The picture of the Ferguson police officer who claims that he was just using the scope of the rifle to zoom in on what was going on. Well don't you have a pair of binoculars? So, all of these post-Ferguson issues come down to trust in the police department and accountability. People have less tolerance and less faith in the police today and a lot of it is because everyone has a phone camera. Everywhere we go, that's what we're getting. Often times police work, even good police work, is very ugly. And so we're having to deal with those ugly images and bad police work is even uglier. When that's captured on film—we all saw the video from North Charleston! (the police shooting of Walter Scott in the back, 2015). That was criminal, absolutely criminal, and you watch the guy pick up the Taser and kick it over next to the man he shot, kick it over next to his body (to plant the Taser next to the victim in an attempt to justify the shooting). I mean, that makes you sick to your stomach. You know what the problem is? The public thinks, "oh well, that goes on all the time." Well no it doesn't go on all the time, but unfortunately it does go on sometimes and that's what we're fighting against.

MB & MB: So the opportunity is to win hearts and minds?

JTM: Yes definitely. That's what we got to do. The first thing you do is put the cameras on officers. You know what happens 10 years from now? People have 10 years' worth of camera data and they go, "you know cops, they have a tough job. If that'd been me I would have shot that guy. If that'd been me, I'd of done this. The cops have a tough job and they're actually doing a pretty good job." The pendulum swings right back. Most probably think that now; but there's a minority that think that everything we do is wrong. I think there's even some people that never even thought about it that are seeing some of these videos. Maybe it's worse than I thought, but believe me it is not, the police do much better than most people realize.

Conclusion

Chief J. Thomas Manger's 38 years of service in law enforcement, 17 of which were as a chief of police, first in Fairfax County, Virginia, and presently in Montgomery County, Maryland, afford him extraordinary firsthand experience of the challenges encountered by law enforcement and changes in the profession over the past four decades. His keen insight into these challenges and changes, and willingness to share his thoughts on a wide variety of critical issues facing law enforcement provide readers a unique opportunity to understand these issues from the perspective of an experienced law enforcement leader. His answers to interview questions shed light on issues of long-standing interest to the academia and the profession, as well as critical issues facing American policing today.

References

Berlin, M. M. 2012. The evolution, decline and nascent transformation of community policing in the United States: 1980–2010. In: Palmer, D., Berlin, M. M., and Das, D. K. (eds.). *The Global Environment of Policing* (pp. 27–48). Boca Raton, FL: CRC Press Taylor & Francis Group.

Eterno, J. and Silverman, E. 2010. The trouble with Compstat: Pressure on NYPD commanders endangered the integrity of crime stats. [Electronic version]. *New York Daily News*, February, 15.

McDonald, P. 2001. COP. COMPSTAT, and the new professionalism mutual support or counterproductivity. In: Dunham, R. G. and Alpert, G. P. (eds.). *Critical Issues in Policing: Contemporary Readings*, 4th ed. Prospect Heights, IL: Waveland Press.

Oliver, W. M. 2004. *Community-Oriented Policing: A Systemic Approach to Policing*, 3rd ed. Upper Saddle River, NJ: Pearson Prentice Hall.

U.S. Census Bureau. 2014. *State & County Quickfacts: Montgomery County, Maryland*. Retrieved August 5, 2016 from http://www.census.gov/quickfacts/table/PST045215/24031.

Ng Joo Hee, Commissioner of Police, Singapore

13

INTERVIEWED BY SUSAN SIM

Contents

Introduction

The Singapore Police Force (SPF) is the Republic's main law enforcement agency tasked with fighting crime and maintaining order; there are separate agencies dealing with illicit drugs, counterterrorism, and corruption. Policing is largely structured around six land divisions, collectively responsible for the safety and security of 5.47 million people, of which 80.4% live in apartment blocks built by a government agency known widely by its acronym "the HDB" (Housing and Development Board), 13.5% in private condominiums and 5.8% in landed properties.* Each land division has about 1,000 uniformed police officers; the largest serves more than 1.4 million residents and the smallest, about 500,000.

Major crimes, complex commercial crimes, cybercrimes, and organized crime are handled by the Criminal Investigation Department (CID), Commercial Affairs Department, and Police Intelligence Department. Other operational units handle specialist functions—Traffic Police, Public Transport Security Command, Police Coast Guard, Airport Police, Special Operations Command, and Security Command. Manpower, finance, logistics, planning, and public affairs are centralized in Police Headquarters. An Internal Affairs Office enforces discipline and investigates public complaints. There is also a state-of-the-art Police Academy with a specialist School of Criminal Investigation that is open to all branches of the government with law enforcement functions.

At the apex of the 15,000-strong force is the Commissioner of Police, who is assisted by three Deputy Commissioners—for Investigations and Intelligence, Policy, and Operations. Of the 13,500 uniformed officers, 8,600 are regulars and 4,900 national service conscripts who serve 2-year rotations. They are joined in patrols by some 1,200 Volunteer Special Constabulary officers who work at least 16 hours a month. In addition, a total of 24,000 police national service reservists (known as Police National Servicemen) report for duty several times a year.

The interview took place on the eve of Ng Joo Hee's retirement from the Singapore Police Force. He was happy to discuss the changes he had initiated as police chief and although not all his plans had been implemented yet, he felt it was time for him to move on and start a new career running PUB, Singapore's national water agency. Ng chose the Home Team Clubhouse in Balestier for the interview to showcase the array of social and sports facilities available to the national service conscripts and reservists serving in the police and civil defense forces, and their families.

Career

Ng Joo Hee was the Commissioner of the Singapore Police Force for five years from 2010 to 2015. A career police officer for almost 30 years, he started out as a criminal investigator before being posted to the Internal Security Department, where he was involved in counter-espionage work. In 1992–1993, he served as a police monitor with the UN peacekeeping mission in Cambodia. On his return, he was tasked to establish and then lead the

---

* Source: Department of Statistics, Singapore, 30 June 2015, http://www.singstat.gov.sg/statistics/latest-data#20.

Special Tactics and Rescue (STAR) Unit, the Singapore Police's elite hostage-rescue outfit. He was given his first land division to command in 2001, before moving to the Criminal Investigation Department as its Deputy Director. He then took on the job of running the Police Intelligence Department. Ng retired from the police in January 2015.

As the recipient of an undergraduate scholarship from the Singapore Police Force to study at Oxford University in the United Kingdom, it was a foregone conclusion that Ng would join the force upon graduating in 1988. But, as a young man, he never dreamed of becoming the police commissioner.

> *NJH:* It was not my youthful ambition to be a police officer. But a place in Oxford changed all of that because my family was poor and I had no money to go. The police came along and paid for my Oxford education. In exchange, I had to do eight years on my return. I liked it, turned out to be a decent police officer and stayed on. That was 29 and a half years ago, and with the last five as Commissioner.

Not only was Ng a "decent police officer," but he was also recruited by the Public Service Commission to join the elite Administrative Service and be groomed for top leadership positions in the Singapore public service. He could have moved to a civilian post in any government department, as several other police scholars did. However, apart from a two-year stint on a policy desk at the Ministry of Trade and Industry, he stayed in the force, where his policing career was, as he often said, a meaningful and "outstanding adventure."

> *NJH:* You don't want to leave as it is just so interesting. One reason is the diverse nature of the work. I had been an investigator, a spy catcher, a UN peacekeeper, a SWAT team leader, a CID detective, and an agent handler. It is just so exciting. You don't know what is going to happen next. And you actually get to help people in this job. The other reason is the officers. Along the way, I started to build strong connections with the men and women who looked up to me for leadership. These are the two main things that made me come to work every day. Of course, we must not forget the bonding that we have as a force and the mission that we share. ... I felt that my work was meaningful as we work to make Singapore safer.

In his 18th year with the force, Ng was offered command of the prison service, which like the police force is one of the Home Team departments under the Ministry of Home Affairs. Inter-agency transfers are common in the Singapore civil service, especially for Administrative Service officers, and Ng's predecessor as Commissioner of Prisons was also a police officer. Ng did not, however, have any correctional experience or training. He was also not told if he would be returning to the police. Nonetheless, he accepted the position and took lessons from the experience.

> NJH: I ran the prison service for a couple of years. It was an eye opener for me. I have always said it is far easier to catch them than to keep them. In policing, we are only interested in the crime and solving the crime. We don't care that much about the individual. But in corrections, it is all about the individual and not the crime. The individual's problem becomes the corrections service's problem. That is almost impossibly difficult work. So I am glad that I am back in policing, with one of the best police forces in the world.

Changes Experienced

A Five-Word Mission

When Ng returned to the police as the Commissioner in 2010, he realized that his officers were not as clear about their mission objectives as he felt desirable. Much of the ambiguity had to do with the strategic shift to community policing that the police had embarked on in 1983. Faced with rising crime rates through the 1970s and the early 1980s, policy makers decided a radical change in policing strategy was required—from one that was reactive, to one that mobilized the community to work with the police to prevent crime. Following the Japanese Koban system, the Singapore Police opened Neighbourhood Police Posts (NPPs) within housing estates, where officers conducted foot and bicycle patrols as well as house visits. The strategy appeared to work and crime rates halved from 1,310 per 100,000 population in 1984 to 650 in 2010 (Sim, 2011).

In the late 1990s, however, the smaller NPPs were merged into larger Neighbourhood Police Centres (NPCs) and officers went back to policing in patrol cars and responding to emergency calls. But police doctrine still required officers to render service to the public, to cultivate the image of the police as friends. The SPF mission statement informed officers that their goal was to protect life and property, as well as to fight crime. Yet, after the discovery of a terrorist network in Singapore with regional ambitions at the end of 2001, and the spread of SARS in 2003, much of the police resources were devoted to battling terrorist threats and pandemics (Khoo, 2003).

The multiplicity of roles led to what Ng considered a false dichotomy between "core, non-core jobs, service versus operations." Many patrol officers did not want to take reports or attend to noise complaints because these were service jobs whereas operations meant crime detection and making arrests. But the reality was that "all these non-core service jobs are part of police operations and actually contribute to a safer Singapore." He wanted "to make Singapore the safest place in the world" and the police needed to do more, not less, to achieve this vision.

> *NJH:* I spent a lot of time trying to get clarity on the mission and we got it down to five words: Prevent, Deter, and Detect Crime. And these words sum up our mission. They also point to Peel's Principles. Policing is all about crime. I think with a crystal clear mission, it is easier for our officers. Everything that they do now, they think about the mission first. I think achieving mission clarity is probably the most important thing that I did for the force. If you think this mission is a good one, then it must drive all of our activities. So you see, we became a lot clearer about what prevention is, and started to invest a lot into preventing crime. One of the problems is that in the past the police were too reactive. We respond only when someone has met harm. Most of our interactions were with victims of crime. We have very few conversations with members of the public when crime hadn't happened. I wanted to change that, to move to a situation where most of our interactions are before a crime has occurred. That is the inspiration for our COPS programme. This is the new Community Policing System where we now put aside manpower which do not respond to 999 (emergency) calls. It is a big investment as we have to put aside manpower just to do this. COPS officers are not despatched to emergency calls. Of course, if they see a crime happening in front of them, they will act. But as a rule, they are not a response force. They walk a beat and their duty is to talk to people they meet. It is all about talking to people before crime happens. These officers may be on bicycles or on foot. To appear friendlier, they wear short trousers and polo t-shirts, but are nevertheless still armed. By and by, they become a fixture in the community and a common sight. Local residents start to recognize them, and our officers start to build a bond and a trust with the surrounding community. Very soon, they start to hear and are the first to be told of questionable goings-on in the neighbourhood, again before something bad happens. I believe this is true community policing.

COPS, the new policing system, was rolled out in May 2012. The official rationale was "to keep pace with the changing operating environment and to meet the shifting safety and security needs of our community." At a time when electronic surveillance—the ubiquitous CCTV—has never been more acceptable to the public, the labor-intensive investment represented by COPS would appear to be paradoxical for a force with limited manpower and facing very low crime rates. Indeed, Singapore's crime rate has been falling consistently below 1,500 per 100,000 population since 1999, and at 555 in 2013, was at its lowest in three decades (SPF, 2013).

Yet it is precisely because of manpower constraints and the changing nature of crime—the rising number of cybercrime cases caused the overall crime rate to rise by 7.4% in 2014—that Ng felt an imperative to make sure his officers truly understood the needs of the people they looked after, and could accordingly equip these citizens with the tools to help the police prevent, deter, and detect crime.

> *NJH:* We have no issues with budget. Not just for the police but for govern-
> ment in general, budget is a secondary concern. The lack of manpower is the
> primary concern. So we have to go back to the old mantra—the community.
> The community must protect itself. We cannot protect Singapore by ourselves.
> We need members of a community to get together and to look after their own
> properties, their own safety, and then join together with their neighbours and
> fellows to safeguard their own immediate neighbourhood and surroundings.
> And then work hand-in-hand with the police to deter and try to make offending
> impossible. Of course, this is easier said than done. For this to work, the hardest
> bit is that people must trust the police. Trust in the police is the secret formula
> for successful community policing. Some of the ideas that led to COPS were
> ground-up, coming from the NPCs as they went after the Ah Longs (unlicensed
> money lenders). Illegal and heavy-handed debt collectors were public nuisance
> number one. When I took over as Commissioner, we were hitting the roof in Ah
> Long arrests. I swore to bring the situation under control and we eventually did.
> I put great pressure on all of our ground units to fight this scourge at the com-
> munity and street level, and challenged them to think of new ways. Many of the
> ideas that came to become COPS came out of our fight against the Ah Longs.

From Fighting Public Nuisance No. 1 to Changing the Game

For years, the Ah Longs or unlicensed money lenders were not only criminal syndicates but also a serious public nuisance in Singapore because their
intimidation of debtors were played out publicly. Loan sharks would typically harass debtors who fall behind on their repayments by sending thugs to
scrawl threatening messages on their front doors or along corridors in public
apartment blocks, alarming not just their victims but their neighbours too.
Cases of loan shark harassment reached a peak in 2009, shortly before Ng
took over as Commissioner of Police. By the end of 2013, the number of cases
had been more than halved (SPF, 2013).

One idea that worked well in this ground war on Ah Longs was the use
of CCTVs to capture the images of the men responsible for defacing property
and threatening debtors. From that grew the Police Camera or PolCam project in public housing estates (generally referred to as HDB flats), which Ng
extended into an island-wide network.

> *NJH:* We have wired up the country. Every HDB apartment block has eight to
> ten cameras. We monitor all ingress and egress, every lift landing and stair-
> case landing. So together with COPS, I think this is a game changer.

He was not worried about privacy issues and foresaw that the government
would have to provide incentives to encourage the private sector to install
CCTVs as well as legislate minimum resolution standards for the cameras.

NJH: We only look at public areas. We will not put up cameras unless residents and the local Town Council agree. Our experience has been that they want it and they want it up fast. We use the cameras for deterrence and for detection. When a crime does take place, we have a better chance of solving it and catching the perpetrator. Although we retain the capability to proactively monitor the cameras if we wanted to, it is obviously impossible to watch a hundred thousand cameras. But if we wanted to, we can, and sometimes we do for selected hotspots. Moving forward, I think the Ministry (of Home Affairs) will have to legislate. We have to make it the law that private buildings have to share footage with us. We will need to create a scheme to incentivize building owners to wire up. That means, we may co-pay or share the costs for installing cameras in buildings, in return for images getting piped to us. There should always be a live link. Whether we watch it or not, we keep it on recording mode. We took the initiative to write a CCTV standard by looking at best practices in the rest of the world. Together with other legislation, we intend to enforce these standards. When public infrastructure is getting built, we tell the owners to stick to our standards. Yes, one way to counter the lack of manpower is to leverage on technology. So CCTV is one technology that we are leaning heavily on.

Prepared for Terrorist Attacks but not Riots

The threat of terrorist attacks has also led to organizational changes in the force as well as changes in the equipment provided to officers and their training. Since the Internal Security Department (ISD) foiled a terrorist network intent on setting off seven truck bombs in Singapore in late 2001, terrorism has been defined as the biggest security threat to Singapore. Ng's revised mission statement therefore states clearly: "Crime in SPF's context include terrorism and public disorder."

NJH: The war on terror has a big impact on us, but that was already so even before I became the Commissioner. The biggest security threat to Singapore is still the terrorist threat. The police are not directly involved in pre-empting a terrorist attack. That is ISD's job, but it is our responsibility to harden the likely targets and we have to work with the community on this. The police also have to manage the aftermath of a successful attack. So post-incident investigation and bringing terrorists to justice are our responsibilities. We have invested a lot into counter-terrorism. You will sometimes see our SOC (Special Ops Command) troopers on Orchard Road (Singapore's famous shopping street). We created a new unit, TRANSCOM, to police the Underground (rail network). That was a direct reaction to the terrorist threat, because of what had happened in London, and also something we had copied from the NYPD. The Mumbai attacks also led us to train every one of our patrol men on how to deal with the initial moments of a swarm attack.

Ng, however, ruled out giving his officers heavier weaponry. The experience of small police forces in the US equipped with military weapons showed they tended to "go overboard" and be too aggressive, he said. He would rather provide his patrol officers with the right protection, although what was right for dealing with a terrorist attack might not work in a street riot, he conceded. The first major riot in 40 years occurred in Singapore in December 2013 when 400 foreign workers in Little India attacked first responders after an Indian national was killed in a vehicle accident. Police and emergency vehicles were overturned and five were torched. Dozens of officers suffered minor injuries from projectiles thrown at them, but there were no fatalities apart from the accident victim. More than 50 people were arrested when the Special Operations Command troops, which are specially trained in quelling riots, arrived on the scene, and began dispersing the mob.

> *NJH:* The Mumbai attacks had set the target for us. We have to defend our-selves against a similar swarm attack. … We gave the patrol officers the required training and the right equipment, especially ballistic protection. Every one of our patrol officers know how to deal with the initial moments of an armed swarm attack, but they were not trained to fight riots. When the Little India riot broke out, patrol officers first to the scene possessed ballistic shields, not riot shields. They were trained to contain swarming terrorists, not rioters throwing rocks and glass bottles. …Should they open fire on rioters who were threatening to torch their patrol cars? I will not risk the safety of my officers for the purpose of defending a burning squad car. We can always buy a new one. I am glad that we used the correct level of force at the riot. … No one got seriously hurt. It was over in two hours. The only damage was to a few police vehicles. I bet you many other police chiefs would be happy to take this riot, any time.

Personal Policing Philosophy

Ng identified closely with Peel's nine principles of policing.

> *NJH:* I think they make for a very good police force. The Anglophone coun-tries have retained the principles. The SPF does not consciously follow the Peelian Principles one by one. But if you look at us as a whole, you will find that we are totally in compliance with what Peel had said that an ideal police force should be. We are in accordance with every one of his principles. The Peelian Principles can be a good checklist for us, and I think we are probably the force that keeps closest to them.

COPS, as he noted, goes back to Peel's Principles, particularly #7: "Police, at all times, should maintain a relationship with the public that gives reality to the historic tradition that the police are the public and the public are the police …."

Ng also believed that the police force should be judged not just by how low it can keep crime rates, but also by the content of its character, and set out to articulate what he called its corporate DNA, the essence of the SPF brand.

Discovering the Police DNA

In his second year as Commissioner, in a somewhat controversial move, he issued a $1 million [US$ 740,000] contract to a branding consultancy to conduct public surveys and run focus group discussions within the force. He positioned the exercise as a rebranding for recruitment purposes.

> *NJH:* We have to encourage people who never thought of policing as a career to join us. In the past, we were able to depend on volunteers. Now we have to actively persuade people who never thought of the police or that they would make a good police officer. Therefore, we have to tell the story of what a police officer does; what our DNA is and what our mission is. That is the reason why we did this rebranding. ... The rebranding helped to crystallize our DNA. We are now able to articulate this DNA in a very clear way to the public. People mostly think of a brand as visuals. There will be some visuals, but the important thing about this branding exercise is that we are now very clear, what the SPF DNA is. It is five things:
>
> > First, we do real work that matters. Not everyone can say that what they do every day affects other people's lives. We can.
> > Number two, we serve a high purpose. Again, not many professions can say this. But, indeed, in the SPF we do serve a high purpose.
> > Number three, we are leaders in the community. Every police officer is a leader in the community that he or she protects.
> > Number four, we value every contribution of our officers. We thank every officer for his or her effort, and reward handsomely those who excel and exceed expectations.
> > Number five, we equip our officers to succeed. We give everyone the kind of training and development that will let him be the best police officer he or she can be. And even when our officers decide to leave us, their experience in the police makes them better people. It makes them better employees and more sought after.

So, this is the police DNA and we want aspiring police officers to join up because of these things. We have never told it to the public quite like this before.

Ng also wanted his officers to uphold a set of values, which he distilled into Courage, Loyalty, Integrity, Fairness, or CLIF in short. To dramatize these as living values, he decided to work with a local TV channel to make a police serial.

> *NJH:* No one can argue about these values. So let's put the values front and center. Everybody must live the values. Then I said, "OK, let's make a Channel

8 serial based on our values—CLIF." It turned out to be the most successful Channel 8 serial ever.

With average viewership of almost one million per episode, two further seasons of the police procedural were commissioned by the TV station after the first ended in 2011.

> NJH: CLIF, being on TV, is made for the general public, of course. But, it is also for our internal public. It is for the ten thousand police officers and their families. And, oh how they loved it! Let me tell you a story. A member of the public watched CLIF, and then decided to surrender himself to the police. After the show, he walked into a police station and confessed his crime. Later, in prison, he wrote a letter to thank us as he felt that we had helped to lift a heavy burden off his shoulders. You see, he had been stealing money at his workplace. He was guilt-ridden but didn't have the courage to own up. Watching CLIF made him come clean.

Ng also had another goal in mind for the TV series—to meet a gender diversity target he had set.

> NJH: One of the things about CLIF was its heavy focus on female officers. The force is seriously short of women. We are barely 15% women. My target is 30%. Women are hard to recruit because the typical Singaporean girl never thinks of herself as a police officer. They think that only mannish women become policewomen. For our advertising now, I find the prettiest and most attractive women officers we have and make them the main features.

Performance is, however, the only consideration in promotion. Two of the top 10 most highly ranked police officers serving in the SPF in 2015 are women, and they run the Airport Police Command and the Police Intelligence Department.

Problems and Successes Experienced

"2013 was a challenging year for the Police," Ng wrote in his Commissioner's Report for the SPF Annual Report for 2013:

> "Corruption trials, protesting Malaysian voters, a police officer accused of double-murder, the Shane Todd inquest,* international football match-fixing,

---

* Shane Todd was an American who was found dead in his apartment in Singapore in June 2012. His family disputed the police finding that he had committed suicide and alleged in the international media that the SPF had failed to properly investigate his death. A Coroner's Inquiry in 2013 ruled that there was no foul play involved in his death.

computer hacking, a kidnapping, a headless corpse, multiple breaches of security at Woodlands Checkpoint, and unrestrained rioting by foreigners on Singaporean streets. Indeed, it has been a turbulent and tumultuous year for us. Certainly, I cannot think of a year, in recent memory, that was more eventful than the one that has just passed." (SPF, 2013)

The Little India riot towards the end of 2013 continued to reverberate through 2014 when a Commission of Inquiry (COI) was convened to look into the causes of the violence and to study the police response. Police leaders were publicly grilled by a panel that included a former police commissioner. He had harsh words for the ground commander, but praised individual officers who pushed back rioters.

Ng, who believed his officers used the appropriate level of force against the mob, had two challenges: keeping morale high and his officers focused on their mission, and ensuring the "rock-solid trust with the communities that we police" was not undermined.

He went back to the principles by which the force built trust with the public:

NJH: First is by being honest. The force must be absolutely honest. We have no toleration for corruption or for any form of abuse. Then, we have to be totally competent. We have to be a good police force which is full of good people. We have to have good training. Our officers need to know what they are doing and what their policing mission is. And then, every one of us has to live our police values.

Good and Bad News Go Out on Facebook

It also meant continuing to embrace transparency, including using social media to highlight the force's zero-tolerance for corruption and incompetence, Ng said.

NJH: We don't cover up bad news. In fact, these days we are the first to go out on bad news, even before the public knows about it. It is not just the police that does this, but also this government. The Singapore government is brutally honest. You can't hide things. If you don't tell first, people will find out eventually, and usually very quickly. If we have messed up, we apologize, suck it up, and move on. In many ways, social media is the biggest check on us and keeps us honest. We are actually quite successful (on social media) for a police force. Our Facebook page has more than half a million friends. We are the biggest Facebook page for the public sector (in Singapore) because we put up information that is interesting and which people find useful. We actively use our Facebook page to prevent and to solve crime. Now, we don't just have a central police Facebook page but one for every NPC. So, police Facebook pages have a more local focus and you can say that it is part of the COPS initiative. Our COPS officers diligently put up local information on their pages. We regularly put up information and photos of suspected persons and ask for public help to keep an eye out for them. It has been very successful, and we have made many arrests and solved numerous crimes that way. There are many times when we would put out statements only on social media and then direct traditional media to them. We are finding that social media can be a powerful tool for crime fighting.

Be Polite, You are Being Recorded

Ng also decided to put cameras on his officers.

NJH: I am personally convinced that the body-worn camera is a powerful technology and a game changer. Not because we can record conversations but because when an officer wears a camera, he becomes a walking sensor. We will be able to see what he sees, hear what he hears, and, maybe someday, even smell what he smells. So, an officer with a camera on him is a walking sensor and that is truly powerful. It has always been the problem that we have men on the ground, and we have limited feel of what they are sensing and little control over what they are doing. We have no feel of what the officers are experiencing. And we are really only relying on verbal communications over the radio.

A pilot project was started in 2014 with patrol officers from several NPCs issued Body-Worn Cameras. There was a notable improvement in civility in public interactions, he noted.

NJH: The pilot scheme proves all that the research has told us. First, civility improves all round, civility of police officers and of the public. The cameras are worn plainly and openly. There is no secret recording. Even if the member of public does not notice the camera, my officer will point it out and tell him that their interaction is being recorded. If a person doesn't want to be on camera, our officer is fully empowered to turn it off. If it is a minor or a vulnerable person, he will turn it off as a rule. Body cameras I think will be another game changer. During the (Little India) riot, if every officer and every vehicle had cameras fitted, radio communications can be down and it wouldn't have been a big problem as we would still be able to see. With cameras, at Central Control, we can see and we can hear. And so, we can command. … Now if all of our officers became walking sensors, we conceivably can have full command.

During the riot, as more patrol officers flooded into the area, the overburdened communications system broke down. Ground commanders could not make sense of the situation, Ng said, and could not re-deploy officers quickly, leaving some stranded in the chaos. Recordings of incidents as they unfolded would also facilitate training.

NJH: Wearing cameras leads to training improvements because you actually get to see what had transpired in a real life transaction in terms of what went right and what had gone wrong. This knowledge fits directly into training. In the past, you depended on people sitting in a circle after an incident, doing an After-Action Review (AAR) and trying to figure out what went wrong. Unfortunately, every personal bias and interpretation then comes into play. With camera footage, there is no argument. So, complaints will also come down. These are the positives of body-worn cameras. Of course, officers will initially complain, saying that they feel very uncomfortable, that the cameras invade their privacy, and that their bosses are always looking over their shoulders. But eventually, they get used to the cameras and even forget that they are wearing them.

All NPC officers have since been issued body-worn cameras when on patrol.

Ng also believed that judicious use of big data technology can provide the police with better sense-making and contribute to crime prevention.

NJH: This sense-making is a new technology. Our new Police Command and Control Centre is like NASA now. There, they are now not just receiving and dispatching 999 calls, but also making sense. With new software and new information getting pumped in from cameras and other sensors on the ground, we can now make better sense (of developing situations). We put intelligence analysts in the 24/7 control center. We have brought our databases together, allowing our analysts to screen against all of the data and information that we possess. We can push information to all of our officers instantly. Although the technology is still not perfect, it is very powerful.

And again, Ng was not worried about complaints from privacy advocates.

NJH: This is Singapore and we have been fortunate. There is great public trust in the police and that is why we can do all these things. The Singaporean public is welcoming of these things.

A Football Team that Never Trains

Indeed, Ng wished that there was a computer program that would enable smart policing, that would "crunch the numbers and then decide where every patrol officer goes." Then perhaps they might require fewer officers on the ground at any one time and allow for more training days.

NJH: This police force does not train enough. I have said this, that if we were a football team, we would be a team that only plays matches and never trains. We really have to change this state of affairs. We simply don't have enough officers to give us the luxury of regular training. Our patrol officers work a 12-hour four-shift system. For them, it is basically morning shift, night shift, rest, day off, repeat. Where is the time for training? What training is done in-service and on an off-day. Typically, our officers get called back one off-day a month for urgent briefings and some training. I have not been able to solve this. Ideally, I would want the entire patrol team to come together after every shift cycle for a whole day of training. Because we currently operate on a 4 team-4 shift system, working in a regular training day would require creating an additional patrol team, and moving to a 5-shift rotation. We just do not have enough people to operate this way. We need to be smarter where the patrol officers go. Right now, our patrol men are confined to assigned patrol sectors as they wait to be despatched in response to 999 calls. There is no method in this and we ought to introduce some for the sake of efficiency. It may well mean that in some places or times, we will have no presence because we know from past experience that nothing is likely to happen in a particular locale. Conversely, there are places and times where enhanced presence is required because we know so. Data-mining and smart software can help us do this.

The independent committee that studied the police response to the Little India riot had recommended sensitivity training for police officers, Ng said.

NJH: One of the challenges is this large presence of foreign laborers in Singapore. It is a policing challenge, a real one. The riot is just an extreme manifestation of this challenge. Basically, these foreigners' expectations of the police force are different from those of Singaporeans. Our expectation is that they will behave like regular Singaporeans, but of course that is mistaken. They don't because they are not Singaporeans and are not acculturized or brought up like Singaporeans. So they will behave quite differently. When some of these foreigners get stopped by our police officers, their first instinct may be to buy their way out. It really happens. A Singaporean would never do that, but a foreigner would because maybe that is the way it is in their home countries. They also try to run away or try to fight with the police. These are the problems that our officers face. I know for a fact that most foreigners are law abiding. They came here to make a living and not to fight the police. In Little India, drinking is a problem and the committee said that it contributed to the riot. How do we prepare our police officers for this difference in expectations? By training. But we have little time for training. This is problematic. So our officers have to learn on the job and by experience. We have to change this.

Policing the Police

Ng was well-aware that in a country where few experienced crime personally, there would be very little tolerance for police incompetence or corruption. Even "the small things" could corrode public trust. For historical and policy reasons, the SPF never had an Ombudsman's Office.

NJH: We thought about it, but we are not going to go for the Ombudsman. I started what we call an Internal Affairs Office. In the past, Internal Investigations and the Service Quality Department were one and the same.

I found it wrong and bizarre. When I became Commissioner, I separated the two functions. We put service quality by itself. The Internal Affairs Office does only internal investigations. It reports directly to the Commissioner, and is staffed only by senior officers and good investigators. I put a very good and steady investigation leader in charge. That is not good enough still. The truth is that the police continues to investigate itself, and that is just not good enough for elected officials or acceptable to the general public. We worked with the Ministry to pass a new law which creates autonomous committees. Independent civilian committees to oversee internal police investigations are now established and report directly to the Minister. For certain major or sensitive cases, these committees will sit and have oversight of the Investigation Papers (IPs). In this way, the Minister can confidently report to Parliament that he is satisfied with police's internal investigation because an independent committee of eminent citizens has looked at our investigations and found no problem with it. It is a model I had copied from Prisons. In Prisons, when an inmate behaves badly and hits a prisons officer, the Commissioner of Prisons can order for him to be whipped. That is a huge power, which can be abused. So we formed committees of prison justices, who are all Justices of the Peace (JPs), and they oversee every corporal punishment. No one gets caned until these committees say that it is OK. We are trying out the same idea for police. If a case involving a police officer is criminal, it will go to court. Many don't end up in court because the Attorney-General's Chambers don't think there are enough grounds to proceed, and wants police to take internal action instead. Serious cases can result in demotion and non-promotion. It can involve dismissal too.

I tell you what the biggest irritant is for the regular person with the police. It is traffic–traffic offences. When someone gets a speeding ticket, he always has a good reason for the bad behavior, and will invariably put in an appeal. The law is clear on traffic offences and we really shouldn't entertain these appeals. But unfortunately, we did in the past. Now, we take a much stricter stance. In fact, I asked Traffic Police to put out in public what the chance of a successful appeal is. It is very close to zero, so no one should bother. Traffic is the most common interaction the public has with the police. We have to work really hard on it (road safety) as it is the most common issue. If not, people would otherwise hate the police just because they get traffic tickets from us.

Theory and Practice

Ng identified Broken Windows Theory as having had a deep impact on his priorities and methods as a Singapore police leader.

The Little India riot was "a black swan event," but the broken window was "the alcohol problem in Little India," he said.

NJH: The very definition of a black swan event is something which you don't expect to happen, but when it happens, on hindsight, you say that you should have seen it coming. In black swan theory, how do you deal with these things? We cannot prevent the next black swan event because, by their nature, black swans cannot be prevented. What you can do is to become more resilient to black swan events. This is our focus. The broken window is that we did not deal adequately with the alcohol problem in Little India. ... It is partly a policing issue as it can lead to public disorder. This is where we learn from experience. We think they will be responsible drinkers. We never thought that a drink can lead to this kind of violence. We never fully understood the behavior.

Since the riots, curbs on public drinking and sale of alcohol have been legislated, adding the enforcement of prohibition hours to the list of police duties.

Ng acknowledged that while theories like Broken Windows and Peel's Principles influenced his practice, the SPF itself did not conduct research.

NJH: We don't do research, not the kind of research you are thinking about. For example, we don't research why crime is so low in Singapore. We don't know and I can't explain. All I know is that certain things we do seem to work, so we keep doing them. There is no criminology faculty in our universities. Singapore is the safest place in the world and no one studies why this is so. One of my ambitions was for police to fund a Chair in Criminology in the National University of Singapore (NUS) but I was never able to get enough interest for the idea.

The SPF has, however, always convened regular teams of officers to study work processes and new equipment with the aim of improving work efficiency and effectiveness, consulting experts as required. Ng continued the practice. Taking a leaf from Silicon Valley, he also implemented Police SkunkWorks, where a team of officers drawn from various frontline units were given six months to develop new products for operational use, the intent being to shorten the R&D cycle of innovation to capitalize on innovative ideas from the ground, he said.

As SPF officers travelled widely and saw what worked elsewhere, they also copied and transplanted ideas to Singapore. Ng himself adapted the New York Police Department's CompStat meeting.

NJH: I learned the CompStat process from the NYPD. Their CompStat process is brutal. It is all about numbers, basically a trial by numbers. In the NYPD, the commanders come in and get assessed by the numbers they are delivering. I like to think that my Compstat process is more collaborative. I sit down with my commanders, who will have their numbers with them. We go through statistics division by division, talk about the more problematic areas and what we can do about them. We share ideas and in spite of the divisional boundaries, the commanders agree to work together for better outcomes. I believe my commanders enjoy their weekly sessions with me tremendously.

They are called the CP's Breakfast Meetings, and take place every Tuesday morning at nine. You may ask why Tuesday. I have them on Tuesdays because I was sure that my commanders, in turn, would be holding their own meetings on Mondays.

Transnational Relations

Asked if he saw value in exchanging ideas with other police forces, Ng said: "Absolutely there is. This is the whole point of initiatives like Pearls in Policing."

In 2012, the SPF hosted the Pearls in Policing meeting, a group of 35 senior police leaders from the English-speaking world who meet once a year in an informal, think-tank setting to discuss strategic and personal challenges facing their profession. Ng also agreed to mentor a group of emerging police leaders as they met for a year to discuss topics chosen for them by the Pearls meeting.

Ng believed that personnel exchanges were helpful for building personal relationships, which facilitate sharing across borders.

> *NJH:* Personal relationships are what matters. That is why the Malaysian Police are my best friends, and I do everything I can to make sure they remain my best friends. Criminals operate in a borderless world. Criminals share all the time, but as police forces we don't share as much as we could. For sure, we have learnt a lot from overseas forces. The SPF has also shared a lot with others. We have shared with the Chinese and Indians. We have ongoing programs with the South Australian Police where we exchange officers for a month. We are training together with Hong Kong and Macau. With Brunei, we help run their senior officers training and, in turn, they offer us valuable training ground for our special forces.

Ng heralded the opening of the Interpol Global Complex in Singapore as "an important development globally" as it would draw police forces closer together to train and jointly fight crime.

> *NJH:* INTERPOL, for the first time, will position capabilities outside of Lyon. It will involve key capabilities like cybercrime and training capabilities. … The training won't be in all areas, but in what they think is required, for example, in response to an emerging threat. It could be terrorism training or cybercrime training, or even pandemic training. They can do it in Singapore as there is now a facility in Singapore and a training unit that can run these programmes. INTERPOL already runs operations out of Singapore. Because of INTERPOL here, we are able to put together operations with other police forces. FIFA World Cup match fixing? Some of the arrest operations were also conducted from here. Policing has got to be done more jointly.

But while police skills were transferable, he cautioned that changing organizational culture and mind-sets were harder.

> *NJH:* The Chinese visit us a lot. For years, they have been coming because they think Singapore presents a good model for China. I always tell them we are not a good model for China because we are a city but also a country. That means we are a national force but policing a city-sized jurisdiction. That is not the case in China. We may be a good model for big cities in China. I also tell them it is not the tactics—Beijing and Shanghai probably have better equipment than we do—but the software. It is about culture and mind-set. A big part of our success is because we have an honest force and are serious about our values. These things are hard to replicate. That is about consistently good leadership across the force, which is also hard to replicate. Every year the Lee Kuan Yew School of Public Policy invites me to lecture its mayor's class (that the school conducts for Chinese mayors). I talk to them about policing Singapore and my message is essentially this: there are no secrets to good policing, textbook after textbook has already been written on the subject, the hard part is putting theory into practice. This applies equally to Singapore.

Democratic Policing

Ng believed that protecting the democratic process was "a sacred duty" for the police and constantly reminded his officers to be politically impartial. That duty was much tested in 2011–2012 when within the space of 12 months, the country went to the polls three times—for the general election in May 2011, the presidential election in August 2011, and a widely-watched and hotly contested by-election in the opposition-held ward of Hougang in May 2012. His officers, Ng conceded, found the long duty hours tiring, especially since they not only had to continue with their usual law and order duties, but also not allow themselves to be drawn into the emotionally charged debates or respond to taunts by unruly elements.

> *NJH:* The police in Singapore is impartial and fair. Politics has nothing to do with us. We have opposition held constituencies to which we extend full co-operation. Crime doesn't care about politics and when it comes to election time it is our mission to protect our democracy. … That is very important to me and I have made it very explicit to the officers that we have to be neutral to the contesting parties. The politics of Singapore is changing and it is far more important than ever that our forces conduct themselves in an impartial way. This is especially important during elections. During election time, I keep telling my officers: "neutrality, neutrality, neutrality." We have to be extra sensitive about the public's perception of police action. At electioneering gatherings, there will always be hooligan elements who try to provoke us, but we have to be slow to anger and be more tolerant than usual. At the last

General Election, the police received wide praise, from all sides of the political spectrum, for the way we carried out our operations.

We make sure the election rallies are safe whether held by the opposition or the incumbent party. Everyone can go to them, have a good time, and then go home safely. In Hougang (an opposition-held constituency), there was only one rally site and it was always full of people. You would have to climb up a big grass slope to get on to the field. When I went to see this site, I gave instructions to have staircases built. And so we scrambled overnight to have temporary staircases and lighting put up in order that no one would fall down on the way to and from election rallies. The police paid for them. We do these things as we want an incident free campaigning process.

The police play a zero factor in how people vote. On polling day, it is the duty of policing officers to man every polling station. For this, we have to call in our reservists in order to make up the numbers. Everyone is involved and the duty hours are long. But we do it happily because we are protecting our democracy and we have to make sure that people can cast their votes in a safe and orderly fashion. When polling is finished, it is the police that guard the ballot boxes and bring them to the counting centers. No one else can do this except us.

I feel strongly that it is our sacred duty to protect our democracy. But until I put it in this fashion to my officers, they never looked at it this way. They've always thought of election duty as the worst detail to be on.

Ng believed that it was the role of the police to uphold human rights, but it also had to enforce the law of the land. Asked if he would ever allow serious protests against the government, he said:

I don't make the laws. I just enforce them. My personal feeling about public protest is irrelevant. If the law allows for street protests, then we will police street protests to make sure they are peaceful and safe. At the moment, our laws only allow for protests at Hong Lim Park (Singapore's Speakers' Corner). So I make sure that Hong Lim Park is safe for every protestor. We do not police Hong Lim Park. When someone books the Park and wants to stage a demonstration, they know the rules. We don't routinely station police officers there unless we sense that there is going to be an imminent threat to public order or if we receive a complaint. We don't police these demonstrations as it is really not our business. ... If there is going to be public disorder, then the police have to be there. That is our job and mission. But, by and large the demonstrations have been peaceful and uneventful.

Looking Ahead

"Crime is the only KPI—key performance indicator—that we report to the public," Ng noted. "We report nothing else except crime twice a year. Of course all police forces report crime, but many also report finance savings. We don't."

As Commissioner of Police, Ng's ambition was to make Singapore the safest place in the world. For the first four years he was CP, the crime rate fell continuously. But he also knew that with crime becoming more complex and borderless, with ringleaders based overseas, the crime rate would eventually rise, as it did in 2014.

Fortunately, or otherwise, public safety was taken so much for granted, he said, that it was a non-issue. "No one talks about it. During elections, public safety is never an issue."

But the flip-side was that the public was also completely unprepared for the scenes of violence that played out during the Little India riot in December 2013. Among the criticisms of the police response was that officers were too gentle in handling the rioters, that they allowed police vehicles to be burnt. Ng disagreed; "it would have been a disaster" had officers responded too forcefully, he argued. As it turned out, nobody was hurt, apart from a few bruises.

The riot was, as he noted, a black-swan event. Nonetheless in its aftermath, the force took corrective measures to revamp its command, control, and communications system. Since the big buses carrying riot control troops were held up in traffic and arrived at the scene late, the SPF formed a mobile riot troop of about 300 men equipped with motorbikes. "It will be the first in the world," he said with some pride.

Ng, however, was cautious about how prepared the SPF might be to deal with international organized crime syndicates, which he believed would be attracted by the successes of the two casinos that opened in Singapore in 2010.

New legislation to deal with organized crime was being worked on, he noted, and indeed The Organised Crime Bill was passed in August 2015 to enhance the ability of law enforcement agencies to disrupt the illegal activities of organized criminal groups. The SPF had also been working with the Macau and Hong Kong police to prevent the entry of known OC elements into Singapore.

> NJH: These people are of common interest to all of us. The danger is that once Asian organized crime comes here and links up with our own disorderly elements—we have gangsters too—we will have trouble.

But as their job scope became more complex, it was becoming very difficult to make sure serving police officers continued to acquire the appropriate training to deal with future problems because there were simply not enough of them.

> NJH: We really have to do more training. We can only do it with more resources. I hope we can solve this. There is actually only one problem that the SPF faces and that is a shortage of officers. This is really the only problem we have.

Conclusion

Commissioner Ng had previously given only one full-length interview to the local newspaper. Even then his goal was to deal with the controversy surrounding his decision to hire a brand consultant for the SPF.

Now at the end of a successful 30-year police career, he was in introspective mood; candid about the strengths and weaknesses of the police force, optimistic about the direction his successor would take it. Articulate and forthright, he was above all proud of what the force had achieved on his watch, proud of his officers and their capacity to learn and adapt. When he declared the Singapore Police Force to be among the best in the world, the strength of his conviction was palpable.

But he believed too that it was time for him to move on and start a new career. "A good opening came up," he said of the timing.

Glossary

Broken Windows Theory: In 1982, criminologist George Kelling and social scientist James Wilson coined the term "broken windows" to refer to their observation that when a building window is broken and left unrepaired, vandals will usually break a few more. An unrepaired broken window, they argued, is a signal that no one cares, and so breaking more windows costs nothing. In environments where disorderly behavior goes unchecked, more serious street crime flourishes. Kelling and Wilson (1982) theorized therefore that if the police deter low-level antisocial behavior, people will behave in a more orderly way, and major crimes will be prevented.

Compstat: CompStat is a data-driven management model introduced by Police Commissioner William Bratton in the New York Police Department in 1994. According to Weisburd et al. (2003), CompStat facilitates accurate and timely analysis of crime and disorder data, which is used to identify crime patterns and problems, and to tailor responses. An accountability structure measures how effective ground commanders are in acting upon the analysis to implement responses that reduce crime and disorder.

Sense-making: The process of clarifying and articulating an organization's understanding of complex situations in order to build situational awareness and shared understanding within the organization. It supports decision-making by establishing an understanding of the interconnections between various elements and actors within a complex system. Sense-making typically begins with sensing processors, for example, crowdsourcing. The feedback gathered from various sensors and stakeholders forms the basis for analysis.

References

Kelling, G. and Wilson, J. 1982. Broken windows: The police and neighbourhood safety. *The Atlantic Magazine*. March, 29–38.

Khoo, B. H. 2003. Sense-Making in Crisis and Complexity. *Ethos* (a publication of the Singapore Civil Service College). Singapore.

Pearls in Policing. 2012. *Policing for a Safer World, Singapore 2012*. The Hague: Singapore Police Force and National Police of the Netherlands.

Sim, S. 2011. *Making Singapore Safe: Thirty Years of the National Crime Prevention Council*. Singapore: Marshall Cavendish.

SPF. 2013. *Singapore Police Force Annual 2013*. Available at http://www.police.gov. sg/prints/annual/2013/#.

Weisburd, D., Mastrofski, S. D., McNally, A., Greenspan, R., and Willis, J. J. 2003. Reforming to preserve: Compstat and strategic problem solving in American policing. *Criminology and Public Policy*, 2, 421–456.

The International Police Executive Symposium

The International Police Executive Symposium (IPES) was founded in 1994. The aims and objectives of the IPES are to provide a forum to foster closer relationships among police researchers and practitioners globally, to facilitate cross-cultural, international, and interdisciplinary exchanges for the enrichment of the law enforcement profession, and to encourage discussion and published research on challenging and contemporary topics related to the profession.

One of the most important activities of the IPES is the organization of an annual meeting under the auspices of a police agency or an educational institution. Every year since 1994, annual meetings have been hosted by such agencies and institutions all over the world. Past hosts have included the Canton Police of Geneva, Switzerland; the International Institute of the Sociology of Law, Onati, Spain; Kanagawa University, Yokohama, Japan; the Federal Police, Vienna, Austria; the Dutch Police and Europol, The Hague, The Netherlands; the Andhra Pradesh Police, India; the Center for Public Safety, Northwestern University, the United States; the Polish Police Academy, Szczytno, Poland; the Police of Turkey (twice); the Kingdom of Bahrain Police; a group of institutions in Canada (consisting of the University of the Fraser Valley, Abbotsford Police Department, Royal Canadian Mounted Police, the Vancouver Police Department, the Justice Institute of British Columbia, Canadian Police College, and the International Centre for Criminal Law Reform and Criminal Justice Policy); the Czech Police Academy, Prague; the Dubai Police; the Ohio Association of Chiefs of Police and the Cincinnati Police Department, Ohio, the United States; the Republic of Macedonia and the Police of Malta. The 2011 Annual Meeting on the theme of "Policing Violence, Crime, Disorder and Discontent: International Perspectives' was hosted in Buenos Aires, Argentina on June 26–30, 2011. The 2012 annual meeting was hosted at United Nations in New York on the theme of "Economic development, armed violence and public safety" on August 5–10. The 2013 Annual Meeting on the theme of "Global Issues in Contemporary Policing" was hosted by the Ministry of Interior of Hungary and the Hungarian National Police on August 4–9, 2013. In 2014 there were two meetings: the Annual Meeting on the theme "Policing by Consent" was hosted in Trivandrum (Kerala), India on March 16–21, and the other on "Crime Prevention and Community Resilience" was hosted in Bulgaria's capital city Sofia (July 27–31). The 2015 summer meeting on the theme of "Police Governance and Human Trafficking: Promoting Preventative and Comprehensive Strategies" was hosted in Pattaya Beach, Thailand, on August 8–12, 2015. The 2016 Annual Meeting will be hosted in Washington, DC on the theme of "Urban Security Planning: Challenges for 21st Century Global Cities."

There have also been occasional Special Meetings of IPES. A Special Meeting was cohosted by the Bavarian Police Academy of Continuing Education in Ainring, Germany, University of Passau, Germany, and State University of New York, Plattsburgh, USA in 2000. The second Special Meeting was hosted by the police in the Indian state of Kerala. The third Special Meeting on the theme of "Contemporary Issues in Public Safety and Security" was hosted by the Commissioner of Police of the Blekinge Region of Sweden and the President of the University of Technology on August 10–14, 2011. The last Special Meeting on "Policing by Consent" was hosted in Trivandrum, India on March 16–21, 2014.

The majority of participants of the annual meetings are usually directly involved in the police profession. In addition, scholars and researchers in the field also participate. The meetings comprise both structured and informal sessions to maximize dialogue and exchange of views and information. The executive summary of each meeting is distributed to participants as well as to a wide range of other interested police professionals and scholars. In addition, a book of selected papers from each annual meeting is published through CRC Press/Taylor & Francis Group, Prentice Hall, Lexington Books and other reputed publishers. A Special Issue of *Police Practice and Research: An International Journal* is also published with the most thematically relevant papers after the usual blind review process.

IPES Institutional Supporters

APCOF, The African Policing Civilian Oversight Forum, (contact Sean Tait), 2nd floor, The Armoury, Buchanan Square, 160 Sir Lowry Road, Woodstock Cape Town, 8000 South Africa. Tel: 27 21 461 7211; Fax: 27 21 461 7213. Email: sean@apcof.org.za

Australian Institute of Police Management, Library, 1 Collins Beach Road RD, Manly, New South Wales 2095, Australia. Tel: +61 2 9934 4800; Fax: +61 2 9934 4780. Email: library@aipm.gov.au

Baker College of Jackson, 2800 Springport Road, Jackson, MI 49202, USA (contact: Blaine Goodrich). Phone: (517) 841–4522. Email: blaine.goodrich@baker.edu

Cliff Roberson, professor emeritus, Washburn University, 16307 Sedona Woods, Houston, TX 77082–1665, USA. Tel: +1 713 703 6639; Fax: +1 281 596 8483. Email: roberson37@msn.com

College of Health and Human Services, Indiana University of Pennsylvania, 216 Zink Hall, Room 105, 1190 Maple Street Indiana, PA 15705-1059 (Mark E. Correia, PhD, Dean), mcorreia 724 357 2555.

Cyber Defense & Research Initiatives (contact James Lewis), LLC, PO Box 86, Leslie, MI 49251, USA. Tel: 517 242 6730. Email: lewisja@cyberdefenseresearch.com

Defendology Center for Security, Sociology and Criminology Research (Valibor Lalic), Srpska Street 63,78000 Banja Luka, Bosnia and Herzegovina. Tel and Fax: 387 51 308 914. Email: lalicv@teol.net

Department of Criminal Justice (Dr. Harvey L. McMurray, Chair), North Carolina Central University, 301 Whiting Criminal Justice Bldg., Durham, NC 27707, USA. Tel: 919–530 5204, 919-530-7909; Fax: 919-530-5195. Email: hmcmurray@nccu.edu

Department of Psychology (Stephen Perrott), Mount Saint Vincent University, 166 Bedford Highway, Halifax, Nova Scotia, Canada. Email: Stephen.perrott@mvsu.ca

De Montfort University, Health and Life Sciences, School of Applied Social Sciences (Dr. Perry Stanislas, Hirsh Sethi), Hawthorn Building, The Gateway, Leicester, LE1 9BH, UK. Tel: +44 (0) 116 257 7146. Email: pstanislas@dmu.ac.uk, hsethi@dmu.ac.uk

Edmundo Oliveira, Prof. PhD 1 Irving Place University Tower Apt. U 7 A 10003.9723 Manhattan - New York, New York, Phone 407.342.24.73. Email: edmundooliveira@cfl.rr.com

Fayetteville State University (Dr. David E. Barlow, Professor and Dean), College of Basic and Applied Sciences, 130 Chick Building, 1200

Murchison Road, Fayetteville, North Carolina, 28301 USA. Tel: 910-672-1659; Fax: 910-672-1083. Email: dbarlow@uncfsu.edu

International Council on Security and Development (ICOS) (Andre Souza, Senior Researcher), Visconde de Piraja 577/605, Ipanema, Rio de Janeiro 22410–003, Brazil. Tel: (+55) 21 3186 5444. Email: asouza@icosgroup.net

Kerala Police (Shri Balasubramaniyum, Director General of Police), Police Headquarters, Trivandrum, Kerala, India. Email: manojabraham05@gmail.com

Law School, John Moores University (David Lowe, LLB Programme Leader), Law School, Redmonds Building, Brownlow Hill, Liverpool, L3 5UG, UK. Tel: +44 (0) 151 231 3918. Email: D.Lowe@ljmu.ac.uk

Molloy College, The Department of Criminal Justice (contact Dr. John A. Eterno, NYPD Captain-Retired), 1000 Hempstead Avenue, PO Box 5002, Rockville Center, NY 11571-5002, USA. Tel: 516 678 5000, Ext. 6135; Fax: 516 2562289. Email: jeterno@molloy.edu

National Institute of Criminology and Forensic Science (Mr Kamalendra Prasad, Inspector General of Police), MHA, Outer Ring Road, Sector 3, Rohini, Delhi 110085, India. Tel: 91 11 275 2 5095; Fax: 91 11 275 1 0586. Email: director.nicfs@nic.in

National Police Academy, Japan (Naoya Oyaizu, Deputy Director), Police Policy Research Center, Zip 183-8558:3- 12- 1 Asahicho Fuchu-city, Tokyo, Japan. Tel: 81 42 354 3550; Fax: 81 42 330 3550. Email: PPRC@npa.go.jp

Royal Canadian Mounted Police (Craig J. Callens), 657 West 37th Avenue, Vancouver, BC V5Z 1K6, Canada. Tel: 604 264 2003; Fax: 604 264 3547. Email: bcrcmp@rcmp-grc.gc.ca

School of Psychology and Social Science, Head, Social Justice Research Centre (Prof S. Caroline Taylor, Foundation Chair in Social Justice), Edith Cowan University, 270 Joondalup Drive, Joondalup, WA 6027, Australia. Email: c.taylor@ecu.edu.au

South Australia Police (Commissioner Mal Hyde), Office of the Commissioner, South Australia Police, 30 Flinders Street, Adelaide, SA 5000, Australia. Email: mal.hyde@police.sa.gov.au

Southeast Missouri State University (Dr. Diana Scharff Peterson, Dean), Criminal Justice & Sociology, One University Plaza, Cape Girardeau, MO 63701, USA. Tel: (573) 651-2178. Email: dbruns@semo.edu

The Faculty of Criminal Justice and Security, (Dr. Gorazd Mesko), University of Maribor, Kotnikova 8, 1000 Ljubl- jana, Slovenia. Tel: 386 1 300 83 39; Fax: 386 1 2302 687. Email: gorazd.mesko@fvv.uni-mb.si

UNISA, Department of Police Practice (Setlhomamaru Dintwe), Florida Campus, Cnr Christiaan De Wet and Pioneer Avenues, Private Bag X6, Florida, 1710 South Africa. Tel: 011 471 2116; Cell: 083 581 6102; Fax: 011 471 2255. Email: Dintwsi@unisa.ac.za

University of Maine at Augusta, College of Natural and Social Sciences (Richard Myers, Professor), 46 University Drive, Augusta, ME 04330-9410, USA. Email: rmyers@maine.edu

University of New Haven (Dr. Mario Gaboury, School of Criminal Justice and Forensic Science), 300 Boston Post Road, West Haven, CT 06516, USA. Tel: 203 932 7260. Email: rward@newhaven.edu

University of South Africa, College of Law (Professor Kris Pillay, School of Criminal Justice, Director), Preller Street, Muckleneuk, Pretoria. Email: cpillay@unisa.ac.za

University of the Fraser Valley (Dr. Darryl Plecas), Department of Criminology & Criminal Justice, 33844 King Road, Abbotsford, British Columbia V2 S7 M9, Canada. Tel: 604-853-7441; Fax: 604-853-9990. Email: Darryl. plecas@ufv.ca

University of West Georgia (David A. Jenks, PhD), 1601 Maple Street, Carrollton, GA 30118, Pafford Building 2309. Tel: 678-839-6327. Email: djenks@westga.edu

Suggested Guidelines
for Interviewers

General Remarks

The general goal of the interviews is to present the views and interpretations of policing developments and current issues by experienced practitioners. What do they see happening in policing in their countries and internationally, and how do they evaluate or interpret developments? We have many analyses and interpretations of policing by scholars and policymakers from outside police organizations. What we would like to have are views and interpretations from within the organizations. What do police leaders who do the work see happening in policing? What are the issues they consider important? What changes do they see as successes or failures? What are likely lasting futures or passing fads? What we are also seeking is to build personal profiles of the judges interviewed: their careers, backgrounds, the influences that shaped their personalities, their successes, failures, joys, temptations, and frustrations in their career and in their job.

The basic goal of the interviews is to capture the views of police officials. Your role should not be to be too critical or to interpret what the officials meant to say, but to write as accurately as possible what the officials have told you. It is their views, based on their experience and thinking, that we are interested in. We know what scholars think about policing, but we know less about what the people who do policing think and how they evaluate trends, developments, and issues in policing. That is the important goal.

The basic reason for doing these interviews in the first place is our firm belief that police officials know a lot and that practitioners can make significant contributions to our understanding of the prospects and problems of policing today. It is that knowledge and their judgments of policing that we are after. But that knowledge is not easily captured.

The practical reason for the interviews is that police leaders do not have the time to write and reflect on their experiences, views, opinions, and perspectives. We think interviews are one means to capture that knowledge and that is why we are requesting researchers like you to record their views.

We want to reemphasize one major point: We *do not want the official rhetoric (or the official success stories)* that high-level people sometimes fall back on during interviews; we want their *personal views and thinking*. If you have the sense that you are getting the formal language and official views of policing and reforms, see if you can get the officials to go beyond that and push them for their own views. The interviewer should seek to get the person interviewed to move beyond simple answers, to get them to analyze and reflect on their experiences and knowledge. That takes skill on the part of the interviewer—but that is why you were asked to do an interview.

Topic Areas Which Should Be Covered

These are the basic areas we would like to cover. In some cases there may be other areas of importance in "your" country or community and you should ask about those areas as well.

For example, questions of police leaders in transitional countries will likely deal more with changes in policing philosophies and organizations than questions for leaders in stable democracies. We know, when asking you to conduct an interview, that you are quite familiar with the policing situations in "your" country and that you will tailor your questions toward the dominant local issues which have had to be dealt with by the leaders. Be creative, but not overly so.

We have listed a number of topics that should be covered in the interview. Please try to cover the topics mentioned below as the conduct and flow of the interview dictates. And add, elaborate, and follow up as you see fit and necessary to clarify points, expand on ideas, or pursue an insight offered.

All the topical areas should be asked, but the specific questions listed below for each topic area are suggestions. Interviews have their own dynamics. Follow them down their most fruitful avenues. Since each of you will be interviewing officials within different organizations, the list and sequence of questions will have to be adjusted in any case.

The wording of questions is, of course, your own. In follow-up questions, try to get specific examples or details of generalizations made. (Examples are probably among the most useful pieces of information to readers.)

Career

Tell us a little bit about your career: length, organizations worked in, movements, specializations, etc. What motivated you to enter/stay in police work?

Changes Experienced

What do you see as the most important changes which have happened within your organization over the course of your career, e.g., in police philosophies, police priorities, management, gender, diversity, training, specializations, equipment, organizational culture, human rights compliance, legal powers?

Have current economic conditions resulted in budget cuts, and if so, how has this impacted the organization?

In regards to external relationships, what changes have you observed, e.g., in police relationships with the public, interagency cooperation, personnel within the criminal justice system, relations with minority communities, political influence, human rights activists?

Personal Policing Philosophy

What do you think is/should be the role and functions of the police? What should be dropped or left to other public and nonstate organizations? What should be done about unpoliced areas?

What facilitates/hinders good relations with the community, with government, with other criminal justice organizations, with nonstate security providers such as community groups, customary, and commercial enterprises?

What should be the priorities of your police service?

Problems and Successes Experienced

What areas have you seen develop during your time, and how has this been achieved? What obstacles have stood in the way of progress?

In your experience, what policies or programs have worked well and which have not? Why?

What would you consider to be the greatest problem facing the police at this time? Are there corruption or lack of resources issues?

How can corruption and human rights abuses be tackled in the service?

Theory and Practice

Would you say theory has played a part in your practice and that of your organization?

What kind of research, in what form, on what issues do you find most useful for practice? Does your organization do research on its own?

Transnational Relations

How have you and the work of your organization been affected by developments outside the country (human rights demands, universal codes of ethics, practical interactions with police from other countries, travel outside the country, new crime threats, "the war on terror," etc.)?

How transferable do you regard your skills to police services in countries of different development levels, and what value is there in advisers and senior officers coming to your service from abroad?

Democratic Policing

What do you see as the key elements of democratic policing?

Does maintaining law and order mean that policing is involved in maintaining the existing social order and power structures, or can it allow serious protests against the government and laws and powerful elites? Can the police resist demands from the government to crack down on opposition and protest?'

What levels of public support does the police service have?

Looking Ahead

What are the most likely developments you see happening? What would you like to see happening?

What to Do Before and After the Interview Before the Interview

Get a sense of how much time you are likely to have and what questions you can get to during that time. In no interview will you be able to ask all the questions you want When you write up the interview, you will have space for about 6,000 to 8,000 words (on the average). Choose your priorities. The top priorities for us are the reflections by the officials interviewed on changes experienced during their careers, how they evaluate those changes, and the interrelations of theory and practice. We also want insights to the person of the leader interviewed. These are high priorities for the interviews.

After the Interview

Please write a short introduction to the interview. The introduction should

- Briefly describe the basic structure of policing in your country. You have to be the judge of how much an informed reader is likely to know about the country and how much should be explained.
- Describe, briefly, the interview itself. Where and when it was conducted; how long it took, or multiple sittings; how honest and open you feel the discussion was.

You should, if at all possible, tape record the interview. For publication, edit the interview to bring out the most important discussion and answers. Chances are you will have much more information than we will have space for your interview in the proposed book.

Write a short conclusion on your impression of the interview. What the major themes were, how well the views expressed accord with the known literature, but do not be overly critical on this point, please. Again, briefly.

Write a glossary of terms or events mentioned in the interview a reader might not be familiar with. For example, if interviewing a German official and *Bundeskriminalamt* is mentioned, describe very briefly what that is; or if in an interview with a South African official and SAARPCO is mentioned, describe that. Just select the most likely items non-experienced readers might not know.

We have had two basic styles in writing up interviews. Both are acceptable, but we prefer the second style.

- One style is to simply transcribe the interviews—questions asked, answers given.
- The second style, which requires more work, is to write short statements about the topic of a question and then insert long excerpts from the interviews. The main point is to have the voice and views of the leaders being interviewed, not your own.

Send the completed interviews to Bruce Baker and Dilip Das at bruce@bakerbrum.co.uk and Dilipkd@aol.com. The total interview, with introduction, conclusion, and glossary should be about 6,000 to 8,000 words.

Finally, each interview will be a chapter which should be useable to teach students in a university class or as a book. It should be a source of knowledge and information to readers interested in policing, including police practitioners, policy makers, police trainers, police researchers, and academics in universities, as well as teachers and trainees in police academies.

Index